CHARITY MOVEMENTS IN
EIGHTEENTH–CENTURY IRELAND

Irish Historical Monograph Series

ISSN 1740-1097

Series editors

Marie Therese Flanagan, Queen's University, Belfast
Eunan O'Halpin, Trinity College, Dublin
David Hayton, Queen's University, Belfast
Fearghal McGarry, Queen's University, Belfast

Previous titles in this series

CHARITY MOVEMENTS IN EIGHTEENTH–CENTURY IRELAND

Philanthropy and Improvement

Karen Sonnelitter

THE BOYDELL PRESS

First published 2016
The Boydell Press, Woodbridge

ISBN 978-1-78327-068-2

The Boydell Press is an imprint of Boydell & Brewer Ltd
PO Box 9, Woodbridge, Suffolk IP12 3DF, UK
and of Boydell & Brewer Inc.
668 Mt Hope Avenue, Rochester, NY 14620–2731, USA
website: www.boydellandbrewer.com

A CIP catalogue record for this title is available from the British Library

The publisher has no responsibility for the continued existence or accuracy of URLs for external or third-party internet websites referred to in this book, and does not guarantee that any content on such websites is, or will remain, accurate or appropriate

This publication is printed on acid-free paper

Typeset by Fakenham Prepress Solutions, Fakenham, Norfolk NR21 8NN

For Mom and Dad

Contents

Figures

Acknowledgements

I am extremely grateful to all the people who have helped and supported me throughout the years that I worked on this project. The genesis of this work dates back to my Masters thesis on the charity school movement in Ireland. I would particularly like to thank Professor David Hayton and Dr Dominic Bryan at Queen's University Belfast and the staff and fellows of the Institute for Irish Studies for their guidance and support. Their interest and consideration propelled that project and helped to inspire this book. I would also like to thank the History Department at the University of Connecticut. Credit for the completion of this project is due to the Department of History at Purdue University and its faculty and staff for all the assistance and encouragement they have offered me over the years. I owe particular thanks to my advisor Melinda Zook. She is exacting in her standards and penetrating in her critiques, but always encouraging. This project, and my writing in general, have benefited greatly from her mentorship. I would also like to thank the rest of my committee, James Farr, Franklin Lambert, and Hilda Smith, for their time and for their insightful suggestions.

A number of archive and library staffs helped me by locating materials, pointing me towards collections, and generously allowing me to use collections that had not yet been catalogued. Thanks to the staffs of the National Archives of Ireland, the National Library of Ireland, Trinity College Dublin, Marsh's Library, the Public Record Office of Northern Ireland, the National Archives of the United Kingdom, and the Royal Dublin Society Library. In particular, Natasha Serne of the Royal Dublin Society, Brian Donnelly of the National Archives of Ireland, and Muriel McCarthy of Marsh's Library. I would also like to thank the staff at the Purdue University Office of Interlibrary Loan, who were essential in providing me with the secondary sources that formed the foundation of this work. The revision of this project into its present form was greatly helped by my participation in a National Endowment for the Humanities Summer Seminar which enabled me to do additional research while rethinking this project with the help of colleagues and new friends. I owe particular thanks to Clare Carroll and Marc Caball for organization. Essential financial support was provided Purdue Department of History, the Purdue Graduate School, the Purdue Research Foundation, Siena College, and the National Endowment for the Humanities.

This project was possible only because of the support I found in the graduate student community at Purdue University. I owe a debt of gratitude to all my colleagues there, past and present, especially Mauricio Castro, Cori Derifield, Kara Kvaran, Erin Kempker, Timothy Lombardo, Erica Morin, Patrick Pospisek, Kate Pospisek, Ron Johnson, Rebecca Venter, and Natalie Latteri, who have commented on drafts, guided me through fellowship proposals, and listened to me vent over many rounds of drinks at Hunter's Pub. The transformation of this project into its current form would not have been possible without my colleagues at Siena College, in particular Mara Drogan, Tim Cooper, Karl Barbir, Jennifer Dorsey, Wendy Pojmann, Fr. Dan Dwyer, Jim Harrison, and Karen Mahar. Mara and Tim especially provided valuable comments and insight at every stage of the process of writing this book. My dog, Maddie, has long resented the way my work takes my attention away from her. However, playing with and walking her were welcome breaks during the long days spent working on this project. My grandmother, Mary McMorrow, did not live to see me graduate college, but she inspired in me a love for Ireland and its history and so deserves to be recognized here. My brother Robert and sister Diane never seemed to lose faith that I would indeed one day finish this project. They have always been willing to lend a supportive ear, even from many miles away. Last, but not least, my parents, Bob and Joan Sonnelitter: this book is dedicated to you because your love and support is what made it possible. The cornerstone of this project and my entire career is your steady, unflappable faith in me. I build from that start in everything I do.

Abbreviations

D.C.L.	Dublin City Library and Archive
N.A.I.	National Archives of Ireland
N.L.I.	National Library of Ireland
P.R.O.N.I.	Public Records Office of Northern Ireland
R.C.B.L.	Representative Church Body Library
R.D.S.	Royal Dublin Society
T.C.D.	Trinity College, Dublin
T.N.A.	The National Archives, Kew

Introduction

Ireland in the Eighteenth Century:
The Case for Improvement

In June of 1746 the earl of Chesterfield, then the Lord Lieutenant of Ireland, wrote a letter to Thomas Prior, the founder of the Royal Dublin Society. Chesterfield praised Prior for the work of the Royal Dublin Society and congratulated him on being awarded a £500 annual bounty from the king to support the work of the society. He urged Prior to 'think of your manufactures about as much as your militia, and be as much upon your guard against poverty as against popery, take my word for it, you are in more danger of the former then of the latter'.[1] Chesterfield was one of many commentators who recognized that the greatest threat to English rule in Ireland in the eighteenth century was not the danger of Catholic rebellion but instead the social and economic problems which plagued the country. By 1746 it was rampant poverty and not Jacobitism that most concerned the Lord Lieutenant of Ireland. In response to this newly recognized threat a wave of reform movements and voluntary societies, of which the Royal Dublin Society was only one, sought to address the social ills plaguing Ireland. These charity movements differed from earlier forms of benevolence in organization, method, and aims. Anglo-Irish philanthropists sought to serve and protect their national interests by developing uniquely Irish adaptations of Enlightened philanthropic models. Through voluntary societies that combined a religious and an Enlightenment agenda they attempted to eliminate destabilizing social issues that beleaguered Ireland and threatened their position.

This book examines those Protestant-led reform movements and voluntary societies that gained prominence in Ireland in the eighteenth century. Movements for reform and improvement existed before the Treaty of Limerick in 1691 and continued to exist after the Rebellion of 1798. However, between these years of relative political stability, these societies were at their most prominent and influential. Following the victory of William III over James II, Protestants had once again firmly established control over Ireland. The Protestant ruling elite of Ireland, more commonly known as the Anglo-Irish Ascendancy, worked to protect themselves from further Catholic insurgence and to solidify their own

---

[1] P.R.O.N.I. T3228/1/26.

monopoly over political power. This period is generally associated with a series of penal laws designed to eliminate the Catholic social and political leadership and to cripple the Roman Catholic Church on the island.[2] The Anglo-Irish, inspired in part by movements in England and on the continent, developed an even greater interest in improving Ireland both socially and economically. This culture of improvement was not unique to Ireland, but the Irish movement did have its own particular characteristics and problems.

Scholars tend to draw a distinction between charities with a strong religious component and the more secular scientific societies,[3] and most studies deal with these reform movements separately. However, these movements have a great deal in common. Religious charities and scientific societies were all part of the same broad movement, driven by the same impetus to reform and improve. Medical and education charities were motivated by both Enlightenment and religious values, while scientific societies were also driven by a commitment to the Anglican faith.

In the early eighteenth century Ireland was emerging from a period of social and political chaos. In his autobiography, William Petty, the second earl of Shelburne and first marquess of Lansdowne, wrote of the state of Ireland at the time of his birth in 1737. He described it as 'a country quite uncivilized, peopled by Catholicks, reduced by frequent rebellions, and laws passed in consequence'.[4] Petty had little affection for Ireland or the Irish, and he deplored his upbringing there. Still, he correctly expressed several of the problems that

---

[2] T. C. Barnard, *The kingdom of Ireland, 1641–1760* (New York, 2004), pp. 42–3, 51.

[3] T. C. Barnard, *Improving Ireland? projectors, prophets and profiteers, 1641–1786* (Dublin, 2008); D. W. Hayton, 'Did Protestantism fail in early eighteenth-century Ireland? Charity schools and the enterprise of religious and social reformation, c.1690–1730' in Alan Ford, James McGuire, and Kenneth Milne (eds), *As by law established: the church of Ireland since the Reformation* (Dublin, 1995); Kenneth Milne, *The Irish charter schools 1730–1830* (Dublin, 1997); Brendan Bradshaw, 'Sword, word, and strategy in the Reformation in Ireland' in *The Historical Journal*, 21, no. 3 (1978), pp. 475–502; Patricia Coughlan, 'Natural history and historical nature: the project for a natural history of Ireland' in Mark Greengrass and Michael Leslie (eds), *Samuel Hartlib and the universal reformation: studies in intellectual communication* (Cambridge, 2002), pp. 298–317; K. Theodore Hoppen, *The common scientist in the seventeenth century: a study of the Dublin Philosophical Society, 1683–1708* (London, 1970); Lindsay J. Proudfoot, 'Landownership and improvement circa 1700 to 1845' in Lindsay J. Proudfoot and William Nolan (eds), *Down: history and society, interdisciplinary essays on the history of an Irish county* (Dublin, 1997); Peter Borsay and Lindsay J. Proudfoot, *Provincial towns in early modern England and Ireland: change, convergence and divergence* (Oxford, 2002); W. H. Crawford, 'The influence of the landlords in eighteenth century Ulster' in L. M. Cullen and T. C. Stout (eds), *Comparative aspects of Scottish and Irish economic and social history, 1600–1900* (Edinburgh, 1977); Laurence M. Geary, *Medicine and charity in Ireland, 1718–1851* (Dublin, 2004); James Meenan and Desmond Clarke (eds), *RDS: The Royal Dublin Society 1731–1981* (Dublin, 1981); J. B. Lyons, *The quality of Mercer's: the story of Mercer's Hospital, 1734–1991* (Dublin, 1991).

[4] Edmond George Petty Fitzmaurice, *Life of William, earl of Shelburne, afterwards first marquess of Lansdowne. With excerpts from his papers and correspondence* (3 vols, London, 1875), i, 2.

beset Ireland and its ruling class, the Anglo-Irish, in the eighteenth century. At the close of the seventeenth century the victory of William of Orange and the re-establishment of a Protestant monarchy in Ireland heralded the rise of the Protestant Ascendancy. The Anglo-Irish were able to entrench themselves as Ireland's ruling class, putting an end to the political unrest of the previous century. Politically, the eighteenth century in Ireland was the age of the Anglo-Irish ascendancy and of the penal laws. Socially, it was a time which saw the Anglo-Irish develop a greater interest in improving the country, which they now firmly controlled. Not surprisingly, this century of turmoil and rebuilding saw the organization of charitable and academic societies dedicated towards that end.[5]

In the seventeenth century Ireland was beset by a series of revolutions and wars that devastated the country for decades and killed thousands. The 1691 victory of William III over James II brought this cycle to an end for a time at least, but the threat of rebellion remained and the Anglo-Irish were keenly aware of their status as a minority. Ireland's population remained relatively static through the late seventeenth and early eighteenth century: according to demographic estimates in 1687 Ireland's population was around 1.97 million; by 1706 it was between 1.75 and 2.06 million; and by 1712 it was between 1.98 and 2.32 million. It did not begin to grow significantly until the late eighteenth and early nineteenth centuries. During this period Protestants controlled most of the land and wealth, but as a numerical minority they felt vulnerable. In 1732, according to estimates, out of 386,902 families in Ireland, only 105,501 were Protestant. These numbers, though, are based on hearth tax returns, the only census taken in the period to classify the number of Catholic and Protestant families living in the districts. Hearth tax returns are not the most accurate measure of population, since they only record those families that had a hearth. They seriously understated the number of households in the country and the extent to which populations were understated varied by denomination. Catholics were more likely to be impoverished and thus more likely not to be recorded. The hearth tax returns also measured only families and not the sizes of families; they treated families and houses as interchangeable. In addition, anecdotal evidence from the period suggests that Catholics may have had larger families. Protestant families were more likely to have servants, but some of these servants were almost certainly Catholic. In all likelihood, Catholics composed between two-thirds and four-fifths of the total population.[6]

There are several reasons for a lack of sustained population growth during the

---

5 Barnard, *Kingdom of Ireland*, pp. 78–89.
6 S. J. Connolly, *Religion, law and power: the making of Protestant Ireland 1660–1760* (Oxford, 1992), pp. 144–5.

eighteenth century. Owing to endemic poverty the population was extremely vulnerable to periodic subsistence crises. Years of difficult growing seasons led to famines in 1674 and again in 1690. The harvests failed again in 1708–9 and in 1721–2, and there were reports of famine in 1728 and 1729.[7] A particularly severe famine hit in 1739–41. That famine was the 'worst human disaster' to hit Ireland in a hundred years and, while demographic data is incomplete, it may have had a higher death rate and greater population impact then even the Great Potato Famine.[8] By examining hearth tax returns, David Dickson theorized that the 1740–41 famine killed approximately 310,000 to 480,000 people out of a population of about 2.4 million; he concluded that there was excess mortality in the range of 13–20 per cent. So, while the Great Potato Famine killed significantly more people and led to mass emigration, it was also affecting a population that was three times larger.[9] Unlike most previous famines, the 1740–41 crisis was not brought on by war or uneven distribution of resources. It was caused by freak weather conditions. Extreme, unseasonable cold followed by months of unusual seasons caused massive crop failure; potatoes that provided a cushion against catastrophic famine were frozen and, once thawed, were inedible.[10] War and a continent-wide harvest failure meant that there was no external food supply to draw on.[11]

One contemporary described it:

> the most miserable scene of universal distress, that I have ever read of in history: want and misery in every face; the Rich unable almost, as they were willing to relieve the poor; the roads spread with dead and dying bodies; mankind of the colour of the docks and nettles which they fed on; two or three, sometimes more, on a car going to the grave for want of bearers to carry them, and many buried only in the fields and ditches where they perished.[12]

This writer estimated that between 200,000 and 400,000 people had perished from both hunger and associated diseases. It was a loss that was 'too great for this ill-peopled country to bear'.[13]

---

[7] Connolly, *Religion, law and power*, pp. 47–8; E. Margaret Crawford (ed.), 'William Wilde's table of Irish famines, 900–1850' in E. Margaret Crawford (ed.), *Famine: the Irish experience, 900–1900* (Edinburgh, 1989), pp. 11–13.
[8] David Dickson, 'The gap in famines: a useful myth?' in Margaret Crawford (ed.), *Famine: the Irish experience, 900–1900. Subsistence crises and famines in Ireland* (Edinburgh, 1989), p. 97.
[9] David Dickson, *Arctic Ireland: the extraordinary story of the great frost and forgotten famine of 1740–41* (Belfast, 1997), pp. 69, 72.
[10] N.L.I. MIC p4679.
[11] David Dickson, 'The other great Irish famine' in Cathal Poirteir (ed.), *The great Irish famine* (Cork, 1995), pp. 53–4; Dickson, 'The gap in famines', p. 97.
[12] *The groans of Ireland, in a letter to a member of parliament* (Dublin, 1741), p. 3.
[13] Ibid., p. 4.

Sir Richard Cox described the cultural impact in a letter:

> Mortality is now no longer heeded; the instances are so frequent. And burying the dead, which used to be one of the most religious acts amongst the Irish, is now become a burther: so that I am daily forced to make those who remain carry dead bodies to the churchyards, which would otherwise rot in the open air; otherwise I assure you the common practice is to let the tree lie where it falls, and if some good natured body covers it with the next ditch, it is the most to be expected. In short, by all I can learn, the dreadfullest civil war, or most raging plague never destroyed so many this season.[14]

Suffering of this magnitude demanded some sort of response for both humane and practical reasons. Food riots broke out in most cities and revolutionary unrest was a significant fear of the Protestant elite. For the most part, the emergency relief provided in 1740–41 was not radically different from earlier responses to similar tragedies, consisting primarily of voluntary efforts by the Church and local elites. Mostly these involved the subsidized or free distribution of food or employment schemes.[15] Katherine Conolly decided to employ the hungry to build a huge obelisk on the north-west skyline a mile from her stately Castletown House.[16] Relief efforts for the 1740–41 famine did require, however, a greater level of coordination and administration than those employed to mitigate past famines. Town authorities intervened in food markets in an attempt to control food prices and stave off rioting, and Church of Ireland parishes created local committees to organize the distribution of relief. In Dublin relief efforts were centralized out of the Dublin Workhouse, a measure which is credited with Dublin's relatively low mortality rate during the crisis.[17] Voluntary societies existed, but none took a leading role in responding to the crisis of those years.

The catastrophic famine of 1740–41 did contribute to the changing nature of philanthropy, and encouraged the development of additional charity societies.[18] Another result, however, as well as of previous famines, was mass vagrancy. In calamitous times, people left small farms and made their way to more populated cities and towns in search of food and work.[19] Ireland had no poor law and so many were left with little choice but to turn to begging.[20] Events

---

14 Armagh Public Library: Lodge MSS, 1741.
15 Dickson, 'The other great Irish famine', pp. 57–8.
16 Dickson, *Arctic Ireland*, p. 42.
17 Ibid., pp. 18–19; Dickson, 'The gap in famines', p. 106.
18 James Kelly, 'Charitable societies: their genesis and development' in James Kelly and Martyn J. Powell (eds), *Clubs and societies in eighteenth-century Ireland* (Dublin, 2010), p. 91.
19 Dickson, *Arctic Ireland*, p. 29.
20 Laurence M. Geary, '"The whole country was in motion": mendicancy and vagrancy in pre-famine Ireland' in Jacqueline R. Hill and Colm Lennon (eds), *Luxury and austerity* (Dublin, 1999), p. 121.

such as famines contributed to the changing demographic make-up of the city of Dublin. Between 1685 and 1725 the city's population more than doubled in size, going from 45,000 people to 92,000. This came during a period when the Irish population as a whole did experience any significant growth. By 1744, in part because of the famine, Dublin had grown to 112,000. It was the eleventh largest city in Europe and the centre of Irish politics, society, and manufacturing.[21] Dublin had always been a Protestant city; outside of the northern counties of Ulster, Dublin was the only place in Ireland where Protestants were in the majority. According to the 1732 hearth tax census Dublin was 68 per cent Protestant, but the Protestant majority was shrinking.[22] By the end of the century, the majority would be Catholic, partly as a result of a higher birth rate among Catholics[23] and partly because of migration from the countryside, an influx of mainly Catholic poor into the city during times of crisis. Many were beggars, but not all, and the influx of Catholic tradesmen caused tensions within the Protestant city.[24] The presence of large numbers of Irish poor was damaging to the prestige of the city and created a variety of social problems.[25]

Despite these problems, Dublin was a thriving city in the eighteenth century. It was the home of the Lord Lieutenant and the Irish parliament; the four central law courts were all situated in Dublin; and the only university in Ireland, Trinity College, was located in the centre of the city. Dublin's population growth did cause problems: overcrowding led to higher rents, making life difficult for the lower classes. The increasing prominence of the city placed burdens on the wealthier classes as well. As the centre of Anglo-Irish society, Dublin was also the centre of the conspicuous consumption that so frequently marked Anglo-Irish society; it was an increasingly expensive city and was regarded as being almost as expensive as London. The increasing grandeur of Dublin's winter season brought the gentry and aristocracy into the city and, of course, required them to spend a great deal of money.[26]

One of the reasons Dublin was so expensive was the obligation the wealthy felt to live a public life. In the eighteenth century Ireland's parliament met more frequently than in the times of unrest in the seventeenth century. Eventually

[21] Connolly, *Religion, law and power*, pp. 43–5.
[22] T. C. Barnard, *A new anatomy of Ireland: the Irish Protestants, 1649–1770* (New Haven, 2003), p. 2.
[23] Patrick Fagan, 'The population of Dublin in the eighteenth century with particular reference to the proportions of Protestants and Catholics' in *Eighteenth-Century Ireland*, 6 (1991), p. 134.
[24] J. T. Gilbert (ed.), *Calendar of ancient records of Dublin in the possession of the municipal corporation of that city* (18 vols, Dublin, 1896), vi, 379.
[25] Michelle Ryan, 'Divisions of poverty in early modern Dublin' in Augusteijn Joost and MaryAnn Lyons (eds), *Irish history: a research yearbook* (Dublin, 2002), p. 132.
[26] T. C. Barnard, *Making the grand figure: lives and possessions in Ireland, 1641–1770* (New Haven, 2004), pp. 282, 89, 302.

a pattern of regular sessions of between five and eight months every second year was established.[27] Ireland, like England, had a House of Lords and a House of Commons, but traditionally the Irish parliament played a limited role in actually governing the country; it met only rarely and did fairly little. This began to change in 1689, with the Glorious Revolution. The Irish parliament of 1692 almost immediately began to assert itself as an independent body that would not be dominated by the executive. The Lord Lieutenant, Henry Viscount Sidney, was shocked to hear discussions among the MPs of removing Poynings' Law.

Poynings' Law had a significant impact on how Ireland was governed before the Act of Union. Dating back to 1494, it stated that all Irish legislation was subject to the approval of the English Privy Council, and was a routine source of conflict between Ireland and England.[28] In the eighteenth century the English administration proved unable to apply the law as strictly as it had in the past and the Irish parliament was eventually able to establish a degree of legislative independence, despite its essentially subordinate position.[29] Poynings' Law was not the only source of conflict, however; the English government felt that it could overrule laws passed in Ireland, and the English parliament felt it had the right to legislate for Ireland as well. Ireland was considered to be subject to English rule because of Henry II's conquest in the twelfth century. The notion that the Irish were a free and unconquered people gained prominence among Irish Protestants in the late seventeenth century, in large part owing to such parliamentary disputes. The fundamental political issue between Ireland and England was whether Ireland had been conquered in the Middle Ages. If it had, then England had the right to legislate over Ireland. If it had not, if Ireland had consented to English occupation, then Ireland ought to retain legislative independence.[30] William Molyneux's 1698 treatise *The case of Ireland's being bound by Acts of Parliament in England, stated* argued that Ireland had, in fact, never been conquered; that Henry II had been invited in and the Irish kings had submitted voluntarily to his rule.[31] It is interesting to note that during these political debates with England Anglo-Irish writers, most of whom were of English descent and had lived in Ireland only a few generations, adopted an Irish identity and laid claim to the traditional rights of the Irish. Molyneux

[27] Connolly, *Religion, law and power*, p. 44.

[28] Ibid., pp. 74–5.

[29] James Kelly, *Poynings' Law and the making of law in Ireland, 1660–1800* (Dublin, 2007), pp. 358–9.

[30] Patrick Kelly, 'Conquest *versus* consent as the basis of the English title to Ireland in William Molyneux's *Case of Ireland stated*' in Ciaran Brady and Jane Ohlmeyer (eds), *British interventions in early modern Ireland* (Cambridge, 2005), p. 334.

[31] William Molyneux, *The case of Ireland's being bound by acts of parliament in England, stated* (Dublin, 1698).

contended that from the earliest instances of English dominion over Ireland all laws were not imposed on the people of Ireland but introduced with their consent.[32] What is to be expected about Molyneux's work is that in this justification of Irish liberty he was not in fact arguing for the liberty of all people in Ireland, but only a Protestant minority. Molyneux asserted that only the Anglo-Irish were the present-day heirs to the system established by Henry II. He did this by drawing distinctions between the 'people of Ireland' and 'Irish papists'. 'Irish papists' were guilty of rebellion against the king and therefore had forfeited their rights.[33]

While the 1692 parliament did not go so far as repealing Poynings' Law, it did assert itself and, because of the financial strain of years of war, had to be appeased by the crown. The Irish House of Commons refused to enact long-term hereditary revenues; instead, they relied on short-term parliamentary duties that had to be regularly renewed.[34] The need for funds required parliament to meet regularly in the 1690s, and eventually the pattern of meeting every second year, that would last throughout the eighteenth century, was established.[35] The conflict over the nature of Ireland's political relationship with Great Britain remained. Anglo-Irish politicians increasingly advocated their independence, but made little actual progress. Ireland was not granted a constitution until 1782. Meanwhile, the English parliament continued to assert its domination over the Irish parliament. In 1720 the British House of Lords passed the Declaratory Act, which stated that Ireland was subordinate to Great Britain, that the final court of appeal in Irish cases was the British House of Lords, and that the British Lords and Commons had power to pass laws over the kingdom and people of Ireland when they chose.[36]

The emerging importance of parliament and the role it played in social reform will be discussed further in later chapters. There were other factors that impacted on the political situation in Ireland, one of which was the rise of political parties. Like Britain in the early eighteenth century, Ireland came to be politically divided between two major political parties: Whigs and Tories. Ireland had its own distinct political issues and so, while the labels Whig and Tory existed in Ireland, they are defined along a slightly different axis. There were several major issues dividing the Irish polity, the first of which was religion. Irish Whigs, like their English counterparts, aligned with Protestant dissenters and Low Church Anglicanism. Irish Tories defended High Church

---

[32] Ibid., p. 39.

[33] Kelly, 'Conquest versus consent', p. 355.

[34] C. I. McGrath, The making of the eighteenth-century Irish constitution: government, parliament and the revenue, 1692–1714 (Dublin, 2000), p. 73.

[35] Connolly, Religion, law and power, pp. 75–8.

[36] S. J. Connolly, Divided kingdom: Ireland 1630–1800 (Oxford, 2008), p. 220.

privileges. The presence of a Catholic majority provided another element to the religious conflict. Irish Whigs supported strong repressive measures against Catholics, while Tories were less hostile, although they were far from being friendly towards Catholics. Catholics, in the instances in which they could vote, tended to support Tories because they were considered more moderate in their anti-Catholic policies. Tories also had the support of the Church of Ireland, while Whigs enjoyed support from Presbyterians centred in the north.[37] The issue of toleration was more problematic in Ireland, where the majority of the population was Catholic. About half of the Protestant population was Presbyterian, in contrast to the less than 10 per cent of the English population that were dissenters. Irish Whigs, unlike their English counterparts, had reservations about granting full political rights to dissenters.[38]

The second major point of contention between the parties was the implications of the Glorious Revolution. Among Irish Protestants there was no contention over the legitimacy of removing the Catholic king. Even committed High Churchmen and Tories did not protest the overthrow of James II. This was explained by William King, later to become the archbishop of Dublin, in his 1691 work *The State of the Protestants of Ireland under the late King James's Government*. King was committed to both Tory politics and High Church principles, but he rejected the traditional English Tory philosophy of passive obedience. James II, he argued, had designed to 'destroy and utterly ruin the Protestant religion, the Liberty and Property of the subjects in general, the English interest in Ireland in particular'. Under these circumstances, King argued, the Protestants of Ireland were left with no choice but to side with William III and Mary II or face 'slavery and destruction'.[39] Protestants in Ireland faced considerably more danger than Protestants in England from James II's policies. The acceptance of William III and Mary II was not an issue – that was agreed upon across party and class divides. Molyneux noted that 'your majesty has not in all your dominions a people more united and steady to your interests, than the Protestants of Ireland'.[40]

Irish Whigs and Tories may have agreed on the establishment of William and Mary, but there were still issues that divided them. Both sides accepted the Revolution and they stayed away from the more extreme elements that appeared in England. Irish Tories lacked the Jacobite element and Irish Whigs failed to embrace radical theories about a contractual monarchy. Irish Whigs

---

[37] Connolly, *Religion, law and power*, pp. 79–80.
[38] Connolly, *Divided kingdom*, p. 215.
[39] William King, *The state of the Protestants of Ireland under the late King James's government in which their carriage towards him is justified, and the absolute necessity of their endeavouring to be freed from his government, and of submitting to their present Majesties is demonstrated* (London, 1691), pp. 4–5.
[40] Molyneux, *The case of Ireland's Being Bound*, ii.

also rejected any association with the overthrow and execution of Charles I.[41] For Irish Protestants, whether Whig or Tory, acceptance of the Glorious Revolution had been about the immediate peril they found themselves in. The Revolution was justified because it rescued them from this danger. The complex ideological debates that arose in England to justify or condemn what had happened were not necessary in Ireland. By the early eighteenth century the divide was based as much on the pursuit of political advantage as it was on any commitment to abstract principles.[42]

One other major political development that defined Ireland in the eighteenth century was the penal laws. The question of how to treat the Catholic majority was a significant issue for members of parliament in the 1690s. The series of restrictive measures passed by the Irish parliament between the 1690s and the 1750s was not considered by Irish Protestants at the time to be penal laws. They preferred the term 'popery laws'. Catholics and dissenters were not legally penalized for practising their religion; the laws made the practice of Catholicism particularly difficult, but not illegal. Instead, Catholics and nonconformists faced a range of legal disabilities for their continued loyalty to churches other than the Church of Ireland.[43]

Irish Protestants feared the Catholic majority that surrounded them, and recent history supported this fear. Beginning in 1691, the parliament of Ireland passed a series of measures designed to restrict Catholic religious practice, property rights, and political participation.[44] These laws did not affect everyone equally, and they had little real impact on the majority of Catholic Irish who were poor, rural, and supported themselves through agriculture. However, Catholic priests, lawyers, gentlemen, and professionals were greatly affected.[45] First, Catholics were disarmed and barred from travelling abroad for a Catholic education. Later bishops, vicars, and members of religious orders were required to leave the kingdom by 1 May 1698; those who did not were subject to transportation and any who returned would be executed as traitors. In 1704 ordained priests were forbidden from entering the kingdom and priests already in the kingdom had to register with authorities and provide securities to ensure their good behaviour in the future. There was also a series of statutes dealing with property rights. Protestants who married Catholics either forfeited their estate to their nearest Protestant relation or faced all the restrictions imposed upon Catholics. Catholics were forbidden from inheriting land from Protestants. They could not purchase land, lend money, or take a lease longer than thirty

---

41 Connolly, *Divided kingdom*, p. 216.
42 Connolly, *Religion, law and power*, p. 83.
43 Ibid., pp. 263–4.
44 Connolly, *Divided Kingdom*, p. 198.
45 Barnard, *Kingdom of Ireland*, p. 53.

years. Catholic estates were to be divided equally among all heirs and could not be kept intact via primogeniture. Any Protestant who became aware of violations to these property laws could file a bill of discovery which entitled them to the Catholic party's share of the proceeds. In 1698 an Irish Act was passed, which repeated the substance of an earlier English act, requiring all members of parliament or those who practised law to repudiate Catholic doctrine. They were also required to educate their children as Protestants. From 1704 on Catholics could vote only if they took the oath of abjuration, denying the exiled James II's claim to the throne. In 1728 an act was passed finally excluding them from voting in parliamentary elections.[46]

It seems clear that there was no consistent agenda on the part of Irish Protestants. The laws were passed over several decades, and over that time the priorities of the Anglo-Irish changed. Early measures were primarily defensive, many reiterating principles already in operation. It had long been the case that Catholics could not sit in the House of Commons or hold government offices. Such measures, though, had been accomplished by executive power and after their recent experience with James II and their fears of arbitrary government it seemed prudent to the Anglo-Irish to set such principles down as legal statutes. Later measures were clearly about eroding the Catholic landed interest that remained, either by forcing their conversion or breaking up their estates.[47]

If the intention of the penal laws was to destroy the Catholic Church then they quite obviously failed, and while the penal laws did make the practice of Catholicism difficult there was no sustained effort by the state to bring the mass of Catholics into the Church of Ireland. As will be discussed later in this study, the Church of Ireland and the Anglo-Irish did engage in several attempts to convert the Catholic population, but none was sustained enough or had broad enough support to be effective. Many Anglo-Irish seemed to rely on the idea that once the Catholic clergy died out, as a result of the penal laws, the people would have little choice but to become Protestant. The true impact of the penal laws is difficult to determine, however. The variety of legal disabilities against Catholics affected the bulk of the Catholic population in only a few ways. They were prohibited from taking long leases, which hurt them and also hurt the land, and the practice of their religion became more difficult. Some wealthier Catholics did conform to the Established Church, though their sincerity in this was always suspect and their conversions were probably a short-term response to immediate circumstances.[48] The penal laws did serve to close various

---

[46] Thomas Bartlett, *The fall and rise of the Irish nation: the Catholic question 1690–1830* (Savage, MD, 1992), ch. 2.
[47] Connolly, *Divided kingdom*, p. 199.
[48] Connolly, *Religion, law and power*, p. 308.

professional avenues to Catholics; there were a limited number of professions considered suitable for gentlemen and the only one available to Catholics was medicine.[49] The impact of the penal laws was not only personal, moreover, but political and economic. They did succeed in at least temporarily eliminating the threat of Catholic Jacobites.

Finally, there is the Anglo-Irish themselves. As the group with a monopoly on power, they were the primary movers in eighteenth-century social reform movements. Catholics, by virtue of their general lack of wealth and the political disabilities of the penal laws, were unable to organize into the same types of voluntary societies to address social issues. Presbyterians did take action over social issues in the local areas where they dominated. The Anglo-Irish as a class, however, were not defined by their reforming interests, as we shall see later in this study, and active reformers were only a small segment of Anglo-Irish society. At a basic level the Anglo-Irish were Church of Ireland Protestants descended from English settlers, most of whom had come to Ireland in the sixteenth and seventeenth centuries. In the eighteenth century, the Anglo-Irish were primarily composed of a group known earlier as the New English, Protestant settlers of English descent, as opposed to the Old English settlers, many of whom dated back to the Norman Conquest and remained Catholic. By and large, the Anglo-Irish were settlers from the Cromwellian era, though technically any conformist Protestant could claim membership of the Anglo-Irish, regardless of their ethnic background.[50] The Protestant population living in the north were neither the Old nor the New English: they were primarily Scottish Presbyterian settlers lured to the north by promises of land as part of the Plantation of Ulster scheme.

The Anglo-Irish identity is a complex one and historians have long found it difficult to define them as a group.[51] Indeed, the Anglo-Irish struggled to define themselves. The issue was whether or not they were English or Irish or in some way both. The eighteenth century was a period in which Anglo-Irish perceptions of themselves underwent a radical transformation, from seeing themselves as primarily English and representing English interests to developing a sense of Irish identity and representing their own interests. It seems that the Anglo-Irish definition of themselves depended on the context; Anglo-Irish writers would refer to themselves as the 'Irish nation', but also laid claims to

---

[49] Patrick Fagan, *Catholics in a Protestant country: the papist constituency in eighteenth-century Dublin* (Dublin, 1998), p. 77.

[50] Connolly, *Religion, law and power*, p. 7.

[51] J. C. Beckett, *The Anglo-Irish tradition* (Ithaca, NY, 1976), p. 11; W. J. McCormack, *Ascendancy and tradition in Anglo-Irish literary history from 1789 to 1939* (Oxford, 1985), p. 88; A. P. W. Malcomson, *John Foster: the politics of the Anglo-Irish ascendancy* (Oxford, 1978), pp. xvii–xix; Connolly, *Religion, law and power*, pp. 103–4.

the rights of English citizens. This developing sense of Irish identity parallels their increasing interest in philanthropy and improvement. Their desire to lay claim to an Irish identity coincided with their desire to transform Ireland and the Irish in tangible ways.

From the English perspective, the Irish were something to be either feared or mocked. By the eighteenth century, most portrayals focused on the Irish as an object of ridicule, a comically backward figure. In this regard the English did not differentiate between Anglo-Irish settlers and the Gaelic Irish.[52] Many Anglo-Irish may have preferred to see themselves as primarily English still, but from an English perspective they were Irish. English contempt for them was only one complicating factor. A variety of political squabbles with England in the eighteenth century led the Anglo-Irish to turn inwards and develop a new idea of themselves. At the same time, they resisted adhering to the emerging British identity, which would have placed them in community with the Presbyterian Ulster Scots.[53]

At the end of the seventeenth century it appears that the Anglo-Irish tended to define themselves as English, and many were strong supporters of a union with England. Economic and political conflicts in the eighteenth century, combined with the rejection by England of a union with Ireland in favour of one solely with Scotland, stimulated Anglo-Irish interest in 'the Irish dimension of Anglo-Irishness'.[54] Part of this interest emerged in a newfound fascination among Protestants with Ireland's ancient past. First, there was a growing interest in the person of St Patrick, the founder of the Christian church in Ireland. In this period the Church of Ireland was eager to downplay the idea that it was an English transplant. To accomplish this, the Established Church espoused the idea that they alone were the proper heirs of St Patrick, that they were the true church in Ireland and their religion represented pure, uncorrupted Christianity, just as St Patrick's did.[55] The Anglo-Irish interest in these aspects of Ireland's past was a way of asserting their right to authority. References to St Patrick supported the legitimacy of the Church of Ireland. References to the

[52] D. W. Hayton, 'From barbarian to burlesque: the changing stereotype of the Irish' in D. W. Hayton (ed.), *The Anglo-Irish experience, 1680–1730: religion, identity and patriotism* (Woodbridge, 2012), p. 22.

[53] D. W. Hayton, 'Anglo-Irish attitudes: shifting perceptions of national identity' in D. W. Hayton (ed.), *The Anglo-Irish experience, 1680–1730: religion, identity and patriotism* (Woodbridge, 2012), p. 43.

[54] Joseph Leerssen, *Mere Irish and Fíor-Ghael: studies in the idea of Irish nationality, its development and literary expression prior to the nineteenth century* (Cork, 1996), pp. 294–5; Colin Kidd, 'Gaelic antiquity and national identity in Enlightenment Ireland and Scotland' in *The English Historical Review*, 109, no. 434 (1994), p. 1201.

[55] Colin Kidd, *British identities before nationalism: ethnicity and nationhood in the Atlantic world, 1600–1800* (Cambridge, 1999), p. 165.

Gaelic past, and to its government, provided support for Anglo-Irish political supremacy.[56]

William Molyneux's *The Case of Ireland Stated* is one of the most famous examples of Anglo-Irish political writing from this period. Molyneux's tract emerged primarily in response to an English Act in 1697 which banned the export of Irish woollen cloth. Molyneux at no point in the piece refers to himself or the ruling class that he represents as Irish, though he does use the term 'people of Ireland' to refer collectively to all inhabitants of Ireland.[57] He contends that most of the 'present people of Ireland' are descendants of the English or British settlers and that there are very few of the 'Ancient Irish' left.[58] Both Henry Maxwell and Sir Richard Cox made similar statements. They wrote defensively of the native Irish to an English audience but still shied away from espousing an Irish identity for themselves.[59] All of these works pre-date the 1707 Act of Union between England and Scotland. Following the suppression of the wool trade many, such as Maxwell, thought a formal union would benefit Ireland's economy.

The idea of a political union with England was widely supported by the Anglo-Irish in the late seventeenth century. The rejection of these overtures by the English parliament, as well as continued conflicts over economic interests, provided the political background for a growing awareness in the Anglo-Irish that they had distinct and separate interests from England. They came to believe that rather than simply representing the English interest in Ireland, their own interests were distinctly different from those of the English government. Underlying this was a complex trade relationship with England, the handling of which by the English parliament led many Anglo-Irish to feel ill-used. Sir Richard Cox wrote of it, 'I wish this be not the case of Ireland, that we desire to get so much from them, till at last we put them out of a condition to pay us anything.'[60] Cox was writing on a bill to prevent the exportation of woollen goods, the same matter which had inspired William Molyneux, and went on to warn that this policy endangered the English position in Ireland, asserting 'by bills of this kind we shall not make the possession of that Kingdom insecure to us'.[61] The Woollen Goods Act was, in fact, the motivation for

---

[56] Ibid., p. 148.

[57] Molyneux, *The case of Ireland's being bound*, p. 39.

[58] Ibid., p. 34.

[59] Henry Maxwell, *An essay upon an union of Ireland with England: most humbly offered to the consideration of the queen's most excellent majesty, and both houses of parliament* (Dublin, 1704), pp. 12–13; Sir Richard Cox, *An essay for the conversion of the Irish shewing that 'tis their duty and interest to become Protestants: in a letter to themselves* (Dublin, 1698), p. 10.

[60] Sir Richard Cox, *Some thoughts on the bill depending before the right honourable the House of Lords, for prohibiting the exportation of the woollen manufactures of Ireland to foreign parts. Humbly offer'd to their lordships. Written in the year, 1698* (Dublin, 1740), p. 6.

[61] Ibid.

a number of similar tracts, works which were crucial to the development of Anglo-Irish identity and a sense of Anglo-Irish patriotism.

James Smyth has argued that the Anglo-Irish mindset, in hindsight, is clearly revealed to be leaning towards an 'affirmation of Irishness' in this period, but that was not apparent at the time. Smyth also speaks about the 'duality of the colonial mind' that influenced Anglo-Irish thinking on these subjects, the ways in which they could be both English and Irish. He cites Samuel Madden, who wrote that Irish Protestants 'are envied as Englishmen in Ireland and maligned as Irish in England'.[62] This raises another issue with regards to the Anglo-Irish: whether or not they had a colonial mindset. This question has some bearing on how the Anglo-Irish saw themselves. Certainly, in the late seventeenth century, they saw themselves as English. Writing in 1698, Cox made it clear that he perceived the Anglo-Irish as English, calling them 'the English of that country'.[63] He attempted to reaffirm the common ties of the English and the Anglo-Irish, writing: 'they are Englishmen sent over to conquer Ireland, your Countrymen, your Brothers, your Sons, your Relations your Acquaintance; governed by the same King, the same Laws; of the same Religion, and in the same Interest, and equally engaged in the same common cause of Liberty'.[64] Cox also referred to Ireland in that same essay as a colony and comments on how it should best be managed. Unlike Molyneux, he had no qualms about regarding Ireland as a conquered nation. In another essay he stated that 'Ireland was at first conquered by the blood and treasure of England, and thereby, and by the repeated oaths and submissions of the Irish, became part of the dominion of England, and a subordinate kingdom to that Crown.'[65]

Cox was writing in 1698, however, and, by 1707, after the passage of the bill on woollen manufactures and the subsequent rejection of a union, many Anglo-Irish had some cause to re-evaluate their position. They now had to base claims for equality on Ireland's rights as a distinct kingdom.[66] Molyneux was an early example of this. In his argument against the woollen Act he wrote that the English parliament ought to have no authority over the Irish one. Cox, meanwhile, accepted the right of the English parliament to make such laws, but attempted to dissuade them from making this particular one. Of course, at the heart of Cox's argument was an explicit acceptance of the status of Ireland as a colony of England.

---

[62] James Smyth, '"Like amphibious animals": Irish Protestants, ancient Britons, 1691–1707' in *The Historical Journal*, 36, no. 4 (1993), p. 787.

[63] Cox, *Some thoughts on the bill*, p. 7.

[64] Ibid., p. 16.

[65] Cox, *An Essay for the Conversion of the Irish*, p. 35.

[66] J. C. Beckett, *The making of modern Ireland: 1603–1923* (new ed., London, 1981), p. 161.

To many Anglo-Irish the greatest insult of the Woollen Act was that it was aimed by the English parliament at its own people.[67] Most arguments against the Act took a similar approach to Cox. They attempted to persuade the English people and parliament that the Act was not in their best interest after all, but few contested their right to make it. John Hovell tried to show that the Act, in hindering the development of the woollen industry in Ireland, was detrimental to the interests of the Anglo-Irish, and therefore to the interests of England.[68] His essay betrays a sense of exasperation at the English treatment of Ireland and its people, writing that one 'would think that the people of this Island were some deadly enemies'.[69] Unlike Cox, he avoided using the word 'colony' and, while he did not explicitly attack English supremacy over Ireland, there does appear to be some frustration with it. He also maintained that Ireland is 'an English Protestant country' with more in common with England than with Wales.[70] Maxwell took a similar stance with regards to Wales several years later in his attempt to argue for a union, saying that 'it was more difficult to unite Wales, then it is now to unite Ireland', largely because in Ireland the 'language, customs, and laws' were all the same.[71] The Gaelic-speaking Irish population features in the arguments of none of these writers; yet, at the same time, there is ample evidence that in their dealings with each other they shared a common anxiety regarding the Catholic population.

These essays also reveal the origins of an Anglo-Irish identity that is neither distinctly English nor distinctly Irish. The term Irish held negative connotations for Anglo-Irish writers, who associated it initially with a barbarous way of life that they held in contempt, as well as with political dissidence. This helps to account for the reluctance during much of the eighteenth century to refer to themselves as Irish, even as they slowly came to construct a new definition of what Irishness was. At the same time that they were redefining Irishness, economic and political conflicts with England led to cracks emerging in that previously close relationship. This increased ownership of and investment in an Irish identity manifested itself not only in political pamphlets but also in the culture of improvement.

It is important to define the terminology that will be used throughout this book. Concepts such as 'reform' and 'improvement' have distinct meanings within an eighteenth-century context. In his study of the development of public welfare in England, historian Paul Slack argues for a gradual shift from

---

[67] Smyth, '"Like amphibious animals"', p. 794.

[68] John Hovell, *A discourse on the woollen manufactury of Ireland and the consequences of prohibiting its exportation* (Dublin, 1698), pp. 1–7.

[69] Ibid., p. 8.

[70] Ibid.

[71] Maxwell, *An essay upon an union of Ireland with England*, p. 12.

'reformation', or radical and comprehensive innovation, to 'improvement', gradual and more piecemeal changes.[72] The term 'improvement' gradually became more prominent than 'reformation'. A. G. Craig, however, has a different conception of the term 'reformation', arguing for a distinction between the term 'reformation', as it was used by late seventeenth-century moral reformers, and 'reform' as it was used by eighteenth-century philanthropists. Craig believes that 'reformation' was marked by the idea of circularity, a return to the almost idealized Tudor past. 'Reform', meanwhile, as it would come to be used by later philanthropists, was more about progress than regression.[73] This book primarily uses 'improvement', the term which was most often used at the time.

In Ireland and in Irish historiography 'improvement' refers to a long-term agenda on the part of Protestants dating from the late sixteenth and mid-seventeenth centuries to 'improve' Ireland. The intention was to Anglicize Ireland: to make its systems of government and law more like those of England and to spread English styles of dress, language, and agriculture. By the eighteenth century the term 'improvement' had broader implications which, this book argues, contained a moral element. What did not change was the basic intention of making Ireland and the Irish more English.

What happened in Ireland during the eighteenth century was not about reformation. Ireland's Reformation of Manners Societies of the late seventeenth century were a distinct movement. The reformers of the eighteenth century did not use the term 'reformation' with respect to their projects or ideals. The term most used at the time, as noted, was 'improvement', a word which had more meanings in the eighteenth century than it does now.[74] Usually 'improvement' referred to very practical changes in agriculture or industry that improved yield or production, making such enterprises more profitable. Peter Borsay contended that 'improvement' in the broadest sense was one of the most influential concepts of the age in the British Isles. It 'resonated most closely with the timbre of the time, and set the agenda for the future'.[75] Borsay defined the improvement movement as containing several basic elements. Most importantly, there was a commitment to change, a belief in the capacity of man to better themselves and the world, and, finally, morality. In the eighteenth century, 'improvement' expanded beyond its economic or political sense to become a moral concept as

---

[72] Paul Slack, *Reformation to improvement: public welfare in early modern England* (Oxford, 1999), p. 2.
[73] A. G. Craig, 'The movement for reformation of manners' (Ph.D. thesis, University of Edinburgh, 1980).
[74] Asa Briggs, *The age of improvement, 1783–1867* (New York, 1959), pp. 2–3.
[75] Peter Borsay, 'The culture of improvement' in Paul Langford (ed.), *The eighteenth century, 1688–1815* (Oxford, 2002), p. 183.

well.[76] This book deals with 'improvement' in its broadest sense and includes charitable schemes such as voluntary hospitals and charity schools as examples of improvement. The philanthropists who founded voluntary hospitals and charity schools were committed to positive and progressive change, believed in the capacity of man to affect that change, and possessed strong moral convictions as to the righteousness of what they were doing.

Toby Barnard once argued that improvers 'tended to be conquerors and colonizers'.[77] Underpinning most ideas of improvement in Ireland was a belief in the basic superiority of the English way of life. The Improvers were not the entirety of Anglo-Irish society, however. Improvement movements, like most philanthropic endeavours, were dominated by the wealthy and well-connected. The Anglo-Irish believed in the superiority of the English way of life and in their right to impose it on Ireland, but this book demonstrates that their actions were motivated by a variety of factors. 'Improvement' in Ireland acquired additional meanings in the course of the eighteenth century; it was not simply a program of Anglicization or of furthering a colonial regime. A complicating factor was the increasingly problematic relationship between England and the Anglo-Irish gentry. For a variety of reasons, many in the Anglo-Irish ruling elite began to develop a new sense of national identity and a new appreciation for some of Ireland's distinctive elements.

This book considers a variety of projects as examples of the age of improvement, some of which have not been traditionally defined as improvement schemes. Using the term 'improvement' broadly, it encompasses charitable as well as economic initiatives. The work of Mercer's Hospital to provide care for the sick does not seem to have been about furthering a colonial agenda, nor did it promote new methods of agriculture and manufacturing. Instead, voluntary hospitals drew upon the same moral and economic imperative that motivated other improvement schemes. Other examples, such as the Dublin Society and the Incorporated Society, connect much more overtly with a narrower definition of improvement. This study demonstrates that there were a variety of connections between these organizations. They shared a common membership and a common language, and in some ways advanced a common agenda.

They also shared a common structure: they were all voluntary societies. The eighteenth-century enthusiasm for voluntary societies was not limited to charity societies. There were clubs and societies for a broad array of purposes and activities, ranging from the political to the social. These associations were an important part of eighteenth-century urban civil society.[78] In Ireland

---

[76] Ibid., pp. 183–4.
[77] Barnard, *Improving Ireland*, p. 13.
[78] Peter Clark, *British clubs and societies 1580–1800* (Oxford, 2000), pp. 141–2.

they were strongest in Dublin, but could also be found outside the metropolis. Voluntary societies were at once an outlet for sociability and conviviality for their members and, frequently, an entryway into civil society.[79] It was only natural to combine the enthusiasm for improvement and philanthropy with the enthusiasm for voluntary societies.[80] Given the level of poverty in Ireland and the lack of a national system of poor relief, charity was a natural field for associational culture to insert itself.[81] Voluntary charitable societies brought a new sort of self-interested benevolence to philanthropy. Members conceived of their actions as altruistic, but at the same time they benefited both tangibly and intangibly from their membership in the associational world and from the activities of their organizations.

Part of that common agenda stemmed from a shared sense of Enlightenment values. For years many historians of the Enlightenment have dismissed or refused to engage with the idea of an Irish Enlightenment. The historian Gerard O'Brien once noted that Ireland 'appeared to have the trappings of an Enlightenment but none of its essence'.[82] Toby Barnard concluded that Ireland had only 'something akin to an enlightenment, but more practical than speculative'.[83] Part of this issue has been how the Enlightenment is defined. In their well-known volume *The Enlightenment in national context*, Roy Porter and Mikulas Teich left out Ireland presumably because they felt it did not have the 'rationality, toleration, humanitarianism, [and] utilitarianism' they felt was common to all national Enlightenments.[84] In recent years Irish historians have become more assertive in arguing for the existence of an Irish Enlightenment, and a great deal of recent work has demonstrated that there was both an Enlightenment in Ireland and an Irish Enlightenment.[85] Graham Gargett and Geraldine Sheridan's *Ireland and the French Enlightenment* has proved the presence of Enlightenment culture in Ireland. Maire Kennedy, in particular, established that Irish readers had access to the major works of the French Enlightenment.[86]

---

79 James Kelly and Martyn J. Powell, 'Introduction' in James Kelly and Martyn J. Powell (eds), *Clubs and Societies in Eighteenth-Century Ireland* (Dublin, 2010), pp. 17–35.
80 T. C. Barnard, 'The Dublin Society and other improving societies, 1731–85' in James Kelly and Martyn J. Powell (eds), *Clubs and Societies in Eighteenth-Century Ireland* (Dublin, 2010), p. 53.
81 Kelly, 'Charitable Societies', p. 90.
82 Gerard O'Brien, 'Scotland, Ireland and the antithesis of Enlightenment' in Sean Connolly, Allan Houston, and Robert Morris (eds), *Conflict, identity, and economic development: Ireland and Scotland, 1600–1939* (Preston, 1995), p. 125.
83 Barnard, *Kingdom of Ireland*, p. 11.
84 Mikulas Teich, 'Afterword' in Roy Porter and Mikulas Teich (eds), *The Enlightenment in national context* (Cambridge, 1981), p. 216.
85 Michael Brown, 'Was there an Irish Enlightenment? The case of the Anglicans' in Richard Butterwick and Simon Davies (eds), *Peripheries of the Enlightenment* (Oxford, 2008), pp. 49–50.
86 Graham Gargett and Geraldine Sheridan (eds), *Ireland and the French Enlightenment, 1700–1800*

It is clear that the Enlightenment reached Ireland; what is more contro-versial is whether or not Ireland had a unique Enlightenment culture of its own and what precisely the nature of that culture was. This book demonstrates the connections between the Irish Enlightenment and new methods of philan-thropy. It illustrates that Ireland possessed a vibrant Enlightenment culture and that this culture changed how the Anglo-Irish approached charity, the economy, and the government of Ireland. Investigating the culture of improvement and philanthropy is one way to approach these issues. Improvement was a core element of the Enlightenment in England,[87] and in Ireland improvement was a way to put Enlightened ideas into action. The culture of improvement and philanthropy was informed by an Enlightened agenda that focused on human betterment. The idea was to use a variety of philanthropic societies to remodel Irish culture to make it more civil, rational, and stable. Like that of England, Ireland's Enlightenment was not secular: Irish improvers maintained close ties with the Church of Ireland. Ireland's Enlightened culture was also practical, however, with Irish improvers focused on finding and enacting rational solutions to a variety of social and economic problems. For the Anglo-Irish philanthropy was not simply a way of selflessly developing Ireland – it was also a way of exercising social control and maintaining a social order that benefited them.

Most studies of improvement and reform in Ireland have focused on its disparate elements. This book argues for the commonalities that existed between different types of reformist organizations and the different strands of this movement. It does not aim to present a comprehensive account of all reform and improvement projects and organizations in early modern Ireland. Instead, it focuses on several examples of the different strands of that movement. Most charity movements were founded and run by a combination of Protestant social elite and Church of Ireland clergy. The Church of Ireland was a major player in the reform and improvement movements and spearheaded several, such as the Incorporated Society. The first chapter focuses more generally on the involvement of the Church of Ireland and its clergy in improvement and reform movements. As the established church, the Church of Ireland had certain community responsibilities, such as poor relief, but many ministers went beyond this in their involvement in philanthropic activity. One of the largest fields of church activity was proselytism.

The following chapter, on educational charity, examines the Incorporated Society for Promoting English Protestant Working Schools in Ireland. The Incorporated Society was chartered in 1733, though it grew out of the earlier

(London, 1999); Maire Kennedy, 'Reading the Enlightenment in eighteenth-century Ireland' in *Eighteenth-Century Studies*, XLV, no. 3 (2012), pp. 377–8.

[87] Borsay, 'The culture of improvement', p. 184.

charity school movement. Charity schools were run privately and established individually, whereas the charter schools were a large-scale attempt to use charitable education as a means of converting the rural Catholic population. The Incorporated Society represents the largest initiative for educational charity in this period. As a major nationwide initiative, it maintained close ties with the Church of Ireland, the Irish parliament, and the Royal Dublin Society.

Chapter 3 explores medical charity. The eighteenth century saw several different forms of medical charity, including county infirmaries and fever hospitals. The earliest was the voluntary hospitals. The focus of this chapter is on Mercer's Hospital in Dublin, which was founded in 1734 and was one of eight voluntary hospitals opened in the city in the eighteenth century. Mercer's Hospital is representative of other voluntary hospitals and faced the same issues of fundraising and finances as these institutions. Its admission policy was not restricted to specific types of cases, unlike the Lying-In Hospital or the Incurables Hospitals, which is why it is taken as the focus of this chapter.

Related to educational and medical charity but also distinct in many ways were scientific societies. The Dublin Society, later the Royal Dublin Society, was founded in 1731 by prominent members of the Anglo-Irish elite and focused on improving agriculture and industry in Ireland. While medical and educational charities were constituted to address specific social problems, generally related to poverty, the Dublin Society was concerned with improving the economic well-being of Ireland. By improving agricultural production it hoped to make Ireland as a nation more generally prosperous.[88] This chapter argues that the Dublin Society's focus was broader then just economic improvement and that it can also be viewed as a philanthropic organization.

The corporatization of philanthropic structures resulted in many profound changes in the way charity work was carried out. It also saw alterations in those who were involved with charity. The creation of voluntary societies caused a recasting of gender roles when it came to charitable and philanthropic works: they were almost exclusively male, allowing few roles to those women who were interested in philanthropy. Chapter 5 examines that change, as well as how women adapted to these new structures and managed to remain active philanthropists. It focuses specifically on the work of Lady Arbella Denny, one of the most respected philanthropists in eighteenth-century Ireland. Lady Arbella worked closely with the Foundling Hospital and founded the Dublin Magdalene Asylum, an organization whose unique operating structure reveals the complex interplay between gender and philanthropy in this period.

[88] James Meenan and Desmond Clarke, 'The RDS 1731–1981' in *RDS: The Royal Dublin Society, 1731–1981*, pp. 1–10.

Insufficient funds were a constant problem for many societies, and they relied to varying degrees on parliamentary support. The idea of government playing an active role, or any role, in the social welfare of its citizens was a new concept. The parliament of Ireland, however, not only routinely awarded grants of money to many prominent voluntary societies in order to support their work, but also sponsored its own initiatives to deal with the problems of rampant poverty. Chapter 6 discusses the role that parliament played in funding the Incorporated Society, Mercer's Hospital, and the Dublin Society. It also deals with state-sponsored philanthropic initiatives such as the Dublin Workhouse and Foundling Hospital and the House of Industry.

While this book will examine many different aspects of Irish social reform movements it does not offer a comprehensive or exhaustive study of the entire movement. A number of voluntary societies arose in the eighteenth century and this study examines only a few of them. Because of its focus on associational charity, less coverage is given to the roles of individuals, both within those organizations and acting alone. There is still a lot of work to be done on the lives of individual 'improvers'.[89] However, the work of certain prominent individuals, such as Thomas Prior, John Putland, and Lady Arbella Denny, is discussed.

This book also focuses on Protestant-led reform movements, and more specifically on Anglo-Irish movements. Presbyterians constituted a substantial portion of the Irish Protestant population, particularly in the north, but in most cases did not cooperate with Anglicans on these endeavours. Presbyterians did involve themselves in philanthropy, and also worked to convert the native Catholic population, but their focus was in the north, where they dominated. The Anglo-Irish ascendancy did not regard Presbyterians as harshly as it did Catholics, but still placed restrictions on nonconformists. The Catholic population of Ireland appear in this book primarily as the objects of charity. The penal laws of the era made it difficult for Catholics to establish the organizational structures for philanthropy work. In addition, fewer Catholics had the financial resources to act as philanthropists. These disadvantages may have actually made it easier for Catholic women than their Protestant counterparts to engage in charity work, a subject which will be addressed.[90] Catholic charity was more individual for much of this period, and Catholics were excluded from involvement in the organizations focused on here.

The research here also concentrates on Dublin. Each of the societies examined was based in Dublin, as were most of the prominent individuals,

---

[89] Andrew Sneddon, 'Bishop Francis Hutchinson (1660–1739): a case study in the eighteenth-century culture of "improvement"' in *Irish Historical Studies*, 35, no. 139 (2007), p. 292.

[90] Rosemary Raughter, 'A discreet benevolence: female philanthropy and the Catholic resurgence in eighteenth-century Ireland' in *Women's History Review*, 6, no. 4 (1997), p. 466.

though not all were concerned exclusively with Dublin's social problems. Dublin was both the largest city in Ireland and the centre of Anglo-Irish society, while exemplifying many of the social problems that the voluntary societies sought to address. While these societies were administered from Dublin, not all of their actions focused solely on the city, however. The Incorporated Society, for example, concentrated on more rural areas and hoped to spread Protestantism in predominantly Catholic areas. The Dublin Society was also concerned with the entire country and did not limit its activities to the Dublin metropolitan area.

As with any study that deals directly or indirectly with subalterns, there are many questions that cannot be satisfactorily answered. Given the limitations inherent in the sources examined here, it is virtually impossible to judge the true effectiveness of the organizations studied. However, the continued growth and participation in social reform movements charted in this study provides compelling evidence for their significance. These organizations represented a unique attempt to serve the interests and aspirations of the nation while furthering a religious and Enlightenment agenda.

Eighteenth-century Ireland was filled with a particular combination of political unrest and economic uncertainty. It is within this context that the Anglo-Irish began to focus on improving Ireland. Social reform movements in Ireland arose out of an Enlightenment belief in the perfectibility of society and out of a paternalistic desire to help the native Irish and the poor. Reform also arose out of a sense of necessity. Many in the Anglo-Irish Ascendancy believed that their government and therefore their lives would never be secure while the country remained impoverished and populated by Catholics. To address these concerns, improvement-minded individuals turned to a new form of social action. They began to found voluntary societies, funded on the joint-stock model. They believed that these organizations offered a solution to the social problems they saw all around them. In the end, eighteenth-century improvers did not eliminate Ireland's social problems, but they did fundamentally change how society addressed those problems.

1

'The Worst in Christendom': The Church of Ireland and Improvement

On 17 July 1690 Queen Mary II of England wrote to her husband, King William III, who was with his army in Ireland. William had recently won a significant victory over his father-in-law, James II, at the Battle of the Boyne and, while final victory over the Jacobite forces in Ireland would take another year, the victory at the Boyne effectively secured William and Mary's reign in Ireland. Mary wrote to her husband of her joy at the news of his victory, but also mentioned to him a matter that deeply concerned her: the Church of Ireland. 'I must put you in mind of one thing, believing it now the season, which is, that you would take care of the church in Ireland. Everybody agrees that it is the worst in Christendom.'[1]

Mary did not expand much on what made the Church of Ireland 'the worst in Christendom' other than the large number of vacant bishoprics at that time. However, she was hardly alone in noting that the Church of Ireland was deeply troubled. Henry Hyde, earl of Clarendon, wrote in 1686, during his tenure as Lord Lieutenant, that 'the state of the church is very miserable … very few of the clergy reside on their cures, but employ pitiful curates which necessitates the people to look after a Romish priest or a Nonconformist preacher, and there are plenty of both'.[2] Clarendon was especially concerned with the large numbers of non-resident clergy at all levels of the Church. He complained that John Vesey, archbishop of Tuam, had been absent for three years, while Thomas Hacket, bishop of Down and Connor, had been absent for six.[3] Non-residency and pluralism were some of the problems afflicting the Church of Ireland at the end of the seventeenth century and, by the eighteenth century, the situation had not changed. The position of the Anglican Church as the legally established state Church of the island was made more secure with William III's victory, but this did little to solve the problems of poverty, pluralism, and non-residence that affected the Church.

The Church of Ireland in the eighteenth century was something of a contradiction. It was the officially established Church of the island, but only a

---

[1] Sir John Dalrymple, *Memoirs of Great Britain and Ireland* (2 vols, London, 1773), ii, appendix ii, 132.
[2] Quoted in J. A. Froude, *The English in Ireland in the eighteenth century* (3 vols, London, 1872), i, 158.
[3] Ibid.

minority of inhabitants were adherents. It had the backing of the state, but its position was insecure and it felt itself under constant threat from Catholics and nonconformists. In a 1737 pamphlet, written as a letter from a gentleman to his son, the anonymous author laid out a number of reasons why young men should not choose the Church as a profession. 'The present Establishment seems to me in a tottering way, and things ripening gradually to its Dissolution.'[4] The belief widely held in the eighteenth century by those both inside and outside the Church of Ireland was that the institution was facing a variety of problems and was in serious disarray. This conviction motivated the actions and beliefs of many of its members. This was also a widely held belief about Ireland as a whole, and one which led to the founding of a number of voluntary societies to address these problems. Despite its own internal problems, the Church of Ireland took an active role in encouraging the improvement of Ireland through both religiously motivated charities and scientific and agricultural societies. This chapter argues that the Church's involvement in philanthropy and improvement demonstrates its institutional insecurity. It focuses on the Church as an object of improvement and how involvement in reform initiatives served to address the problems troubling it. The involvement of the Church in improvement was motivated by benevolent concern for the country and the people of Ireland, as well as a pragmatic desire to improve its own position and situation.

The events of the seventeenth century are essential to an understanding of the Anglican mindset in Ireland during the eighteenth century. The rebellion of 1641and its aftermath convinced Irish Protestants that they were in grave physical danger from Catholics. This was also a period which put the established Church at risk of losing its position and authority. The Church of Ireland did recover from these events, and was re-established as the official state Church in 1660, following the ascension to the throne of Charles II. However, shortly afterwards the Church faced another crisis. The period of James II's reign and the subsequent war in Ireland between 1685 and 1691 came to represent for many Irish Protestants, particularly Anglicans, a second Irish rebellion.[5] James II landed in Ireland in March 1689, intent on recovering his crown. In May he convened the so-called 'Patriot Parliament', which met only briefly and among other actions repealed the Act of Settlement and threatened Anglican control of the state. William King, bishop of Derry, who would go on to become archbishop of Dublin in 1703, catalogued James' actions in his 1691 book *The state of the Protestants of Ireland under the late King James's government.*

---

4   *A letter from a gentleman in the country to his son at the university, dissuading him from going into holy orders* (Dublin, 1737), p. 13.
5   T. C. Barnard, 'The uses of 23 October 1641 and Irish Protestant celebration' in *English Historical Review*, CVI, CCXCXXI (1991), p. 894.

King himself was imprisoned in 1689, along with other Protestant notables who represented a threat to James' control of Ireland.

King's book was intended primarily as a justification of the Glorious Revolution from the perspective of Irish Protestants. He contended that any monarch who attempts to destroy his people abdicates, and that James II intended to sabotage the Protestants of Ireland through both political and economic repression. King recounted James II's many supposed crimes against his Protestant subjects and was particularly vehement regarding the king's actions against the Church of Ireland and its clergy. James II refused to fill vacant bishoprics; rescinded funds for maintenance of the Protestant clergy; confiscated Protestant churches and gave them to Catholics; and encouraged the ill treatment of Protestant clergy, which included their being beaten and robbed.[6] King is hardly an unbiased source, but most of his charges had merit; during his time in Ireland James II did attack the privileges of the established Church of Ireland. It is within this context that Mary II wrote of her great concerns over the Irish Church.

The eighteenth century and the establishment of the Anglo-Irish ascendancy brought back a measure of stability to the Church of Ireland. However, fears about the stability of the state Church, given the many problems it had to contend with, remained widespread. The removal of James II and the estab-lishment of a firm Protestant monarchy had addressed the immediate threat to the Church, but not the many underlying issues. In 1697 Anthony Dopping, bishop of Meath, surveyed the state of the Church of Ireland and proposed several remedies for the situation in a document originally intended to be shown to Thomas Tenison, archbishop of Canterbury. Dopping contended that the Church of Ireland was never in a particularly strong condition, though after the turbulence of James II's reign its condition was even worse. He concluded that the Church of Ireland had four chief afflictions that needed to be addressed: a lack of ministers; non-resident clergy and the problem of pluralities; an inadequate number of churches and the poor condition of those in existence; and a lack of Protestants.[7] While some of these issues were the result of the wars of the preceding sixty years, none of them were easily or expeditiously solved. Writing decades later, Richard Woodward, bishop of Cloyne, cited three factors which impeded Church of Ireland clergy in discharging their duties. He cited the continued lack of churches, the lack of glebe land for parsons to reside on, and the continuing prevalence of the Irish tongue.[8] Although Dopping and

6   King, *The state of the Protestants of Ireland under the late King James's government*, pp. 195–218.
7   John Brady, 'Remedies proposed for the church of Ireland' in *Archivium Hibernicum*, 22 (1959), p. 164.
8   Richard Woodward, *The present state of the church of Ireland: containing a description of its precarious situation; and the consequent danger to the public* (5th ed., Dublin, 1787), p. 87.

Woodward were writing decades apart, they cited several of the same problems. It was clear to many that the Church of Ireland needed to be fixed and reform movements offered a way to address these problems. In eighteenth-century movements for improvement, the Church of Ireland thus took on two roles: it was both an active participant in and encourager of many different organizations, as well as an institution that was in need of improvement itself.

Dopping felt that the first problem he listed, a lack of properly trained Anglican ministers, could be easily fixed by importing such ministers from England. He supported the appointing of English bishops to vacant seats, who would in turn appoint English ministers at the parish level. He assumed that this solution would serve the interests of the crown while also increasing the number and quality of ministers in Ireland. 'By this means not only the number of the clergy would be mightily increased, but their diligence quickened; because the necessity of choice would in great measure be taken off, and room left to advance men more according to their deserts.'[9] Dopping was generally critical of clergy and bishops educated at Trinity College Dublin, which is surprising given that he himself was educated there.[10] He felt that Irish-educated bishops were too complacent and did little to address the problems of the clergy in Ireland. He criticized them for being to 'contented to bear with the disease'.[11]

The eighteenth-century Church of Ireland made a standard practice of appointing English ministers to some of the most desirable positions, as Dopping had recommended. It was a practice, however, with which many of Dopping's fellow Irish-educated churchmen disagreed. William King, archbishop of Dublin, complained in 1724 of seeing 'men who have spent their strength and youth in serving the church successfully left destitute in their old age, and others, who never served a cure, have heaps of benefices thrown upon them'.[12] This policy did not lead to an increase in the number of English clergy, particularly in the many small poor rural parishes where competent ministers were most wanted. English clergymen were generally not lured to Ireland for the poorer parishes that mostly made up the Church. Even Dopping admitted that Ireland's reputation for frequent wars and the smallness of church livings made it an unattractive prospect for many Englishmen.[13] Reverend William Preston, an English transplant to County Carlow, complained both of the expensive repairs he had to make to the church and parish house but also of his surroundings. He

---

[9] Brady, 'Remedies proposed for the church of Ireland', p. 165.

[10] Joseph Irvine Peacocke, 'Anthony Dopping, bishop of Meath' in *The Irish Church Quarterly*, 2, no. 6 (1909), p. 120.

[11] Brady, 'Remedies proposed for the church of Ireland', p. 165.

[12] Quoted in J. L. McCracken, 'The ecclesiastical structure, 1714–1760' in T. W. Moody and W. E. Vaughan (eds), *A new history of Ireland: eighteenth-century Ireland 1691–1800* (Oxford, 1986), iv, 87.

[13] Brady, 'Remedies proposed for the church of Ireland', p. 165.

could not abide the native Irish in the area, describing them as 'such bloody vermin'. Eventually he placed a curate in his position and returned to England.[14]

The policy of appointing Englishmen to important and rich offices may also have acted as a deterrent to Irishmen considering a clerical career. The 1737 pamphlet by a fictitious country gentleman cited, among other reasons, the lack of opportunity for advancement and the difficulty in living off a small clergyman's income to dissuade young men from entering the Church. 'Consider then, first, that you were born and bred in this sorry Kingdom of Ireland, where there is neither Learning, Virtue, nor Merit of any King to qualify a Man for more than a Vicarage of 60 or 70 pounds a year, and that, not till towards the close of his Life.'[15] Wealthier offices were part of the patronage system and were generally reserved for the well-connected.[16] The pamphlet warned of the prevalence of nepotism in the doling out of Church offices and cautioned its audience that only the well-connected made a decent living as clergymen: 'all the highest and best Preferments are enjoyed by a few, and the rest suffered to drudge in penury and contempt'.[17] Another commentator in 1757 noted the difficulty of recruiting good men for the Church. The cost of the necessary education and of maintaining a standard of living appropriate to the position required far more than the potential salary of forty or fifty pounds a year.[18] Regardless of their means, clergymen were expected to live as gentlemen, to be agents of civility among the native Irish, and to set a good example for their parishioners.[19] Given these realities, it is not surprising that many felt the Church was an undesirable career, compounding the perceived problem of a parish ministers.

The greater problem for the Church of Ireland was a lack of money. This was connected to the third and fourth of the problems cited by Dopping – pluralities and the non-residence of many clergy and the poor material condition of many churches. As the established Church, the Church of Ireland was, in theory, richly endowed and supported by tithes paid by the entire population.[20] In practice, tithing was a complex issue and a constant source of resentment for the laity, most of whom were Catholics or nonconformists. The value of individual parishes in Ireland varied widely, but many were worth very little. The parish may have been the most basic unit of ecclesiastical organization, but in Ireland

---

14 Barnard, A new anatomy of Ireland, pp. 86–7; D. W. Hayton, 'Parliament and the established church: reform and reaction' in D. W. Hayton, James Kelly, and John Bergin (eds) The eighteenth-century composite state: representative institutions in Ireland and Europe, 1689–1800 (Basingstoke, 2010), pp. 78–9.
15 A letter from a gentleman in the country to his son at the university, p. 13.
16 McCracken, 'The ecclesiastical structure', iv, 86–7.
17 A letter from a gentleman in the country to his son at the university, p. 14.
18 A Protestant's address to the Protestants of Ireland (Dublin, 1757), p. 20.
19 Barnard, Making the grand figure, pp. 109–11.
20 McCracken, 'The ecclesiastical structure', iv, 84.

what mattered more was the benefice, or the group of parishes held by a single clergyman. It was generally only through groups of several united parishes that a clergyman could make a living. During Dopping's tenure as bishop of Meath, 47 per cent of parishes there were worth less than thirty pounds a year.[21] Archbishop King of Dublin reported that in some cases ten parishes had to be united to make up a benefice worth fifty pounds a year.[22] The problem of pluralities in the Church of Ireland was complex. There were instances where ambitious men strung together a number of Church offices for personal profit, but it was also quite commonly the case that a number of parishes had to be united simply to provide a reasonable income.[23] Dopping blamed three factors for the low incomes of many Irish parishes: unequally divided parishes, lack of tillage, and the large number of impropriations where neighbouring properties annexed land that technically belonged to the benefice. These factors meant that many parishes did not receive the full amount of tithes that they were due. Dopping proposed restructuring the traditional parish boundaries, uniting smaller parishes and restructuring larger ones with arbitrarily drawn boundaries.[24]

Eighteenth-century commentators routinely pointed out that many of these issues dated back further then the conflicts of the previous century. In 1711 Convocation agreed that part of the blame lay with the monarchy's policy during the Reformation of awarding to laymen the tithes that once belonged to abbeys and monasteries. While the problem of impropriations had grown since then, 'these impropriations being a considerable part of the tyth of the whole Kingdom, makes it necessary for the Bishop to unite several adjoining Parishes, to make up a small Provision for a Minister'.[25] In 1724 Jonathan Swift estimated that the clergy in Ireland received only about half of what they were legally due in terms of tithes.[26] The Convocation also cited a lack of glebes in most parishes, and those that did have them were small and scattered. The members agreed with Dopping that there was a lack of churches and houses as well, all of which made 'the local residence of the clergy in many places impracticable'.[27]

Despite Dopping's concern over the lack of the Protestant clergymen by the eighteenth century, others felt that Ireland had the opposite problem. By 1727 Hugh Boulter, archbishop of Armagh and primate of all Ireland, could write to the archbishop of Canterbury that there were about 800 incumbents and curates

---

[21] Barnard, *A new anatomy of Ireland*, p. 83.
[22] McCracken, 'The ecclesiastical structure', iv, 86.
[23] Barnard, *A new anatomy of Ireland*, pp. 84–91.
[24] Brady, 'Remedies proposed for the church of Ireland', p. 166.
[25] *A representation of the present state of religion, with regard to infidelity, heresy, impiety and popery: drawn up and agreed to by both houses of convocation in Ireland* (Dublin, 1711), p. 11.
[26] Jonathan Swift, *Some Reasons against the Bill for Settling the Tyth of Hemp, Flax, Etc by a Modus* (Dublin, 1724), p. 8.
[27] *A representation of the present state of religion*, p. 11.

of the Church of Ireland all told, and while this pales in comparison with the estimated 3,000 Catholic priests, it was still beyond the resources of the Church of Ireland to support. Boulter complained that 'A great part of our clergy have no parsonage houses, nor glebes to build them on.'[28] Another commentator in 1732 observed that there were perhaps 700 beneficed clergymen in the country, but only seven benefices worth at least £300 per annum.[29] While some commentators felt these numbers inadequate to compete with Catholic clergy, it was presumably sufficient enough to minister to the small portion of the population that adhered to the Church of Ireland. While Church of Ireland clergy were outnumbered by Catholic priests, they still had many advantages over them. Toby Barnard has called the Anglican clergy one of the largest and most influential professions on the island in that period.[30]

Historians might describe the Anglican clergy as powerful and influential, but ministers did not share that opinion. Instead, they overwhelmingly saw themselves as under attack, and not simply from the Catholic or nonconformist competition, but from the Church of Ireland laity. The eighteenth century was a period in which the established Church in both Ireland and England became convinced that they were in 'an age of danger'.[31] The concerns of the English clergy, and perhaps to a lesser extent the Irish clergy, were probably overstated, but this deeply held conviction and the clerical defensiveness that it entailed influenced how the clergy saw and interacted with the world around them. A central issue in the Church of Ireland was tithes or, from the perspective of the clergy, impropriations. The Church of Ireland and its clergy argued that the laity had infringed and continued to infringe upon Church land, leading to long-term loss of revenue for parishes. This contributed to many of the Church's problems – the smallness of benefices, the poor condition of churches, the necessity of pluralism, and the frequency of non-residency. From the standpoint of the laity, tithes were a source of resentment; even Church adherents resented the loss of income that tithes entailed. The Catholic peasantry hated tithing to the Church of Ireland. Resentment over tithes fuelled peasant groups such as the 'Whiteboys', who violently rioted in western and south-western Ireland from the 1760s.[32] Jonathan Swift complained that 'the payment of tythes in

---

28 Hugh Boulter, *Letters written by his excellency Hugh Boulter, D.D. Lord Primate of all Ireland, to several ministers of state in England* (2 vols, Dublin, 1770), i, 169.

29 *A letter from a lord to a commoner, concerning the two church bills lately rejected* (2nd ed., Dublin, 1732), p. 22.

30 T. C. Barnard, 'Improving clergymen, 1660–1760' in Alan Ford, James McGuire, and Kenneth Milne (eds), *As by law established: the Church of Ireland since the Reformation* (Dublin, 1995), p. 136.

31 Donald A. Spaeth, *The church in an age of danger: parsons and parishioners, 1660–1740* (Cambridge, 2000); Peter Virgin, *The church in an age of negligence: ecclesiastical structure and problems of church reform 1700–1840* (Cambridge, 1989).

32 R. B. McDowell, 'Colonial nationalism and the winning of parliamentary independence,

this Kingdom, is subject to so many Frauds, Brangles, and other Difficulties, not only from Papists and Dissenters, but even from those who profess themselves Protestants'.[33] In this instance, Swift and the rest of the clergy came into conflict with improvers. The bill that Swift's pamphlet was protesting was designed to reduce the tithes on flax, hemp, and hops as a means of encouraging the cultivation of these crops and encouraging the linen manufacture. In most cases clergymen, including Swift, were ardent supporters of improvement for both practical and spiritual reasons. Clergymen theoretically benefited from agricultural prosperity in the form of increased tithes, or increased income from their own lands (if they had any), and so many clergymen experimented with new crops and improved farming methods and enthusiastically embraced the Dublin Society, an organization dedicated to improving agriculture and manufacturing, upon its founding. In this case the interests of clergymen were not all that different from those of any other member of the landed order,[34] and the tithe bill that Swift was protesting placed the financial interests of the clergy at odds with the financial interests of the kingdom. As a self-interested clergymen, Swift sided with the clergy in attacking any infringement upon their privileges. Clerical support for improvement projects was motivated by more than just financial gain, but it was a blow to many to see their incomes potentially reduced in the name of improvement.

The issue of tithes was one of several which frequently caused conflict between the clergy and the landed gentry, contributing to an uneasy relationship between two classes with a number of broadly similar interests.[35] In a 1728 letter to the bishop of London Boulter observed 'The gentlemen of this country have ever since I came hither been talking to others, and persuading their tenants who complained of the excessiveness of their rents, that it was not the paying too much rent, but too much tythe that impoverished them.'[36] There were many clergy who felt that landlords were frequently too interested in their own profits and in exploiting their tenants. Boulter wrote:

> I cannot accuse the bulk of the protestants except the Scots in the north here, of being enemies to episcopacy and the established clergy as such, but some gentlemen have let their lands so high, that without robbing the clergy of their just dues, they are satisfied their rents can hardly be paid; ... and the controversy here is, not whether the farmer

---

1760–1782' in T. W. Moody and W. E. Vaughan (eds), A new history of Ireland: eighteenth-century Ireland 1691–1800 (Oxford, 1986), iv, 201.

[33] Swift, Some Reasons against the Bill for Settling the Tyth of Hemp, Flax, Etc by a Modus, p. 5.

[34] Barnard, 'Improving clergymen, 1660–1760', p. 137.

[35] Hayton, 'Parliament and the established church', pp. 79–82.

[36] Boulter, Letters written by his excellency Hugh Boulter, i, 232.

shall be eased of an unreasonably burthen, but whether the parson shall have his due, or the landlord a greater rent.[37]

William King, as archbishop of Dublin, shared this opinion, writing in 1712 that the 'poverty of the people and neglect of education do not always proceed from the Laziness of the people or their unwillingness to give the learning, but much more from the cruelty of the Landlords who rack their Tenants so that they can neither render to God, to the publick or to their children what is due to them'.[38] This tension was exacerbated by the belief that Protestant landlords stirred up resentment of tithes among the lower classes. The clergy frequently felt they were being persecuted by parliament as a result of such conflicts, citing any legislation that restricted tithes as an unwarranted attack against their traditional right.[39] There was a general impression that the laity was united against them. Boulter reported that the gentry in Ireland had entered into associations agreeing not to pay any agistments (the tithes on pasture lands) and to financially support any members who were sued to pay theirs.[40]

These routine conflicts over tithes, which continued throughout the eighteenth century, complicated the Church's relationship with agricultural improvement. In general, the clergy and the Church supported efforts to encourage manufacturing and improve agriculture in Ireland. They did not, however, support any restrictions on their traditional liberties. There were advocates of improvement in both England and Ireland who viewed tithes as hindrances to their work and as 'taxes upon industry'.[41] This controversy placed the Dublin Society in an awkward position. It was an organization dedicated to improving husbandry and agriculture, but it had a number of clergymen among its active membership. The solution for the Dublin Society was to remain silent on the issue; it never expressed any negative opinions on tithes.

In his prolonged defence of clerical privileges, *The present state of the Church of Ireland*, written in 1787, Richard Woodward admitted that in some ways tithes operated 'like a tax on industry' and that 'if the farmer could really put the value of the Tithes in his own pocket ... it would be an encouragement to the Plough'.[42] Woodward, however, remained adamant that tithes were a traditional right of the clergy, and one that was essential to their livelihood and that of the Church. Furthermore, the livelihood of the established Church,

37 Boulter, *Letters written by his excellency Hugh Boulter*, i, 184.
38 Andrew Carpenter (ed.), *Letters to and from persons of quality* (Dublin, 1976), p. 17.
39 Swift, *Some Reasons against the Bill for Settling the Tyth of Hemp, Flax, Etc by a Modus*, p. 4.
40 Hugh Boulter, *Letters written by his excellency Hugh Boulter*, ii, 182.
41 James Adam, *Practical essays on agriculture: containing an account of soils, and the manner of correction them* (2 vols, London, 1789), ii, 507.
42 Woodward, *The present state of the church of Ireland*, pp. 57–8.

he contended, was essential to the stability of the nation.[43] Woodward was shrewd enough to recognize that Ireland required more than just an established Church, and that economic improvement was also important. But as a Church of Ireland bishop he was convinced that eliminating tithes to fund improvements was not the way to accomplish this. 'The fairest prospect of Improvement will not justify the risk of Innovation in a system, which in a Religious view, has no equal, and in a Political one, is essential to the preservation of the best Constitution that ever was framed.'[44] Rather than increasing prosperity, alterations to the traditional system would produce chaos and ruin and would 'soon overturn the Protestant Ascendancy'.[45] As far as Woodward was concerned, improvement was to be encouraged, but not at the risk of the political system.

The abilities of individual clergymen to effect improvements in agriculture were limited. Owing to the lack of glebe lands available, most Church of Ireland clergy were able to do little more than exhort parishioners to improve on their own lands. Some clergymen, in possession of glebe lands, did experiment with new agricultural techniques, but they were a minority.[46] While the acquisition of glebe land, to support and encourage clerical residency, was a major goal of the Church of Ireland, routine conflicts over tithes meant that they were mostly unsuccessful. The Church had lost a significant amount of land in the turmoil of the seventeenth century, and it proved difficult to recover. Dopping felt that it was the duty of the king to pass a law restoring all impropriations to the Church, but such an act was extremely unpopular with the laity. Dopping advocated setting up a fund and using the interest to purchase back impropriations.[47] A fund was established, but it did little to ease the problems of the clergy. Shortly after becoming archbishop of Armagh in 1724, Hugh Boulter wrote that the fund was about £1,500 in debt. He proposed encouraging a subscription among bishops and other clergy to try and bring the fund out of debt. Those who possessed preferments of at least £50 a year were to subscribe a small percentage of their income to the fund, the profits of which were to be used to purchase glebes or to buy back impropriations.[48] During Boulter's time the Church also made several efforts to encourage the granting of glebe land through legislation.[49] In these conflicts with parliament and the laity over tithes and glebes, the Church implicitly presented itself as yet another worthy object

---

43 Ibid., p. 56.
44 Ibid., p. 76.
45 Ibid., p. 76-7.
46 Barnard, 'Improving clergymen, 1660-1760', p. 137.
47 Brady, 'Remedies proposed for the church of Ireland', p. 166.
48 Boulter, *Letters written by his excellency Hugh Boulter*, i, 4-5.
49 Ibid., 262.

in need of charity and improvement. The Church stressed the importance to the welfare and security of the nation of a national, established, and episcopal Church, while also stressing their own need for assistance in improving their circumstances.

Both glebes and tithes were major issues for the Church of Ireland: each contributed to the problems of plurality and non-residency of the clergy, and to the major problem of clerical poverty. A career in the Church did not generally lead to wealth or financial security. Even beneficed clergy had relatively small incomes and there were a number of curates in Ireland who made very little. In 1721 William King estimated that out of 600 clergymen in Ireland half were curates whose income was a mere £30 a year.[50] Another commentator lamented the plight of 'the old worthy Curate' who was forced 'to pine away his Life upon the miserable pittance of half an Ensign's pay'.[51] The problem of clerical poverty in Ireland was a severe one. Related to it was a proliferation in the number of impoverished widows and children of clergymen. King was sympathetic to the plight of curates, but felt that those who married and had children were irresponsible. Their children, he wrote, 'prove beggars and commonly their wives are poor contemptible creatures, a disgrace to themselves and their function'.[52] Sir Francis Hutchinson noted in a 1783 bill intended to address this problem that many clergymen died without being able to leave any provision behind for the support and mainte-nance of their wives and children.[53] This was not a new problem: Robert Nelson, in his account of worthy charities in the country to which persons of quality ought to donate, cited the existence of the Society for the Relief of Distressed Widows and Children of Clergymen of the Diocese of Dublin. The Society was founded in 1749, and by the time Nelson published his address in 1752 it had 220 subscribers from both laity and clergy. Nelson provided little information as to how the society operated or rewarded its objects, save for occasional benefactions of between £20 and £30 to the women, which were insufficient for many.[54] In 1769 Elizabeth Madden, the widow of Reverend John Madden, applied to the Dublin Society for assistance in establishing a thread manufacture in County Londonderry. Madden, who was left with thirteen children to support, was granted £100 by the Society to enable her to establish the manufacture.[55]

---

[50] Charles Simeon King (ed.), *A great archbishop of Dublin William King D.D., 1650–1729. His autobiography, family, and a selection from his correspondence* (London, 1908), p. 228.

[51] *A Protestant's address to the Protestants of Ireland*, p. 19.

[52] quoted in Barnard, *A new anatomy of Ireland*, p. 83.

[53] Sir Francis Hutchinson, *A bill for raising and establishing a fund for a provision of the widows and children of the clergy of the church of Ireland* (Dublin, 1783), p. 3.

[54] Robert Nelson, *An address to persons of quality and estate* (Dublin, 1752), pp. 118–19.

[55] RDS Minute Books vol. 10.

According to John Garnett, bishop of Ferns and Leighlin, clergymen's widows were ideal objects of charity. In a 1756 charity sermon on the subject Garnett argued that the citizens of Ireland had a Christian duty towards charity. The country was full of charitable objects, yet he contended that few of them actually deserved assistance. It was a duty of the charitable to carefully consider the proper objects and consequences of charity, and widows and children stood 'clear of each of these exceptions'.[56] Garnett was kinder than King when it came to commenting on the clergymen who had left behind these impoverished families.

> They, we see, had their faults, and their indiscretions, at hard straights sometimes to make provisions for their families, at others involved in debt. Poverty, however, was not adopted into a religious order in their church, nor celibacy in their priesthood. They betrayed no distrust of providence, for the support of an offspring, which nature prompted, and every dictate of reason and religion encouraged. The tenderest of all connexions they cultivated with this honest view. Their fault, perhaps the fault of the times, it was; they paid not sufficient attention to the future provision of either.[57]

Regardless of the faults of their spouses, clergymen's widows were still worthy objects of charity. Patrick Delany, dean of Down, argued that it was the duty of the congregation to assist a clergymen's family. 'His brethren, for whom he laboured out his life, should have a due and conscientious care of the family so left indigent and unprovided for.'[58] The issue of impoverished clerical widows was not unique to the Church of Ireland. In 1678 Charles II granted a charter in England to a Corporation for the Relief of Poor Widows and Children of Clergymen.[59] There were similar organizations in Wales, numerous English counties, and even in Philadelphia, all devoted to providing financial assistance to clerical widows and orphans. Nor did these sermonizers distinguish much between clerical widows in England and in Ireland, except to note that Ireland ought to follow the example of 'our mother-country' in establishing a similar fund.[60]

To some among the laity, the clergy were themselves to blame for many of their problems. An anonymous commentator noted that the spectre of impoverished clerical widows and orphans 'must lessen you in the eyes of us laymen'.[61]

---

[56] John Garnett, A sermons preached at the ordinary visitation of the two dioceses of Ferns and Leighlin. Recommending a subscription for clergymen's widows (Dublin, 1758), p. 10.

[57] Ibid., p. 14.

[58] Patrick Delany, Eighteen discourses and dissertations upon various very important and interesting subjects (London, 1766), p. 234.

[59] An Abstract of the Charter Granted by the Late Majesty King Charles II. For Erecting a Corporation for Relief of Poor Widows and Children of Clergymen: Dated July 1, 1678 (London, 1711).

[60] Delany, Eighteen discourses and dissertations, p. 242.

[61] A letter from a layman, to the clergy of Ireland (Dublin, 1749), pp. 3–5.

Another pamphleteer accused clergy of 'quitting your Cure, and running up to Dublin to spend your Time in Idleness, or to hunt after Preferment, by attending the Levies of the Great'.[62] There was some merit to this accusation. Many Church of Ireland clergymen disliked living in rural parishes, surrounded primarily by the Catholic Irish, and preferred to reside in Dublin if they could afford to.[63] Some clergymen collected a number of parishes for income while largely neglecting them. In certain cases this was a necessity, given the small incomes of many parishes, but some clergymen were able to profit from such schemes.[64] Many felt that the Church of Ireland needed to first reform itself from within to rid itself of bad elements within the clergy and episcopate and to properly reward 'virtue, diligence, abilities, and knowledge' in the awarding of preferments.[65] No longer should the 'highest and richest preferments' be awarded to those who have shown no merit but 'are the Sons or Relations, or are married to some Relations, or it may be to a favourite Maid of the Family'.[66]

Perhaps the greatest problem affecting the Church of Ireland, then, was, as Anthony Dopping put it, 'want of Protestants'.[67] One pamphleteer accused Irish bishops and clergy of spending too much time on improvement projects such as linen manufacture and navigation and not enough time on propagating the Protestant religion.[68] Decades later Richard Woodward would complain of the continuing prevalence of the Irish language, regarding it as a hindrance to the Church.[69] Woodward's issue with the Irish language was that its use among the native Irish made the work of converting them all the more difficult. As a group the Anglo-Irish objected to Gaelic on many grounds: it was associated not only with Catholicism but also with ignorance and barbarism. The Incorporated Society for Promoting English Protestant Schools in Ireland represented one large-scale attempt on the part of the Church of Ireland and the Anglo-Irish laity to bring about mass conversions. However, the decision to focus so many resources on charitable education came at the end of years of debate over the proper method of ministering to the Irish. A 1731 parliamentary report alarmed many Irish Protestants by showing an increase in the number of Catholics. This report, which sparked the founding of the Incorporated Society, reiterated what most Irish Protestants were already aware of: namely, that they were grossly outnumbered by Catholics. Increasing the number of Protestants in Ireland was seen as essential to improving the position of the Church and the stability of the

---

62 A Protestant's address to the Protestants of Ireland, p. 12.
63 Barnard, A new anatomy of Ireland, pp. 86–7.
64 Ibid., pp. 88–90.
65 A Protestant's address to the Protestants of Ireland, p. 20.
66 Ibid., p. 19.
67 Brady, 'Remedies proposed for the church of Ireland', p. 164.
68 The pedlar's letter to the bishops and clergy of Ireland (Dublin, 1760), p. 5.
69 Woodward, The present state of the church of Ireland, p. 87.

kingdom.[70] The founding of the Incorporated Society in 1733 meant that most of the Church's energy and resources for proselytism were focused on the charter schools. Before 1733 there was considerable debate within the Church over the best methods to encourage conversion among the native Irish. All agreed that more Protestants were needed for the health and stability of the Church and the security of the nation, but there was considerable disagreement as to how this ought to be achieved. Proselytism represented the most active part of the Church of Ireland's improvement agenda, but the need to proselytize in such large numbers also illustrates the weaknesses of the Church and how it hoped to help itself by helping Ireland.

While the Church of Ireland fought with the state over issues such as tithes, the two parties agreed on the subject of the Catholic majority. Dopping concluded that the assistance of the state was essential if they were to increase the number of Protestants. The 'prudence of the state' was needed to pass and enforce laws which 'may establish and secure the peace of Ireland for the future'.[71] Dopping, writing in 1697, had few constructive ideas as to how to encourage conversions, although he was a supporter of penal laws. He advocated building English schools, decades before the charter schools, but felt that it was impractical to build a school in every parish. Instead, he proposed establishing public workhouses in every county of Ireland where the children of the poor Irish would be taken while young and educated as Protestants until they were 18–20 years old. Their names would be changed to English names, and they would be transplanted to counties far from where they were born so that their parents would not be able to visit them.[72] Sending missionaries to preach to the Irish in their own language was dismissed, as it would only encourage the continued use of Irish.[73] Instead, Dopping proposed following a scheme of Oliver Cromwell and transplanting the Irish to one province, isolating them from the rest of the country, and giving them an equivalent amount of land to what they had before. While this method would not encourage conversion among the Irish, it would prevent English settlers from being converted by them. One of the overriding fears of many of the Anglo-Irish was that the number of Catholics was growing because Protestants, particularly in poor and rural areas, were abandoning their religion and essentially 'turning native'. As Dopping put it, 'an English planter coming to live amongst Papists, where he hath not sometimes a Protestant neighbour within 2 or 3 miles of him; by degrees dwindles into their language and manners if not into their religion'.[74] Over time, he or his family might also adopt their religion as well.

---

[70] Brady, 'Remedies proposed for the church of Ireland', p. 167.
[71] Ibid., p. 165.
[72] Ibid., p. 169.
[73] Ibid., pp. 167–8.
[74] Ibid., p. 168.

Thus the Anglican Church had to contend with two problems: converting the population, and preventing their own people from becoming corrupted by their surroundings. To many, the danger to the Protestant population came not just from the native population but also from their own religious practices. One 1757 commentator criticized both the clergy and the laity for their lack of religious ardour. He condemned the 'coolness of temper, or rather indeed, an Indifference about all religious Matters' which characterized the Church. The Protestant cause in Ireland would never advance unless ministers endeavoured to educate themselves better on matters of theology and develop a greater zeal for their faith.[75] Conversion was generally viewed with suspicion: one commentator doubted the ability of the Church of Ireland to affect genuine conversions. 'I cannot but lament, that for want of this learning in our clergy, or zeal for our cause, many of our most ignorant converts remain so ill instructed, that it is to be feared, their hearts have never thoroughly been turned to us.'[76] The lack of enthusiasm was especially apparent when contrasted with 'that zeal which rages in [Catholics'] breasts with such a pernicious fury'.[77] While the anonymous pamphleteer placed a great deal of blame for this on the clergy and hierarchy of the Church of Ireland, he also apportioned some blame to the laity, particularly the gentry, who encouraged bad practices within the Church and who 'never shew any great regard to the reformation, than by a number of Protestant Bumper Toasts, to get Drunk in the cause'.[78]

There were certainly members of the gentry for whom this was true. However, some of the gentry were deeply involved in reform initiatives, and it seems clear that many members of the Anglo-Irish Ascendancy possessed genuine religious conviction. It was this conviction which in part drove their interest in charitable and improvement causes. It is true that the Church of Ireland was not known in this period for evangelizing. However, as the energy expended on the charter schools demonstrates, the Church of Ireland's clergy and laity were willing to expend considerable energy and time on conversion. Prior to the founding of the Incorporated Society in 1733 there were no wide-ranging Church-sponsored attempts to encourage conversion, but this was not the result of a lack of religious zeal. Instead, it was the result of a preoccupation on the part of the Church with improving itself and its existing laity, and a lack of consensus over the best means to enact such conversions.[79]

---

[75] *A Protestant's address to the Protestants of Ireland*, pp. 6–8.

[76] Ibid., p. 12.

[77] Ibid., p. 11.

[78] Ibid., p. 13.

[79] D. W. Hayton, 'Creating industrious Protestants: charity schools and the enterprise of religious and social reformation' in D. W. Hayton (ed.), *The Anglo-Irish experience, 1680–1730: religion, identity, and patriotism* (Woodbridge, 2012), pp. 171–2.

Church of Ireland clergymen had to be careful about how much zeal they showed for their faith. Too much religious enthusiasm was regarded suspiciously and might lead them to lose their livings, since religious enthusiasm was associated with nonconformists. In 1776 Edward Smyth, a curate in County Down, found himself called before his bishop, James Traill, on charges of unorthodox opinions. Smyth's parishioners accused him of associating with 'swadlers', meaning Methodists. They feared allowing their children to attend worship with Smyth less they be 'infected with enthusiasm'.[80] Smyth managed to escape the charges, but the accusation demonstrates the tenuous positions that many clergy of the Established Church occupied.

There was considerable interest in the eighteenth century in conversion schemes, particularly among the many English-born bishops of the Church of Ireland. Mass conversion served multiple ends.[81] First, it was essential for the security of the Anglo-Irish Ascendancy. Henry Maule, bishop of Dromore, stressed the 'destructive principles of the Romish church' in his 1735 sermon commemorating the rebellion of 1641. He emphasized that the danger would never be over, because 'men of that persuasion will be too often tempted to act according to those Principles, and again endeavour to throw us into new convulsions'.[82] Another commentator noted that in Ireland 'we have no other Distinction but Protestant and Papist to signify a loyal or disaffected person'.[83] Second, it was a moral duty on the part of all good Protestants to rescue the Catholic population from ignorance and damnation. Edward Synge, archbishop of Tuam, urged Protestants to show 'love, tenderness, and compassion' towards Catholics and help to save them from the 'errors of Popery' which were fundamentally 'destructive of eternal salvation'.[84] On another occasion, Synge praised the great satisfaction that all Christians must feel upon rescuing a neighbour from damnation.[85] Finally, it was essential for improvement. Conventional wisdom of the time held that Catholicism was inherently hostile to economic

---

[80] Edward Smyth, *An account of the trial of Edward Smyth, late curate of Ballyculter, in the diocese of Down* (Dublin, 1777), pp. 17–18.

[81] Andrew Sneddon, '"Darkness must be expell'd by letting in the light": Bishop Francis Hutchinson and the conversion of Irish Catholics by means of the Irish language, c. 1720–4' in *Eighteenth-Century Ireland*, 19 (2004), p. 40.

[82] Henry Maule, *God's goodness visible in our deliverance from popery. With some fit methods to prevent the further growth of it in Ireland. In a sermon preached at Christ-Church, Dublin, &C. On the twenty-third day of October, 1733. By Henry, lord bishop of Dromore* (London, 1735), p. 61.

[83] *A new scheme for increasing the Protestant religion and improving the kingdom of Ireland* (Dublin, 1756), p. 11.

[84] Edward Synge, *A brief account of the laws now in force in the kingdom of Ireland, for encouraging the residence of the parochial clergy, and erecting of English schools* (Dublin, 1723), pp. 4–6.

[85] Edward Synge, *The reward of converting sinners from the error of their ways. A sermon preached in the parish church of St. Bridget, Dublin* (Dublin, 1719), p. 3.

development.[86] Francis Hutchinson, bishop of Down and Connor, felt that Protestantism was inherently better suited for a trading nation, which Ireland aspired to be. Catholicism had too many holy days, monks and nuns were seen as a drain on resources, and it was filled with 'expensive vanities and idle errands to take them off from their business'. He argued that making Ireland thoroughly Protestant was as essential for improvement as was encouraging agriculture and industry.[87]

The central problem for the Church's conversion initiative was a lack of consensus on how it was to be achieved. Converting the Gaelic Irish was a complex issue. The native Irish differed from the English in more than just religion, and linguistic and cultural barriers were routinely cited as barriers to the mission. It was important, too, to ensure sincere conversion. The penal laws provided ample encouragement for industrious Catholics to convert at least nominally, and the Anglo-Irish feared that many conversions were less than sincere. Bishop Francis Hutchinson warned against accepting 'snakes into our bosom'. Yet he also acknowledged that the Anglican Church made conversion a difficult process, and feared that as a result they lost many potential converts to the Presbyterian Church.[88]

Attempts to encourage conversion through preaching to the Irish in their own language never met with the same kind of success that the Incorporated Society achieved. Preaching in Gaelic was popular among improvement-minded clergymen and a few laymen, and in the 1680s Robert Boyle, the noted chemist, financed the printing of an Irish-language Bible to be distributed among the native Irish. Works along this line were praised by some, who charged that the continued use of Protestant material in the Irish language would 'wholly remove from ourselves what we charge the Romanists withal, the locking up of our religion in an unknown tongue'.[89] The basic principle of evangelizing to a population in their vernacular had scriptural precedent, but opponents felt it an unwise method to use among the Irish. One reason is that printing in Irish was seen as impractical. Most printers felt that Irish-language printing required a special typeface, of which there were only a few copies, and one had already been lost,[90] while few printers were willing to invest in casting a special type to

86 Connolly, *Religion, law and power*, pp. 294–5.

87 Francis Hutchinson, *A letter to a member of parliament, concerning the employing and providing for the poor* (Dublin, 1723), pp. 10–11; Andrew Sneddon, *Witchcraft and Whigs: the life of Bishop Francis Hutchinson, 1660–1739* (Manchester, 2008).

88 Francis Hutchinson, *Advices concerning the manner of receiving popish converts* (Dublin, 1729), pp. 2–3.

89 Robert Boyle, *The works of the honourable Robert Boyle* (5 vols, London, 1744), v, 619.

90 The only exception was Theobald Stapleton's Irish-language Catechism, which was printed in Roman typeface. Raymond Gillespie, 'Irish printing in the early seventeenth century' in *Irish Economic and Social History*, 15 (1988), pp. 86–7.

print works that would have only a small market.[91] Nathanael Foy, bishop of Waterford and Lismore, charged in 1698 that Irish-language publications were simply a means of 'continuing them in their obstinacy'. Such schemes would be unsuccessful, he argued, because most of the native Irish could not read, and even if they could they would be discouraged from reading the Scripture by their priests.[92] For Foy, the problem with the Irish was not simply their Catholicism, it was their 'barbarous' and 'heathenish' way of life. He argued that

> Tis manifest to a considering person, that most of their barbarous usages and customs, their depredations and outrages, their profound ignorance, gross superstitions, and old idolatry, are all owing if not as to their original, yet as to their long continuance amongst them, of their wild savage way of living in single cottages, and similar uninhabitable places, at great distances from another.[93]

Foy called for the Irish to be forced into urban colonies. To be truly converted, the Irish had to adopt English customs and language as well as their religion. They had to in all things be 'conformable to our Customs and Usage, and forsake their own'.[94]

Attacks on Irish-language preaching became more prevalent in the eighteenth century. Conversion became associated rhetorically with a broad-based cultural and economic improvement agenda in which Gaelic, as a remnant of a traditional way of life associated with barbarism, was to be abandoned.[95] There were still those who advocated the use of Irish, who did not see it as at odds with an improvement agenda. The most vocal was John Richardson, rector of Belturbet, a mid-level clergymen with a parish in County Cavan. He had been educated at Trinity College before entering the Church and dedicated much of his energy to rallying support for evangelizing in Irish. In his writings, he noted not just the spiritual benefits of conversion but also the political and economic ones. Converting the Irish would serve 'to augment the Wealth and Improvement' of the country, and would improve the Church of Ireland specifically by adding a great number of new members.[96]

In most of his writings, Richardson advocated the use of the Irish language simply as a conversion tool. He answered earlier critiques of the practice, such

---

[91] Raymond Gillespie, *Reading Ireland: print, reading and social change in early modern Ireland* (Manchester, 2005), p. 57.

[92] Nathanael Foy, *A sermon preached in Christs Church Dublin; on the 23rd of October 1698. Being the anniversary thanksgiving for putting an end of the Irish Rebellion* (Dublin, 1698), pp. 28–30.

[93] Ibid., p. 27.

[94] Ibid., p. 30.

[95] T. C. Barnard, 'Protestants and the Irish language, c. 1675–1725' in *Journal of Ecclesiastical History*, 44 (1993), p. 253.

[96] John Richardson, *A proposal for the conversion of the popish natives of Ireland, to the established religion* (Dublin, 1711), ii, 46.

as Foy's, by arguing that, once converted, the Irish would have no need to continue in their traditional language and would in time adopt the English language along with English customs. Unlike earlier writers who advocated a traditional view of the Irish as barbarians, Richardson advocated a generally kinder view of the Gaelic Irish. He commended their 'many valuable qualities', such as affection, charity, hospitality, strong constitutions, and their teachable nature. The Irish lacked only the opportunity for improvement, but were otherwise perfectly capable.[97]

This is a significant contrast to traditional portrayals of the native Irish as objects of fear or mockery.[98] Richardson argued that the true enemy was not the culture or language of the native Irish but rather the Catholic religion.[99] Like most of his contemporaries, Richardson was virulently anti-Catholic. He regarded Catholicism as a religion which promoted waste, led the Irish to acquire 'a habit of idleness and laziness', and contributed to the poverty of its adherents and the nation as a whole.[100] He differed in that he did not regard these qualities as inherent in the Irish. Their way of life was inferior and the Irish language was in many ways 'barren and defective', but it was still a valuable tool in the mission of improvement.[101] Use of the Irish language, he argued, was the most efficient and enlightened means of ensuring a mass conversion of adults. Richardson wrote that 'it is too great a task, to abolish a religion and a language at once'. The ingrained habits of generations could not be abandoned so easily, and the best method of ensuring genuine conversion was through 'mild and gentle' means.[102]

Richardson managed to win some support for his programme in England, particularly from the Society for Promoting Christian Knowledge. However, his ideas were unpopular in Ireland. He envisaged his scheme as working in concert with plans for English-language schools for children. Charity schools were increasingly popular in the eighteenth century and their potential to serve as a tool for evangelization was also widely recognized. In the minds of many of his contemporaries, charity schools had the advantage of unabashedly promoting the English interest by providing a means both to convert and civilize Irish children. To many, Irish-language preaching retarded the progress of cultural assimilation. Moreover, it was possible to use 'mild and gentle' means without resorting to the Irish language, since the Irish 'are all desirous to read, write,

---

97 Ibid., p. 46.
98 Hayton, 'From barbarian to burlesque', pp. 1–24.
99 Richardson, *A proposal for the conversion of the popish natives of Ireland*, p. 21.
100 John Richardson, *The great folly, superstition, and idolatry, of pilgrimages in Ireland* (Dublin, 1727), p. 103.
101 Richardson, *A proposal for the conversion of the popish natives of Ireland*, p. 27.
102 John Richardson, *A short history of the attempts that have been made to convert the popish natives of Ireland, to the established religion* (London, 1712), p. 11.

and to speak the English Tongue'.[103] Henry Maule, then bishop of Dromore and later bishop of Meath and Cloyne, also advocated using proactive means to deal with the Catholic majority. In his 1733 sermons given to commemorate the 23 October uprising of 1641 Maule argued that it was the responsibility of Irish Protestants to rescue them from 'Popish darkness' in order to avoid 'those troubles and calamities, which were so fatal to our Protestant Forefathers'.[104] As far as Maule was concerned, education in 'true religion' went hand in hand with education in the English language. It was unnecessary to make concessions to the traditional Gaelic language or lifestyle since the Irish had recently 'become quiet and civilized'. Having abandoned their previous barbarous, wandering habits, 'they taste the sweets of English Society, and the advantages of civil government'.[105]

Richardson envisaged his scheme of Irish-language preaching as working separately, but in concert with, a national network of charity schools. He concluded that it was only by preaching to adults in Irish and thus simultane-ously converting them that the threat of charity-school children being drawn back to Catholicism was removed.[106] Years later the Incorporated Society recognized this same threat, but chose to address it by transporting children to distant schools and thus permanently removing them from their families. Other reformers combined more closely the use of the Irish language with charity schools more closely. Francis Hutchinson remained committed to the use of Irish as a tool for proselytizing well into the 1720s, after Richardson's ideas had fallen out of favour. Hutchinson founded charity schools in remote parts of his diocese and used a phonetic Irish alphabet of his own invention to teach the children a Protestant catechism printed in Irish; he taught the children at his charity school to read first in Irish and then in English, thus avoiding the traditional critiques of Gaelic instruction.[107] Based on this experience, he did not believe that the Irish were ready to abandon their native language. He did, however, believe that their commitment to Catholicism was limited. At least, this was the case on the isolated island of Rathlin where he instituted his plan.[108] Like Richardson, Synge, and others, Hutchinson believed that gentle methods, not coercion, were the best means to ensure successful conversion. He urged Protestants to 'scatter charity and alms as well as light and knowledge' among the Catholic population.[109] The native Irish were essentially ignorant of religion

103 Maule, God's goodness visible in our deliverance from popery, p. 66.
104 Ibid., p. 63.
105 Ibid., pp. 64–5.
106 Richardson, A proposal for the conversion of the popish natives of Ireland, pp. 27–9.
107 Sneddon, "'Darkness must be expell'd by letting in the light'", pp. 37–45.
108 Ibid., pp. 39, 45.
109 Francis Hutchinson, A sermon preached in Christ-Church Dublin, on Thursday the 30th of January 1723. Being the anniversary fast for the martyrdom of King Charles the First (Dublin, 1723), p. 18.

and its principles and were kept that way by Catholic priests. Hutchinson argued that the Reformation in England had been accomplished by translating the Bible into English, freeing the people from the subjugation of ignorance. Attempts to force conversion by laws were bound to be ineffectual, as were laws that attempted to wipe out the Irish language. 'Darkness must be expell'd by letting in light; and old languages must be taken away by teaching new ones.'[110] Hutchinson hoped that his method would be adopted by other charity schools around the country.[111] In his own diocese, he applied this method of charity schools and Irish literacy only on Rathlin. However, there were few concentrated Catholic populations in his Ulster diocese.[112]

Hutchinson was not alone in equating Catholicism with ignorance. Edward Synge, archbishop of Tuam, also portrayed Catholic priests as preying upon the ignorance of the people.[113] Synge and most others believed that education was the ideal means of ensuring sincere conversions. In 1707 he published the account of a young Irishman named Daniel Herly, who was first sent to an English school where he was taught to read and write. Because he was educated, he came to question the precepts of the Catholic faith and read the Bible on his own, despite being warned against this by a local priest. After reading the Bible the errors of Catholicism became clear to him and he converted.[114] While Synge celebrated the ability of education to convert Herly he also expressed sincere sadness for Herly's parents, whom he described as good, moral people, but condemned to ignorance, idolatry, and damnation.[115]

Most attempts at converting the Irish took for granted that the bulk of the Catholic population were poor and uneducated. Providing them with an education seemed an ideal way to ensure conversion, hence the widespread popularity of charity schools in Ireland. However, there was some acknowledgement that this did not describe every Catholic in Ireland. Hutchinson noted that Protestants must be careful not to 'despise all Papists as ignorant and unlearned in comparison of ourselves; but rather take it for granted that there must be something amongst them very plausible and right, or otherwise there would not be so many learned and brave Nations adhere to them and be fond of them'.[116] Hutchinson proposed special provisions to encourage the conversion of Catholic priests. Edward Synge, in his *Charitable Address to all who*

---

[110] Francis Hutchinson, *The church catechism in Irish* (Belfast, 1722), pp. 6–8.

[111] Ibid., p. 12.

[112] Sneddon, '"Darkness must be expell'd by letting in the light"', p. 46.

[113] Edward Synge, *A charitable address to all who are in communion with the church of Rome* (London, 1727), p. 112.

[114] Edward Synge, *A sincere Christian and convert from the church of Rome, exemplified in the life of Daniel Herly, a poor Irish peasant* (London, 1707).

[115] Ibid., pp. 5–9.

[116] Hutchinson, *Advices concerning the manner of receiving popish converts*, p. 18.

are of the communion of the church of Rome, addressed himself primarily to learned Catholics, whom he attempted to persuade logically to question their faith. However, his arguments did generally rest upon the belief that even learned Catholics suffered from a 'religious lethargy' and did not generally question the rationale behind their faith.[117]

In almost all literature, the conversion of the native Irish population was explicitly linked with the national improvement agenda. Increasing the number of Protestants, it was argued, would naturally lead to the improvement of the country. One anonymous commentator viewed things differently, however, and argued that Ireland needed to be improved before the number of Protestants could increase. He argued that the best way to expand the Protestant population was through encouraging earlier marriage and thus increasing the birth rate. This could be done only by providing these new young families with a means of supporting themselves, so manufacturing and increased tillage was to be encouraged.[118] This was a unique take on the situation, but it still linked the fate of Ireland's economy and government with its religious situation. What was less overtly expressed, though still present, was the linking of the fortunes of the Church of Ireland with the fate of conversion efforts. The Church would be strengthened financially and institutionally by increasing the number of adherents.

Clerical residency, the establishment of glebes, and the condition of churches would all be aided by increasing the Anglican population of the country. Individual members of the clergy were motivated by a sincere desire to aid the Catholic population, who they perceived as in desperate need not just of conversion but also of education and civilization. While individual opinions on how best to approach the topic of conversion varied, the necessity of conversion was agreed by all. However, it is clear that the eighteenth-century Church of Ireland suffered from greater problems then just its numbers. The Church supported improvement efforts for the nation because it was in need of improvement itself. It was hoped that strengthening the nation would go hand in hand with strengthening the established Church.

[117] Synge, *A charitable address to all who are in communion with the church of Rome*, pp. 4, 112.
[118] *A new scheme for increasing the Protestant religion and Improving the kingdom of Ireland*, pp. 24–5.

2

Education and Charity:
The Incorporated Society for Promoting
English Protestant Schools in Ireland

The Incorporated Society for Promoting English Protestant Schools in Ireland, more commonly known as the charter schools, has often been criticized by scholars. All agree that the project was a tremendous failure, although interpretations of this failure differ. Michael Ahern called the charter school movement 'one of the most iniquitous and disgraceful experiments in Irish education'.[1] R. B. McDowell described the Society as 'ill-managed by committees of languid, educationally inexpert amateurs, and its schools, staffed by incompetent and unscrupulous teachers'.[2] W. E. H. Lecky accused it of using 'the guise of the most seductive of all charities, to rob [Catholic] children of the birth right of their faith'.[3] Lecky attributed the failure of the Society's proselytizing initiative to the intense resentment it inspired among Catholics. On the other hand, J. A. Froude described the schools as 'the best conceived educational institutions which existed in the world'.[4] He attributed their failure primarily to mismanagement. According to Froude, charter schools had the potential to be a great gift to the impoverished people of Ireland. Instead, the schools were neglected and failed owing to the incompetence of the Incorporated Society and its members.[5] Although they were contemporaries, it is not surprising that Lecky and Froude took different approaches to the Incorporated Society. Lecky's A history of Ireland in the eighteenth century was a direct reaction to Froude's The English in Ireland in the eighteenth century; Lecky was generally sympathetic to Irish Catholics, while Froude was an imperialist who regarded it as England's moral duty to rule the Irish.[6]

The foundation of all these accusations is well documented in the historical record. The Incorporated Society failed to permanently convert large numbers

---

[1] Michael Ahern, 'Clonmel charter school' in *Tipperary Historical Journal*, 5 (1992), p. 148.
[2] R. B. McDowell, 'Ireland on the eve of the famine' in R. D. Williams and T. D. Edwards (eds), *The great famine: studies in Irish history, 1845–52* (Dublin, 1994), p. 55.
[3] W. E. H. Lecky, A history of Ireland in the eighteenth century (5 vols, London, 1892), i, 235.
[4] Froude, The English in Ireland, ii, 450.
[5] Ibid., ii, 451.
[6] Donal McCartney, *W.E.H. Lecky: historian and politician, 1838–1903* (Dublin, 1994), pp. 64–5; Ciaran Brady, *James Anthony Froude: an intellectual biography of a Victorian prophet* (Oxford, 2013), pp. 265–6.

of Catholic children to the established Church. Furthermore, in the late eighteenth and early nineteenth centuries the Society was plagued with numerous reports of extremely poor conditions in the schools. This chapter does not dispute the idea that the charter schools failed to live up to the high expectations they initially inspired. Most historical interpretations take for granted a sentiment articulated by Ahern: 'the primary aim of the Charter schools was political, not philanthropic'.[7] This chapter, however, contends the opposite. It argues that the Incorporated Society and its members were motivated by genuine philanthropic and religious concerns, and that the attempts of the Society to institute a widespread system of education were part of broader series of Enlightenment-inspired initiatives to improve Irish society.

In 1731 a committee headed by Hugh Boulter, archbishop of Armagh, presented a report to the Irish House of Lords on the state of the Roman Catholic religion in Ireland. To many in the Anglo-Irish ascendancy, the report was truly frightening. The *Report on the state of popery in Ireland* revealed that, despite decades of penal legislation designed to curb the practice of the Catholic faith, the Church of Rome was still a vibrant and, in many ways, a thriving institution in Ireland. Parish clergy and bishops from all over Ireland reported back to the committee on the prevalence of Catholic priests, wandering friars, Mass houses, and 'popish' schools in their regions. Even within Dublin, a Protestant stronghold, new Mass houses were being built throughout the city to service the spiritual needs of the growing Roman Catholic population. Twenty-four new Mass houses had been built in Dublin alone since the beginning of King George I's reign. There were twenty-nine schools to provide for the Catholic population of the city.[8] Within the repressive confines of the penal laws, the practice of Catholicism continued relatively unhindered. There was no need for the Catholic Irish to turn to Anglicanism when they could continue to practice their ancestral faith. In many areas, there were more Catholic priests than Anglican ministers in residence, all of which was a cause of great concern to Irish Protestants, who associated Catholicism with rebellion.

The Gaelic Irish were considered a naturally rebellious people and, with religious and political differences fuelling their animosity, were even more dangerous. This is why the penal laws had been enacted in the first place, but, as the 1731 report revealed, they had been ineffective in curbing the practice of Catholicism. The report confirmed what some already suspected – that there might be better ways to encourage the conversion of the Catholic population. The origins of the charter schools, indeed, stretch back farther

---

7   Ahern, 'Clonmel charter school', p. 152. With the exception of Milne's *Irish charter schools*, the standard work on the charter schools.
8   'Report on the state of popery in Ireland, 1731' in *Archivium Hibernicum*, 4, no. 10 (1915), p. 174.

than 1731. Charity schools arose first in England in the late seventeenth century, before being adopted in Ireland. In many ways, the charity school movement grew out of the earlier interest in the Reformation of Manners, but while the Reformation of Manners was essentially a conservative movement that focused on adult behaviour, the charity schools were more progressive and focused on forming children's comportment rather than on reforming adult conduct.[9]

Charity schools appeared first, and were most successful, in major urban areas such as London and Dublin. Large cities were host to a range of social ills which troubled reformers. The problems of urban poverty and the behaviour of the urban poor were a major source of concern for reformers. Charity schools sought to correct adult behaviour by inculcating in the young correct religious principles. Like the earlier moral reformers, advocates of charity schools tended to be middling laymen and low churchmen. Part of what drove their interest in charity schools was the ease and lack of expense with which they could be established. The foundation of a school traditionally required a large initial outlay of money, both to build the school and to establish an endowment to run it. Charity schools did not necessarily require a special building or even facilities to house the students, and they did not operate from endowments. Most charity schools funded themselves through the new joint-stock method of finance. Concerned individuals could subscribe a certain amount of money annually to support the schools and funds were also raised through special collections such as charity sermons.[10]

The development of charity schools in Ireland was much like the development of the Reformation of Manners Societies in Ireland. Pious, concerned individuals took the example of a movement already begun in England and brought it to Ireland. Officially, a system of universal education was meant to exist already in Ireland. During the reign of Henry VIII laws had been passed which mandated each parish in the country to also have a school for educating children in the English language. However, few such schools actually existed; most parishes did not have sufficient funds to establish them and there was difficulty in locating qualified schoolmasters who were not Catholic.[11] Initially, many charity schools were more concerned with the Protestant poor than with Catholics. However, it is difficult to generalize on this topic because each charity school was founded on individual initiative and the kinds of student accepted varied from school to school. In 1711 an organization was set up in

9   Craig, 'The movement for reformation of manners', p. 6; M. G. Jones, *The charity school movement: a study of eighteenth century puritanism in action* (Cambridge, 1938), p. 9.
10 Ibid., pp. 12–13.
11 Catherine Murray, 'English schools in Ireland in the seventeenth and eighteenth centuries' (MA thesis, Queen's University Belfast, 1954), pp. 10–13.

Dublin to encourage charity schools in Ireland, which corresponded with the Society for Promoting Christian Knowledge in England. This organization left almost nothing in the way of records, but it appears to have operated in a similar manner as the SPCK; it did not actually govern any charity schools, but merely encouraged their founding.[12] Children admitted were generally 'of the lowest condition and the meanest rank'. They received a basic religious education and were generally taught at least to read, but it was considered important not to educate them beyond their station in life. The charity school Society was concerned with making the children useful, so that they did not grow up to be a burden upon the nation.[13]

In many Irish charity schools preference was given first to orphans, second to the non-orphaned poor, and, finally, if any vacancies remained, to the children of Catholic parents.[14] Since many charity schools were attached to and run by Anglican parishes, so it was only logical that they focus their limited resources on members of the congregation. However, from the outset the possibility of using charity schools as a means of converting Catholics through education was recognized. In Dublin two private charity schools were established in 1712 that were intended to educate Catholic children, one for girls and one for boys. These schools operated separately from other charity schools attached to the same church, St Patrick's Cathedral, and were maintained privately.[15]

Dublin in the eighteenth century had seventeen parishes and there were charity schools in sixteen of them. With few exceptions, each of these schools was established at the behest of the minister and run by the parish itself. One notable exception was the school for girls in St Pauls' parish, which was erected and maintained for the purpose of training domestic servants by private gentlewomen who lived outside the parish.[16] This parish-based structure of the charity schools might explain the low enrolment of Catholics in the early years of the movement. Because most charity schools were maintained on a parish level, they were probably viewed as simply an extension of parish responsibilities to the poor. The eighteenth century was a period which saw increased civic responsibilities being brought to parishes in Ireland.[17] The parish was the

---

[12] Hayton, 'Creating industrious Protestants', p. 153.

[13] Marsh's Library: 'Letter concerning the society for promoting charity-schools, from St. Andrews Vestry' (1725).

[14] Edward Nicholson, *A method of charity-schools, recommended, for giving both a religious education, and a way of livelihood to the poor children in Ireland* (Dublin, 1712), p. 41.

[15] Edward Synge, *Methods of erecting, supporting & governing charity-schools: with an account of the charity-schools in Ireland; and some observations thereon* (Dublin, 1721), pp. 16–25.

[16] Ibid., p. 25.

[17] Rowena Dudley, 'The Dublin parish, 1660–1730' in Elizabeth Fitzpatrick and Raymond Gillespie (eds), *The parish in medieval and early modern Ireland* (Dublin, 2006), p. 279.

most important unit of local government as well as the basis for poor relief.[18] While technically Ireland in the eighteenth century did not have a poor law like England's, which mandated poor relief be handled by parishes, in practice the system was much the same and parishes by tradition had responsibilities to the poor living within them.[19] Because of the limited resources Anglican parishes had to work with, the general trend was to limit the number of people eligible for aid. Even Church of Ireland adherents were not always eligible for the limited amount of aid that some parishes could afford.[20] Charity schools, when run by a parish, were generally supported separately from other forms of relief. Special collections were marked for the schools and the money raised from charity sermons, subscriptions, and legacies generally provided the funds for schools, but there were still only a limited number of spaces available. On average, each charity school in Dublin supported twenty-four children.[21]

The conversion of the Catholic population was not the primary purpose of these early charity schools in Ireland. Irish charity schools intentionally copied the structure and operation of charity schools in England, which were concerned with providing a basic academic and religious education to the children of the poor. Edward Synge, archbishop of Tuam, a major proponent of improvement movements and charity schooling, noted that the primary aim of charity schools was 'the charity of educating poor children, tending not only to the good of themselves both in soul and body, but also to the preservation of others from those numerous evils they might be expos'd to, from such children not being instructed in the duties of religion and civil life'. Synge and other Irish proponents of the movement did recognize early on that charity schools could also be used to educate Catholic children, who were doomed to ignorance because of the penal laws prohibiting Catholic schools.[22] Synge was vocal in his belief that the penal laws would do little to encourage conversion. He advocated reform within the Church of Ireland and the use of philanthropic methods such as charity schools to bring Catholics into the fold. Conversion of the Catholic population was not the only concern of reformers. The Protestant poor presented just as much of a problem and there was a real fear that Protestants left to ignorance and poverty would become Catholics.

Henry Downes, bishop of Elphin, noted that schools had the potential to ensure that the children became 'true Christians, good Protestants, sincere

---

[18] T. C. Barnard, 'The eighteenth-century parish' in Elizabeth Fitzpatrick and Raymond Gillespie (eds), *The Parish in Medieval and Early Modern Ireland* (Dublin, 2006), p. 297.

[19] Rowena Dudley, 'The Dublin parishes and the poor, 1660–1740' in *Archivium Hibernicum*, LIII (1999), pp. 80–81.

[20] Barnard, 'The eighteenth-century parish', pp. 313–15.

[21] *An account of charity schools in Great Britain and Ireland* (London, 1712).

[22] Edward Synge, *An account of the erection, government and number, of charity-schools in Ireland* (Dublin, 1717), pp. 3–4.

Members of the Church established by Law, and faithful subjects to our Gracious Sovereign King George, and zealous for the Protestant succession of his illustrious House'.[23] Still, this was never a primary function of most independent charity schools. It was not until the report of 1731 that Protestants were alarmed enough to try and institute a large-scale attempt to convert the Gaelic Irish population. Most of the credit for the founding of the Incorporated Society belongs to Hugh Boulter, archbishop of Armagh. Boulter was an import from England who took office in 1724. Before Boulter's endorsement none of the earlier attempts to expand charity schooling for this purpose came to fruition. The support of the powerful archbishop of Armagh as well as the concern engendered by the 1731 report helped to push through a petition for establishing a society to erect and govern free schools throughout the country that would provide a basic academic and religious education to the children of poor Catholics.[24]

The charter, which received royal approval in 1733, laid out the concerns of the founders: primarily, that large areas of Ireland were populated almost entirely by Catholics.

> That the generality of the Popish Natives appear to have very little sense or knowledge of religion, but what they implicitly take from their clergy, to whose guidance, in such matters, they seem wholly to give themselves up, and thereby are kept, not only in gross ignorance, but also in great disaffection to our person and government, scarce any of them appearing to have been willing to abjure the Pretender to Our Throne.[25]

The Incorporated Society charter recognized something that had become clear to many by that point: namely, that the penal laws did little to curb the actual practice of Catholicism. A new method was needed for dealing with the problem, and the charter school project promised to deal effectively and efficiently with several problems at once. It would provide a basic education for a number of impoverished children, preventing them from growing up to become beggars or criminals. It would convert large numbers of Catholics who spoke primarily Gaelic, and transform them into loyal English-speaking members of society. The charter also specified something else: namely, that while the children of Catholic parents were a first priority, the Society would also cater to 'other poor Natives of Our said Kingdom'.[26]

---

[23] Henry Downes, *A sermon preach'd in the parish church of St. Warbrugh, Dublin: May the 7th 1721* (Dublin, 1721), p. 19.

[24] Milne, *Irish charter schools*, pp. 9–22.

[25] *A copy of His Majesty's royal charter, for erecting English Protestant schools in the kingdom of Ireland* (Dublin, 1733), p. 4.

[26] Ibid., p. 4.

The Incorporated Society began operation with the formal approval of its charter at Dublin Castle on 6 February 1733. Commissioners, consisting of the lord lieutenant and some of the chief nobility and gentry of Ireland, were appointed to put the charter into action, and officers were elected. The lord lieutenant – Lionel Sackville, duke of Dorset – was the first commissioner and was elected president of the new Society; the archbishop of Armagh was vice-president and treasurer; and John Hansard, esq. was the secretary.[27] The Commissioners made up the first members of the Incorporated Society. The general body of the Society was to meet quarterly, but in addition there was a Committee of Fifteen composed of members who resided in or near Dublin. The Committee of Fifteen was to meet on the first Monday of every month. They were empowered to execute all rules and orders of the Society.[28] It was this Committee which was responsible for overseeing day-to-day operations. As schools were established there were also local committees which were intended to supervise operations at each individual school. The Society was aided by a Corresponding Society in London, which supervised fundraising in England for the benefit of the charter schools.[29]

The charter school project was not solely about proselytism. It was also about improvement. The Society maintained close relationships with organizations such as the Dublin Society and the Linen Board, which dedicated themselves to strengthening Ireland's economy through improvements to agriculture and manufacturing. The members of the nobility and gentry who joined and supported the Incorporated Society were also for the most part members of the Dublin Society. The project was informed by both an Enlightenment and a religious agenda. They sought to turn the children into good Anglicans, but also into good citizens, reasonably well educated and trained in skills that would allow them to contribute to the Irish economy. The proselytizing initiative was in some part motivated by practical concerns over political and social stability. However, the Society's members also believed that converting Catholic children to the Church of Ireland would improve their lives in innumerable ways, by ensuring their personal salvation, removing the restrictions of the penal laws, and allowing them greater economic and social opportunities.[30]

The language of proselytism allowed improvers to implement a social agenda. Concerns over religion were explicitly linked in the minds of many

[27] Incorporated Society in Dublin for Promoting English Protestant Schools in Ireland, *A brief account of the proceedings of the Incorporated Society in Dublin, for Erecting and Promoting English Protestant Schools in Ireland* (London, 1735), p. 6.

[28] *A copy of His Majesty's royal charter, for erecting English Protestant schools in the kingdom of Ireland,* pp. 12–4.

[29] Incorporated Society, *A brief account of the proceedings of the Incorporated Society in Dublin,* pp. 6–7.

[30] Ibid., pp. 6–7.

with concerns over Catholicism. The Incorporated Society routinely stressed the practical utility of its endeavour in its publications.[31] However, by overly stressing the conversion initiative the reformers may have done themselves a disservice in the long term, although in the short term such language certainly helped them in obtaining official approval and in raising funds. The emphasis on the charter schools as solely a conversion project permitted them to be seen by historians and nineteenth-century observers as an abject failure. Certainly, conversion was an important part of the Society's agenda, but it was not the sole purpose of the charter school project. While the members of the Corresponding Society in London always stressed the narrow agenda of Catholic conversion as the goal of the schools, there is evidence that active members of the Society in Ireland saw their organization as serving a broader purpose. This is not to say that they did not value the proselytizing initiative. They certainly did, but they did not conceive of the charter schools as being solely a tool for converting Catholics; rather, they felt that the network of free schools which they had at their command could be used to address a variety of social ills.

One example is illustrated by a 1762 discussion of the issue of soldiers' children. The Society proposed to open up one of its nurseries to 100 destitute children fathered by soldiers. All children were to be under the age of six, and the Society proposed to take a further 100 boys and eighty girls into charter schools. Preferably the Royal Charter School on the Strand would house the boys, while the girls would go to Santry school. The idea of taking in soldiers' children, whose fathers were Protestant, was seen as simply another way of fulfilling the obligations of its charter. Many of these children had Catholic mothers and, even if they were not destitute, they were considered in danger of becoming Catholic. Furthermore, they were a drain on the resources of the parish where they resided; St Paul's in Dublin was supporting 392 children of soldiers at the time,[32] and the foundling hospital in Cork was overburdened with destitute children abandoned by their soldier fathers.[33] Providing assistance to the destitute children of soldiers was not outside the letter of the charter, which instructed the Society to focus on 'the children of the popish, and other poor

---

[31] Incorporated Society, *An account of the proceedings of the Incorporated Society in Dublin, for Promoting English Protestant Schools in Ireland, from February 6th. 1733, on which day the royal charter was opened, to the 6th. of March following* (Dublin, 1734); Incorporated Society, *A continuation of the proceedings of the Incorporated Society in Dublin, for Promoting English Protestant Schools in Ireland, from the 25th of March, 1740, to the 25th of March, 1742* (Dublin, 1742); Incorporated Society, *A brief review of the rise and progress of the Incorporated Society in Dublin, for Promoting English Protestant Schools in Ireland. From the opening of His Majesty's royal charter, February 6th, 1733, to November 2d. 1748* (Dublin, 1748).

[32] P.R.O.N.I. DIO/4/8/12/1.

[33] T.C.D. 5225.

natives of our said kingdom'.[34] Still, it was outside what was publicly acknowledged as the primary aim of the Society, the aim that was routinely stressed in fundraising efforts: the conversion of Catholic children. Members in Dublin agreed to the plan, but it was also important to them to have the support of the members of the Corresponding Society in London. In its letter in May of 1762 the Society seems to be asking permission of the Corresponding Society to institute this minimal change in policy. It acknowledged that, while its charter granted it the right to admit Protestant children, it had done so only rarely. It further stated the three instances in which it had granted admission to Protestant children: first, when there were insufficient Catholic children to fill the schools, which it claimed happened only rarely, in times of economic prosperity; second, when Protestant children had fallen into the care of Catholics who would presumably raise them as such, although it reiterated that all impoverished children, regardless of their parents, were in danger of becoming Catholic; and, finally, when the children's fathers were soldiers. The Society's plan in 1762 was simply to broaden a policy already in place and grant admission to a number of soldiers' children. The members in Dublin perceived such a course of action as having a broad utility. It would protect such children from the dangers of Catholicism; the boys would be favourably inclined to join the army – and here they referred to the potential of the charter schools to serve as 'a seminary' that would supply troops; and, furthermore, they could marry charter school girls and help to perpetuate the Protestant religion in Ireland.[35]

To the members in Dublin this seemed like a reasonable use of their charity, one technically allowed by its organizational charter and a valuable public service. That they felt the need to consult with, and almost to ask permission of, the Corresponding Society, reveals something about the nature of the relationship between the institutions. In some ways, for reasons either financial or administrative, the Incorporated Society felt itself subservient to the Corresponding Society, which had been formed only to help it raise funds. While the Corresponding Society in its response began by politely mentioning that it did not presume to know more about such issues than did members in Dublin, it made clear its apprehensions about the plan. 'What may be done legally by letter of the charter, may not therefore be expedient, nor agreeable to the spirit of the design, and we need not appeal to history for the danger of deviating from the principle intention of any institution.'[36] They warned the Dublin members against expanding their prerogative, as it might damage their fundraising ability. The financial distress of the Society, which by this time was

[34] A copy of His Majesty's royal charter, for erecting English Protestant schools in the kingdom of Ireland, p. 4.
[35] P.R.O.N.I. DIO/4/8/12/3.
[36] P.R.O.N.I. DIO/4/8/12/3.

a routine problem, is mentioned, but the corresponding members argued that more subscribers could be gained by focusing intensely on a single goal: the elimination of Catholicism. It is only in this way that others will 'catch the fire from you'.[37] The possible long-term benefits of the admission of soldiers' children were dismissed as being too remote. The Corresponding Society reiterated that it ought to focus on immediate gains and benefits. As for the soldiers' children, if they are left in the care of Catholic mothers then their admission can be considered. But, 'as to the children of Protestants, whatever their distress may be, the truly zealous and political part of our fellow subjects in both kingdoms should relieve them from off their own backs, or from their own tables, rather than take anything from the Protestant schools'.[38] In response to such concerns, the decision was made to abandon the plan to admit soldiers' children as a matter of policy,[39] though, over the years, a number of soldiers' children were admitted to charter schools.

That the Incorporated Society felt the need to consult with and follow the advice of the Corresponding Society indicates how dependent it was on London for fundraising. By the 1760s the Incorporated Society, which had been founded amid a number of generous bequests, was struggling financially. Allegations about abuses and poor conditions within schools had not yet been made public, but the Society was struggling to raise money and keep even the schools it had in operation. The relationship between the societies was a complex one, in some cases deferential and in others not. In a 1740 letter to the Incorporated Society the Corresponding Society stressed that it desired to be deferential to the former in its suggestions, as the Society 'on many accounts must be the best judges whether at all, or how far, such methods may be reasonable or practical'.[40] However, it is clear that, despite their good intentions, the members of Corresponding Society had little real understanding of conditions in Ireland and the difficulty entailed in convincing Catholic families to surrender their children permanently to be raised in a different religion. For example, they suggested that the Society should encourage wealthier Protestants to hire only Protestant servants, which might encourage Catholics to convert. In its reply the Incorporated Society noted that this plan was impractical for several reasons: Protestant servants were scarce and therefore costly, and the sheer number of poor Catholics meant that many of them were willing to work simply for food, and often pretended to be Protestants to gain positions with wealthy families. The Society could only hope to change the

---

[37] P.R.O.N.I. DIO/4/8/12/3.
[38] P.R.O.N.I. DIO/4/8/12/3.
[39] T.C.D. 5225.
[40] T.C.D. 5302.

general practice by creating an available workforce of Protestants who could be hired into service.[41]

Money from the Corresponding Society in London was certainly valued, however. In 1743 the Incorporated Society wrote explicitly to thank it for funds it had raised which allowed the Society to erect nurseries. The Society noted, however, that it was unable to carry out plans for additional schools because of want of funds.[42] The sums that the Corresponding Society managed to raise and convey to the Society in Dublin varied considerably over the years, but were never its primary means of financial support. In 1741 it recorded having raised £ 557 14s. 2d. in benefactions and subscriptions. The Corresponding Society spent £170 14s. on its own expenses, such as salaries and printing costs; the rest was sent to Dublin.[43] In 1742 the Society recorded having received £826 3s.4d. in contributions and subscriptions from England between 1739 and 1741; this, however, was considerably less than the £1007 17s. 4½d. it raised in Ireland. Money from England was only about 21 per cent of its total revenue for those years, and only about 16 per cent of its total expenses for the period in which they ran a deficit of £1088 15s. 2¾d.[44] The amount of the corresponding Society's benefactions did not grow considerably over time either. By 1773 it was reported that it had contributed £953 6s. 9d. for the years 1771 and 1772. Meanwhile, the Incorporated Society's expenses had grown considerably and increasingly it had to rely on money granted to it by the Irish parliament.[45] Given the routine financial difficulties faced by the Incorporated Society, it is understandable that it relied so much on even small benefactions and treated the Corresponding Society with deference. In general, the existing political situation between England and Ireland conditioned the Anglo-Irish to be deferential, to some extent, to their English counterparts.

As for the attitudes of the members of the Corresponding Society towards the Incorporated Society, while they claimed to defer towards their colleagues' greater knowledge and experience of Ireland, it is also clear that they thought of the charter schools mostly in terms of how they could be used to benefit England. The first, and to many the most obvious, benefit was the conversion initiative. Sermons before the Corresponding Society stressed that the Catholic Irish were a violent people with a deeply ingrained hatred of the English as 'invaders and plunderers; as usurpers of the land itself, which, they imagine was

---

[41] T.C.D. 5302.

[42] T.C.D. 5302.

[43] T.C.D. 5302.

[44] Incorporated Society, A Continuation of the Proceedings of the Incorporated Society in Dublin, for Promoting English Protestant Schools in Ireland, from the 25th of March, 1740, to the 25th of March, 1742, p. 33.

[45] P.R.O.N.I. DIO 4/8/12/11.

their forefathers'.[46] While the population of Ireland remained primarily Catholic the danger of rebellion was always present. The benefits of the conversion of the Irish to a contented Protestant population would be felt in England as well:

> The benefits that would accrue to this Kingdom need no explaining: Had all the inhabitants of the British Isles the same Friends, and the same Enemies; were they brought to act with joint hands, and with one heart, what credit and stability would that be to our times? What an accession of glory and strength to the happy Government we live under?[47]

The primary benefit that was always stressed in both Corresponding Society and Incorporated Society literature was the political stability that would result from widespread conversion. This benefit was easily explained to a public in London concerned about national security. However, there were other ways in which the Incorporated Society could serve English interests. Putting aside the theoretical constitutional question of whether or not Ireland in the eighteenth century was actually a colony, it seems clear that the English effectively viewed it as something akin to one. The Corresponding Society's members certainly felt genuine charitable concern for the Irish children they hoped to assist. However, they were also concerned with how the charter schools could be used to benefit England. The concept of the schools as working schools was an important part of their public image, and it was believed early on that, ideally, individual schools might become largely self-sufficient because of the proceeds from the labour of the children.[48] What the children produced varied from school to school, but even early on the members of the Corresponding Society wanted to encourage the production of materials that would benefit England. They wrote to the Incorporated Society as early as 1737 to encourage it to produce fine sewing thread and coarse brown linen in its schools – both items that England imported in large quantities from other countries.[49] While the encouragement of such industries was seen as a benefit to Ireland as well, it would also make Ireland more dependent on England as her sole trading partner.

The encouragement of linen manufacture was in keeping with the broader English policy towards Ireland in the eighteenth century. A thriving Irish linen industry was seen as an appropriate replacement for the woollen industry that had been suppressed at the close of the seventeenth century. In 1698 William III

---

[46] Joseph Wilcocks, *A sermon preach'd before the society corresponding with the Incorporated Society in Dublin, for Promoting English Protestant Working-Schools in Ireland, at their anniversary meeting in the parish-church of St. Mary Le Bow, on Saturday, March 17. 1738–9* (London, 1739), p. 17.

[47] Ibid., p. 19.

[48] Incorporated Society, *An account of the proceedings of the Incorporated Society in Dublin, for Promoting English Protestant Schools in Ireland, from February 6th. 1733*, pp. 7–10.

[49] T.C.D. 5302.

wrote to the Lords Justice of Ireland 'that the growth and increase of the woollen manufacture there, hath long and ever will be looked upon with great jealousy by all our subjects of this kingdom and if not timely remedied may occasion very strict laws totally to prohibit and suppress the same'.[50] Instead, the Lords Justices were instructed to encourage the people of Ireland to turn to the manufacture of linen, an industry that the government of Ireland did everything it could to encourage. This was formalized in 1699 when England's parliament passed the Irish Woollen Export Prohibition act, which blocked the export of Irish wool.[51] The trading relationship between Ireland and England was a contentious one, as a 1710 report noted: 'there can be no trade whatsoever in Ireland but will in some degree or other effect the trade of England'.[52] Irish linen was deemed to be less damaging to the English economy than other goods the country might produce, since the English already had to import linen from abroad. So the government of Ireland, left with little choice, and apparently fearful that it would be debarred from all trade, tried its best to encourage the growing of flax and the manufacture of linen.[53] The charter schools, which relied on their close relationship with the political establishment, also encouraged the linen manufacture. The Society's rules from 1734 stated that 'particular regard' should be shown to teaching the children aspects of linen manufacture, including raising flax and hemp, spinning yarn, and the knitting, sewing and marking of linen.[54] The Linen Board of Ireland, established in 1711, was a valuable supporter of the charter schools, granting gifts such as wheels and looms to the schools and to some children who had completed their apprenticeships in linen weaving.[55] The Newmarket school in County Cork made a deal with the Linen Board to supply it with apprentices and servants when needed, in exchange for the utensils needed to train the children effectively for the linen industry.[56] The close relationship between the Incorporated Society and the Linen Board was encouraged by government. In 1785 a committee appointed by parliament informed the Society that it ought to encourage their children towards the manufacture of cloth such as linen, as this 'will not only be very advantageous to themselves but if industriously and honestly pursued become of general

---

[50] Marsh's Library: 'King William III's letter to the lords justice concerning the linen manufacture of Ireland' (Dublin, 1698).

[51] Patrick Kelly, 'The Irish Woollen Export Prohibition Act of 1699: Kearney re-visited' in *Irish Economic and Social History*, VII (1980), pp. 22–3.

[52] Marsh's Library: 'Report to Queen Anne concerning linen manufacture in Ireland 1710' (Dublin, 1710).

[53] Ibid.

[54] Incorporated Society, *Rules established by the Incorporated Society, in Dublin, for Promoting English Protestant-Schools in Ireland* (Dublin, 1734), pp. 6–7.

[55] T.C.D. 5225, 5236.

[56] T.C.D. 5237.

utility to this kingdom'.[57] This simply confirmed existing policy: prior to 1785 the two organizations were linked through their overlapping memberships, and the Incorporated Society always encouraged linen manufacturing in its schools.[58]

Charter school children were educated in various aspects of linen production. Nonetheless, the Society still worried that too many children were being trained for linen manufacturing and that it was damaging to boys to be educated in the production of cloth and yarn. Constant spinning was considered 'unwholesome' and 'too effeminate' for charter school boys. The local committees were asked to recommend 'some kind of masculine labour' which would be 'better adapted and more serviceable to them' as they matured.[59] In 1773 the master of the Galway schools was informed that, because the linen trade was in decline, he was to find some other 'useful branch of industry' in which to employ the children.[60]

That children were trained in some 'useful branch of industry' was a large part of the Incorporated Society's mode of operation and an important part of how it portrayed itself publicly. The concept that charter schools were working schools was stressed almost as much as the proselytizing initiative; it was emphasized even in its name, which, in most material issued by the Society, including regular reports and sermons, is given as The Incorporated Society, for promoting English Protestant Schools in Ireland. However, in sermons given before the Corresponding Society, which were published and distributed primarily in England, its name was given as The Incorporated Society in Dublin, for promoting English Protestant Working-Schools in Ireland. Nor was this a coincidence. The Corresponding Society decided in 1738 to always title the schools specifically as working schools, as this might 'help to promote the good views thereof'.[61] While the Incorporated Society itself did not feel the need to stress the working aspect in its name it did stress the importance of the children's labour in the text of sermons and other material and in the Society's official seal, which appeared on the cover of all its printed material (Figure 2.1). The seal contained the Society's motto, 'Religione et Labore', and contained images of a Bible, as well as of farming instruments and a spinning wheel.

One significant way in which the Incorporated Society and the Corresponding Society moulded the public image of the charter schools was through the public charity sermons that were given on their behalf. These charity sermons were an important opportunity not only to publicize the charter schools but

---

[57] T.C.D. 5238.

[58] Incorporated Society, An Account of the Proceedings of the Incorporated Society in Dublin, for Promoting English Protestant Schools in Ireland, from February 6th. 1733, p. 14.

[59] T.C.D. 5301.

[60] T.C.D. 5236.

[61] T.C.D. 5302.

Figure 2.1. The seal of the Incorporated Society, from *An Account of the Proceedings of the Incorporated Society in Dublin, for Promoting English Protestant Schools in Ireland* (Dublin, 1734).[62]

also to convince people to support them financially. They emphasized not only the proselytizing initiatives of the schools but also their other, practical benefits. Children were made to work. Poverty was equated with idleness, and the Catholic Irish were particularly associated with indolence. The sermons stressed the ability of the schools to curb these habits.[63] Training children for labour and industry was also seen as an important benefit to the Irish nation, something that would contribute to bettering the economy. Thomas Rundle praised the schools because they would 'inure them to labour' and thus improve the nation and the children.[64] Robert Howard, bishop of Elphin, noted in 1738 that 'nothing can furnish universal plenty and happiness, but universal labour and industry'.[65] Howard felt, as did many improvers, that Ireland was not poor because it lacked resources, but because the natural potential of the land was

[62] Incorporated Society, *A brief review of the rise and progress of the Incorporated Society in Dublin, for Promoting English Protestant Schools in Ireland*.

[63] Michelle Ryan, 'Divisions of poverty in early modern Dublin' in Joost Augusteijn and MaryAnn Lyons (eds), *Irish history: a research yearbook* (Dublin, 2002), p. 134.

[64] Thomas Rundle, *A sermon preached in Christ-Church Dublin, on the 25th Day of March 1736. Before the Incorporated Society for Promoting English Protestant Schools in Ireland* (Dublin, 1736), p. 22.

[65] Robert Howard, *A Sermon Preached in Christ-Church Dublin before the Incorporated Society for Promoting English Protestant Schools in Ireland* (Dublin, 1738), p. 22.

not being utilized. The charter schools and other organizations, such as the Royal Dublin Society, particularly devoted themselves to correcting this failing. Howard argued that the lack of cultivation in Ireland was not due entirely to the natural failings of the native Irish, as most people assumed. Instead he contended that 'many circumstances and accidents have conspired to depress and keep down the genius of this nation'. Ireland and the Irish were poor because of a lack of opportunity and encouragement, not a lack of work ethic or discipline.[66] The charter schools would help to correct this by educating the children of the Irish natives in the principles of 'labour and industry'.[67] Focusing on the working aspect of the schools was one way in which the charter schools, particularly in their early years, could differentiate themselves from charity schools. Joseph Wilcocks, bishop of Rochester, praised the good intentions of charity schools, but thought the curriculum of charter schools was superior because it allocated only two hours a day to academic study and for the rest of the day the children worked: 'two hours in a day are full enough for those who are to live by the labour of their hands'.[68] Charter schools represented not only a proselytizing initiative but also an attempt to put into action new ideas for improving cultivation and industry in Ireland.

Most of a child's day was spent neither at academic nor religious education, but rather in the instruction of those 'those trades and occupations, that are most useful and profitable to the Community, of which the Linnen Manufacture is undoubtedly, the most considerable, and next to that Agriculture and Gardening'.[69] Child labour was meant to be an additional source of income for the schools. It was never a large one: in 1773 it was estimated that the labour of the then 2,100 children in fifty-two schools was worth £800 a year.[70] The schools were not expected to be totally self-sufficient, but the children's work was a valuable commodity to the schoolmasters, whose wages were debited according to the number of children in their school and the calculated value of their industry. The value of each child's employment was set in 1768 at 20s. each per year.[71] The Society insisted that the children should not be allowed to be idle, but the fact that masters were financially invested in the labour of children did cause problems. One master complained in 1774 that he was unfairly censured for reporting too many children as unable to work. He criticized the Society

---

[66] Ibid., p. 20.

[67] Ibid., p. 23.

[68] Wilcocks, A sermon preach'd before the Society Corresponding with the Incorporated Society in Dublin, for Promoting English Protestant Working-Schools in Ireland, p. 16.

[69] Incorporated Society, An account of the proceedings of the Incorporated Society in Dublin, for Promoting English Protestant Schools in Ireland, from February 6th. 1733, p. 4.

[70] P.R.O.N.I. DIO/4/8/12/11.

[71] T.C.D. 5301.

for sending him nothing but 'miserable cripples'.[72] Schoolmasters may well have overworked the children in order to meet the 20s. requirement expected of them, or in the hope of exceeding it. Children worked seven hours a day and the Society believed that 'A master or mistress of any degree of cleverness and industry will in that time make such child earn much more than will pay 20 shillings yearly for its work.'[73] Simultaneously, the Committee of Fifteen also condemned masters and mistresses who overworked children contrary to the rules of the Society and to the detriment of their health and education.[74] Nonetheless, such abuses did occur. In 1772 it was reported that several children from Inniscarra School in County Cork were 'in a manner cripples having almost lost the use of their limbs'. This was concluded to be the result of their being kept constantly at their spinning wheels without rest.[75] While the Society did not endorse the overworking of children, it did insist that all children be able to work, strictly enforcing an admissions policy whereby children who were too young to work (six was considered an appropriate age) or who were not certified by a physician as healthy enough for industry were not admitted.[76]

Teaching the children the value of labour was a part of the charitable service provided by the Society. After their time at school was completed they were sent out to be apprentices to Protestant masters. The Incorporated Society prided itself on turning the children not just into Protestants but also into adults capable of contributing to society and supporting themselves by honest labour. The degree to which it was successful at this, however, is debatable. While the Society served a number of charitable purposes, the proselytizing initiative was never forgotten. Of course, to the Anglo-Irish of this period proselytism was a charitable impulse. The charter schools were performing an important service to the Catholic population not only by providing job training but through conversion, which would enable them to become full citizens and would free them from the restrictions of the penal laws.

The many possible positive effects of charter schools were described in published materials. The Incorporated Society sought to appeal to the charitable impulses of the population, as well as to their basic fears and concerns over safety and the economy. Charter schools would contribute to the security of the Protestant population of Ireland by removing a large, discontented, and rebellious population. They would contribute to the economy by encouraging important industries such as linen and by producing a well-trained and educated workforce. And, of course, there were the spiritual rewards to be reaped from

[72] T.C.D. 5225.
[73] T.C.D. 5236.
[74] T.C.D. 5236.
[75] T.C.D. 5236.
[76] T.C.D. 5236.

rescuing 'the souls of thousands of poor children from the dangers of popish superstition and idolatry, and their bodies from the miseries of idleness and beggary'.[77] What was even better about the charter schools was their method of achieving these ends. The methods of the charter schools 'cannot be liable to censure or objection, not by force or terror, not by penal laws and prosecutions, which can only make hypocrites, but by the innocent and gentle means of enlightening and instructing the ignorant minds of children in the pure truths of the gospel'.[78] This sentiment was in keeping with the long-term objections that many had to the penal laws and their potential effectiveness in terms of encouraging conversion among Catholics. In 1723 Edward Synge, archbishop of Tuam, encouraged the use of 'love, tenderness, and compassion' to encourage genuine conversions among Catholics.[79] The positive social and economic effects that would emerge from both conversions and education were what the Society stressed itself. However, even in its earliest years it did not conceive of the charter schools as merely a conversion tool. Positive economic and social benefits would be felt not simply by making children good Protestants but by providing them with an education and training them in a trade and in good habits. Even if these approaches were unsuccessful the Society provided a valuable service 'in Feeding, Clothing and Comforting many poor distressed Children, Orphans and Foundlings, exposed to Want and Misery, and in qualifying them for getting their Bread in an honest Way during their Lives'.[80] It is thus clear that at that point the Incorporated Society did not conceive of itself as purely a proselytizing tool. In published promotional material the Society tended to gloss over the difficulties of ensuring genuine and permanent conversions to Protestantism, preferring to advance the viewpoint that it could, within a few years, permanently solve the problem of the religious division in Ireland, if only it had the funds to open enough schools.[81] Since it never did have sufficient funds to open schools for every Catholic child this sort of statement is impossible to corroborate. Such statements also gloss over the difficulty of enrolling every Catholic child. Children were supposedly only entered into the charter schools with the voluntary consent of their parents, if they had them. Despite their belief that their goals were impossible to criticize, the charter schools were always the objects of some censure from Catholics. Catholic

---

77 Incorporated Society, A brief review of the rise and progress of the Incorporated Society in Dublin, for Promoting English Protestant Schools in Ireland, p. 9.

78 Ibid., pp. 9–10.

79 Synge, A brief account of the laws now in force in the kingdom of Ireland, pp. 3, 6.

80 Incorporated Society, An abstract of the proceedings of the Incorporated Society in Dublin, for Promoting English Protestant Schools in Ireland: from the opening of His Majesty's royal charter, on the 6th day of February, 1733. To the 25th day of March, 1737 (London, 1737), p. 5.

81 Incorporated Society, A brief review of the rise and progress of the Incorporated Society in Dublin, for Promoting English Protestant Schools in Ireland, p. 8.

priests threatened to refuse sacraments to parents who gave their children to the charter schools.[82] The Society took numerous steps to make sure that those children who it educated remained Protestants all their lives.

In its first years most children who were handed over to the Incorporated Society remained in the geographic area where they were from. However, the Society feared that this policy left the children exposed to the influence of their Catholic families, and changed its policy in 1740. Apparently, the members had always been aware that this could prove to be an issue, but in their first years were more concerned with establishing their schools and ensuring they had enough students, so they chose not to implement any policies which might discourage parents from voluntarily surrendering their children. By December 1740 it was decided that the time had come to correct this oversight.[83] The Incorporated Society was doing well in late 1740, thanks in large part to a devastating famine that was beginning to affect the nation. They struggled financially as a result of rising food prices, but children in the schools were spared the worst catas-trophes of the famine because they, at least, had food. In a 1740 letter to the Corresponding Society the secretary noted that charter school children were 'better nourished than others of their low rank' and had managed to avoid the diseases which racked the rest of the nation's poor. This fortunate development was attributed to 'the distinguishing favour and protection of the Almighty'.[84] In its correspondence the Incorporated Society only acknowledged that the relatively good conditions in the charter schools discouraged children from escaping during this difficult time. However, it is safe to assume that desperate economic conditions did allow some Catholic families to overcome the fervent objections of priests and give at least one child to the charter schools in such situations.[85] The Society's registry of children does not survive for the first decades of operation, so it is difficult to determine if the famine of 1739–41 actually led to an increase in children being admitted. Certainly, by this point, the Society felt itself on sufficiently stable ground to begin instituting a policy that had long been its design. The transportation of children to charter schools far from their home was a practical method intended to ensure the long-term success of conversions. Children had to be removed from their families and Catholic relatives lest they relapse into popery. In its early years the Society feared that such a policy would discourage parents from willingly giving their children and that Catholic priests would present it as a sort of kidnapping, in which parents would never hear from their children again. That part at least

---

[82] Joseph Robins, *The lost children: a study of charity children in Ireland, 1700–1900* (Dublin, 1980), p. 69.

[83] T.C.D. 5301.

[84] T.C.D. 5302.

[85] Robins, *The lost children*, p. 69.

was true; the separation between parent and child was meant to be permanent. But by 1740 the Society was confident that it had established a reputation for treating the children well and providing for them.[86] It was several decades before its reputation of doing quite the opposite appeared. The transplantation scheme was costly to the Society, however. Children were lodged first in the Dublin workhouse at the Society's expense before being transported to a school that was considered a safe distance from their Catholic relatives.[87] Schools were built in all four provinces, with the hopes of building at least one in each county. All were built in predominantly Catholic areas, but near towns, so that their good effects could be observed by locals and also, in theory, so as to make oversight easier for local committees.[88]

As far as the Incorporated Society was concerned, the children that were given to it to be educated were given up permanently. They were never to be reunited with their families for fear that they might be corrupted. To accomplish this permanent separation, the Society instituted the transplantation scheme and also sought to discourage parents from removing their children, or children from leaving the schools. In 1734 it was decided to subject parents to a £5 penalty in the event that they remanded their children from either a school or an apprenticeship.[89] Even before the transplantation scheme was put into effect, it was concluded that to prevent any kind of relapse children must spend at least four years in charter schools before being apprenticed. Then they must be sent to apprenticeships some distance from their families.[90] Nor could children be recovered once given to the Society, at least not without a great deal of difficulty. To get children back, parents could apply to the Society to have them returned, and they were subject to the £5 penalty. Apparently this was not a sufficient deterrent, and in 1772 it was agreed to require the parent, relation, or whoever recommended the child to pay for the cost of maintaining the child during their time in the schools. From then on their food, clothing, and transportation costs had to be paid in full before the child would be returned.[91] The reason for this shift was a marked increase in number of applications for children to be returned, which the Society attributed to parents either not considering the consequence of 'parting with their children and delivering them into the society's care' or having 'fraudulent' motives to begin with, and wishing only to have their children fed and clothed at another's expense for a

---

86 T.C.D. 5302.

87 T.C.D. 5302.

88 Incorporated Society, *An abstract of the proceedings of the Incorporated Society in Dublin, for Promoting English Protestant Schools in Ireland*, p. 16.

89 T.C.D. 5301.

90 T.C.D. 5301.

91 T.C.D. 5225.

time while they were in economic difficulty.[92] The expense of a £5 bond, plus the additional money owed for food, clothing, and transportation, was too much for many petitioning parents. Records show that in only a few instances were children returned through official channels. Related to this was the problem of children escaping or, as the Society seemed to fear at one point, being stolen by secret Catholic schools. In either case, the Society decided to take legal action against anyone caught assisting or harbouring anyone involved in either rescuing or stealing children.[93] The Society took this quite seriously, offering a £10 reward in 1761 for the apprehension of one James Healy, who had assaulted the Society's carrier, Thomas Pollard, and taken two children, Charles and James Molowney.[94] Healy's relationship to the children is not known, but in some instances such rescues were undertaken by family members, as in the case of a mother rescuing her son in 1789.[95]

Rescues were fairly rare. Far more common were children eloping on their own initiative, which is why the Society promised legal action against those who knowingly harboured escaped children. Elopement was considered a serious infraction, but the Society did not want to lose students. The question of how to punish escapees was an issue of some controversy. In 1775 schoolmasters and mistresses were directed to readmit children who had eloped with only moderate punishment.[96] The next year brought a change of heart and it was decided that readmitting children who had eloped only encouraged them to run away, so they were not to be readmitted without a special order from the Committee of Fifteen.[97] Prior to this order, the Society was known to devote considerable resources to tracking down escaped children, publishing advertisements in newspapers and paying for them to be pursued and retaken.[98] Even after its directive not to readmit such children it continued to advertise information about escapees and offer rewards for their return.[99] The following is one example of an advertisement placed by the Society with regards to the growing problem of elopement in the 1780s:

Whereas the Incorporated Society in Dublin for promoting English Protestant schools in Ireland have received information that the elopement of several of the boys and girls from different schools and nurseries under their care, have of late become very frequent and alarming, occasioned as they apprehend by the encouragement of their parents, as well as by their easy reception into such schools or

92 T.C.D. 5225.
93 T.C.D. 5301.
94 T.C.D. 5225.
95 T.C.D. 5240.
96 T.C.D. 5225.
97 T.C.D. 5226.
98 T.C.D. 5236.
99 T.C.D. 5239.

nurseries as their inclinations may prompt them to be placed in, And the society being determined as much possible to prevent the like in the future. Do hereby caution the masters and mistresses of the said schools and nurseries and all other persons whatsoever from harbouring or entertaining any boy or girl who may hereafter elope from the said schools or nurseries as they are determined to prosecute with the utmost rigour of the law all such person or persons as shall seduce from, conceal harbour or entertain any of the boys or girls belonging to any of the said schools or nurseries.[100]

The reasons for elopement varied. In 1771 a boy who had been transported to a new school eloped back to his previous school. Certainly, some escaped to rejoin their families. Most were escaping poor conditions at either schools or apprenticeships. In 1787 several boys eloped from Newmarket school, where they were apprenticed to Charles Chadwick. Their escape prompted the Society to investigate allegations that Chadwick's 'severity and ill usage' had prompted many children to escape.[101] Elopement became a growing problem for the charter schools, the number of children who escaped or were 'stolen away' increasing between 1765 and 1792. Meanwhile, the number of those children who were eventually recaptured fell.[102]

While at the charter schools, children were not to be exposed to any Catholic influences. The Society strictly enforced rules that stated that only Protestants could work for the schools in any capacity.[103] To encourage children to remain Protestant after their education, in 1748 the Society decided to award £5 marriage portions to charter school children upon the completion of their apprenticeship and marriage to a Protestant.[104] Apprenticeships were to be served only with Protestant masters and the children were expected to be given time to attend church services.[105] Such measures were designed to make sure that, once children received a charter school education, they remained Protestant for the rest of their lives.

Publicly the charter schools were meant to focus primarily on educating the children of Catholics. While the members of the Society certainly felt genuine concern for the Catholic children of Ireland, the Society's emphasis on proselytism was also a judicious one. It spoke to the political and security concerns felt by many Protestants in both England and Ireland, who might not otherwise be inclined to donate to charity. Many involved in the charter schools felt that the schools could also be helpful in assisting the broader population of orphaned and distressed

---

[100] T.C.D. 5240.
[101] T.C.D. 5239.
[102] T.C.D. 5668.
[103] T.C.D. 5301.
[104] T.C.D. 5301.
[105] T.C.D. 5285.

children in Ireland.[106] However, the Society chose to emphasize publicly that the schools existed only to convert the children of Catholics. In 1740 it ruled that the number of Protestant children admitted into any school should not exceed one-fifth of the population of the school. In 1745, under a recommendation from the lord lieutenant to be cautious about admitting Protestants, it was decided to further limit the number of Protestants to one-tenth and that those of Protestant parentage admitted had to be orphans.[107] A month later, the Committee of Fifteen resolved to admit only the children of popish parents. In 1752 it wrote to the local committees ordering them to fill vacancies in the school with the children of Catholics in the neighbourhood who would be transplanted to different schools. In 1775 it restated its criteria for admission and warned local committees against not following them: only children with one or more Catholic parent or orphaned children left in the care of Catholics were to be admitted.[108] In publicly circulated material produced by the Society it reiterated constantly its focus on 'popish' children. To ensure this, children were not admitted without a standard form that stated their circumstances and the circumstances of their parents.

Despite such routine declarations, the registry of children bears out a different account. While the registry does not survive for the earliest years of the Society's operations, from 1765 onwards it is clear that the Incorporated Society was actually admitting considerably more Protestant children than its rules allowed. Between 1765 and 1766 280 new children were admitted into the Society's care, 30 per cent of whom had two Protestant parents. These numbers fluctuated with time, but the percentage of children with Protestant parents was always considerably more than either one-fifth or one-tenth of the total number of admitted students. The overall trend for this period, illustrated in Figure 2.2 below, saw a decline in Protestant admissions, but not even close to the extent that the Society advertised.

Officially, the Society's policy on Protestant admission remained unchanged until 1803; unofficially, Protestants or children being raised by a Protestant parent continued to be admitted in significant numbers.[109] While the Society's rhetoric publicly emphasized the schools as a tool of conversion only, the members did not give up their vision of 'feeding, clothing and comforting many poor distressed Children, Orphans and Foundlings' regardless of the religion of their birth.[110] The Society's registry also contains information about the

---

106 Incorporated Society, An abstract of the proceedings of the Incorporated Society in Dublin, for Promoting English Protestant Schools in Ireland, p. 5.
107 T.C.D. 5301.
108 T.C.D. 5301.
109 T.C.D. 5668.
110 Incorporated Society, An abstract of the proceedings of the Incorporated Society in Dublin, for Promoting English Protestant Schools in Ireland, p. 5.

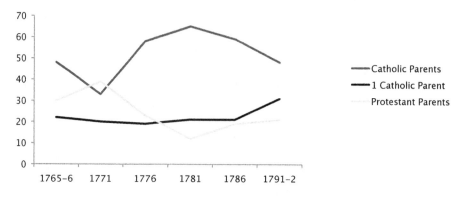

Figure 2.2. Religious background of admitted children.

background of admitted children, and very few of the Protestants admitted are listed as orphans. Most children, of either background, did have at least one dead or otherwise absent parent. Figure 2.3 illustrates the various backgrounds of admitted children throughout the eighteenth century.

These numbers varied a little year by year, but the overall trend is towards varying degrees of financial hardship on the part of parents of charter school children. Each child admitted to the charter schools had to be recommended by someone. Given the close ties between the Incorporated Society and the Church of Ireland it is not surprising that in the majority of instances children were recommended by a clergyman. Non-related laymen, many of whom were prominent individuals, either nobles or members of the gentry, were also responsible for a number of recommendations. In some cases, people recommended the children of their tenants or servants, but in most instances their exact relationship to the child is unknown. A few children recommended themselves for entry into the charter schools. Children listed as being given at the direct request of their parents were fairly uncommon. In 1771, 28 per cent of new children admitted were given by a parent, a much higher than average percentage. Of those children, two-thirds were given up by single parents and 68 per cent by a Protestant parent.[111]

As time went on the Incorporated Society began to encounter other difficulties. Stories of poor conditions at the schools became public. The headquarters of both the General Board and the Committee of Fifteen were in Dublin, and they relied on routine reports from local committees and schoolmasters and mistresses to keep abreast of conditions at individual schools. Local committees were meant to inspect schools routinely, but the evidence

[111] T.C.D. 5668.

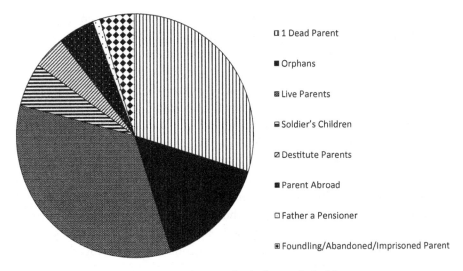

Figure 2.3. Background of admitted children.

indicates that they were not especially vigilant on this account. Over time, this lack of oversight into school conditions would come back to haunt them. John Howard, the prison reformer, began to report on the conditions he observed in the schools in the 1780s. Conditions varied between schools, and some were worse than others. Howard described the children of Castlebar school in County Mayo as, 'puny, sickly objects, almost naked'.[112] In general, he reported that many schools were crumbling physically, the children ill-fed and poorly educated.

The Society had dealt with concerns over conditions in the schools before, but prior to the 1780s it had been able to keep such issues private. Concerns that children were overworked or undereducated at various schools routinely appear in the minute books of the General Board and the Committee of Fifteen, but became more common in the 1780s. In July 1786, in response to negative reports that were surfacing, it was decided that more oversight was needed, and the board appointed Richard Underwood, previously an agent of the Society overseeing its licensing of hawkers and peddlers, as an inspector of several charter schools. Underwood did not last long in the position. He was dismissed in December 1786, having filed an extremely negative report regarding conditions at the Newmarket school under the master Charles Chadwick. Upon further investigation the Society decided that it was

112 John Howard, *An account of the principal lazarettos in Europe, etc.* (Warrington, 1789), p. 108.

Underwood who had acted improperly, perhaps bribing the children, and that Chadwick was not guilty of any particular misconduct.[113] In the next year Chadwick was accused of 'severity and ill-usage' by several boys who had escaped from his school. He once again protested his innocence and was apparently believed by the Society, as he was kept on and even rewarded in 1788 with a premium for his 'good care of the children and the school for the year'. Later that year, though, a report alleged that the children in Newmarket school were behind academically, and he was instructed to spend more time teaching them.[114] Chadwick was able to keep his position despite such accusations, but the Society did dismiss schoolmasters who were found to be guilty of misconduct. In 1772 the master and mistress of Santry school were dismissed, 'the honour credit and very being of the society having been affected by the said master and mistress' bad behaviour to the children by stinting them of their food and the indecent and cruel manner of correcting them with improper instruments'.[115]

The Society investigated accusations of incompetence or poor conditions in schools, but does not appear to have taken action very often. In 1790 the Committee of Fifteen was alarmed by a report from the local committee of Strangford school in County Down about an outbreak of venereal disease among the boys. The infection seems to have been brought in by Thomas Boland, a student who had been apprenticed and was then allowed back into the school. Boland was immediately dismissed from the school, but while the master and mistress were suspected of negligence in allowing the infection to spread they kept their places.[116]

The degree of vigilance by local committees seems to have varied greatly, and most reports of poor conditions seem to have come from outside visitors, such as Francis Hutchinson and prison reformers such as John Howard and Sir Jeremiah Fitzpatrick. The Society did attempt to address such problems by recruiting new members to local committees and expanding the involvement of women. The Incorporated Society is a prime example of a voluntary society that operated through a corporate structure which worked to exclude women from active participation in most roles. Women could subscribe to the Society, but they could not become official members, so could hold no offices within the Society, nor could they attend meetings or vote on resolutions. The Society was run from Dublin, but local schools were meant to be overseen by a local committee of Society members who resided in that area. The local committee would routinely inspect the schools and report back to the committee of fifteen

---

[113] T.C.D. 5226, 5238, 5239.
[114] T.C.D. 5239.
[115] T.C.D. 5326.
[116] T.C.D. 5240.

in Dublin.[117] Since women could not become members of the Society they also could not serve on local committees. However, by the 1760s it was clear that women's participation and ideas were needed in certain areas, particularly those correlating with the practical domestic skills associated with womanhood in the period. In 1765 the Incorporated Society, which had recently concluded that greater oversight was needed over local schools, issued an order requesting the assistance of ladies and gentlewomen in the areas of their schools who 'would be willing to visit the respective schools and inspect the diet, cloathing, bedding, cleanliness, work and behaviour of the children and also the economy and order of the house and give proper directions time to time in those and all other articles which may conduce to the good of the schools'. This step was taken because the Society had realized that 'there are many articles of domestick economy and management in the several charter schools which fall properly under female direction'.[118]

The Society had both male and female students and sought to ensure that young girls were brought up as good Protestants with decent employment prospects in proper female industries. Contributing to the need for greater involvement from philanthropic women was the decision in 1765 to segregate several of its schools by gender, a policy which would gradually increase as the century continued. Given all this, it is not surprising that the members of the Incorporated Society decided to extend to women the opportunity for greater participation. They felt they needed women's expertise on matters seen to be directly related to the domestic sphere.

In theory, the local committees on which women were eventually able to serve had a great deal of authority over the individual schools that they oversaw. Their duties were to routinely visit and inspect individual schools and to attest that proper progress was being made in the children's academic and religious education. Local committees were to be kept abreast by schoolmasters and mistresses on the progress of every child in the school and their circumstances. They had the power to approve the schoolmasters and mistresses and to have them dismissed, and could recommend children for admission.[119] In practice, the Society lacked thorough oversight of its individual schools. Some local committees were almost certainly guilty of neglecting their duties, given the reports of extremely poor conditions at charter schools late in the eighteenth century. To its credit, the Incorporated Society was aware that it needed to do more to oversee individual schools and particularly that it needed the insight

---

[117] Incorporated Society, An abstract of the proceedings of the Incorporated Society in Dublin, for Promoting English Protestant Schools in Ireland, pp. 16–17.

[118] T.C.D. 5301.

[119] Incorporated Society, An abstract of the proceedings of the Incorporated Society in Dublin, for Promoting English Protestant Schools in Ireland, pp. 16–20.

and reports of women observers to determine the true state of conditions at some schools. Also, by this point, a new burst of energy and enthusiasm was needed for the work, which local women would be able to provide. The Society issued several more requests for women to inspect schools and send back reports and recommendations. In 1785 it expanded this and permitted any charitably inclined ladies to visit and inspect schools and to make detailed observations on conditions and how they could be improved.[120] In 1786 the Committee of Fifteen was so impressed with the report sent back to them by a Lady O'Brien and Mrs Creagh on the misconduct of one schoolmaster that it requested Lady O'Brien to look into several reports regarding another school not too distant from her.[121]

Despite the existence of female visitors, many schools still lacked sufficient oversight. By 1788 reports of poor conditions, particularly from John Howard, motivated a parliamentary inquiry into the state of the schools. The Society had for years been dependent on large sums of money awarded to it by the Irish parliament to remain operating, so the outcome of this report was extremely important. The investigation noted, among other things, contradictions between local committee reports and the reports of Sir Jeremiah Fitzpatrick. While it heard considerable evidence from Howard and Fitzpatrick about poor conditions in many schools it also relied mostly on reports from the Incorporated Society itself, which concluded that, while there were some instances of abuse, conditions in most schools were favourable.[122]

By the nineteenth century attitudes towards Catholicism had softened considerably, while the reputation of the charter schools declined precipitously. Robert Stevens' An inquiry into the abuses of the chartered schools in Ireland (1818) would irreparably damage the reputation of the Society: an organization once considered a well-intentioned charity became perceived as a religious organization bent on taking advantage of Irish Catholic poverty. Stevens accused the charter schools of kidnapping Catholic children and raising them in horrible conditions. His inquiry, which relied mostly on the reports of Howard and Fitzpatrick regarding poor conditions in many of the schools, portrayed the Incorporated Society as a fundamentally mismanaged institution, one funded by public money where officers drew large salaries and lived in luxury while the schools crumbled and the children lived in rags.[123] Stevens' report was

---

[120] TCD 5226.

[121] TCD 5238.

[122] 'Report on the state of the Protestant charter schools of the kingdom, reported by the Right Honourable Mr. Secretary of State' in The Journals of the House of Commons of the Kingdom of Ireland from the Eighteenth of May 1613 to 1794, 25 (Dublin, 1788), dii–dxliii.

[123] Robert Steven, An inquiry into the abuses of the chartered schools in Ireland (2nd ed., London, 1818), p. 7.

highly influential. In 1820 correspondence between the lord lieutenant and the Society revealed that the government no longer felt the schools represented an efficient use of public money. Since they no longer restricted themselves to Catholic children by this point, and had formally disavowed the proselytizing initiative, they could not justify their funding in that way. It was argued that the charter schools did not provide a sufficient return on their investment in that they did not educate nearly enough children given the amount of parliamentary grants they had received.[124]

Despite such scandals, the Incorporated Society did not die out in the nineteenth century, but it did change direction radically, shifting its focus from elementary education for Catholics to secondary education for Protestants. It retains that focus to the present day, though its methods of operation have evolved.[125] While they failed in many ways, the eighteenth-century charter schools represented an attempt at unifying Enlightenment principles of improvement with religious principles of proselytism. In the long run their emphasis on conversion opened them up to intense criticism from many different quarters, but the charter schools were based on a genuine desire to improve both the lives of the poor in Ireland and the social and economic conditions of the country.

[124] P.R.O.N.I. DIO/4/8/12/32, 33.
[125] Milne, *Irish charter schools*, pp. 333–5.

3

To Cure and Relieve: Voluntary Hospitals in Eighteenth-Century Dublin

In 1758 a young man named William Carey arrived at Mercer's Hospital in Dublin. He was recommended for admission by the Reverend William Henry. It was a long journey for the nineteen-year-old Carey, who had lived up until then on an isolated island in Lough Melvill in County Leitrim. A year earlier he had begun to experience bizarre symptoms. At first it was a sudden swelling in his right wrist. Soon the swelling turned hard and that hardness began to spread up his arm. Carey's muscles were ossifying. Reverend Henry observed that a kind of jelly first oozed out of his joints, which then gradually turned into bone. The severity of his disorder required more advanced medical treatment than was available in Carey's remote island home. He had to travel to receive any treatment, which brought him first to Castle Caldwell in County Fermanagh, to be evaluated by Reverend Henry and Sir James Caldwell. From there Henry transported him to Dublin and had him admitted to Mercer's Hospital for treatment. There the physicians and surgeons of the hospital treated him with mercury, both orally and as plasters applied to his skin. The course of treatment seemed to help stop the spread of the ossification and to ease his joints, but little could be done about those areas already affected. Carey was instructed to bathe twice daily in the ocean near his home and to continue using the mercurial plasters on the affected areas.[1]

The eighteenth century brought many medical advances, but there was still little physicians could do to actually cure the sick, particularly with a case as unusual as Carey's. There was a widespread belief in the medical benefits of mercury and the therapeutic value of the seaside and, for Carey at least, they seemed to provide some relief.[2] Carey, and others like him, had few options when it came to receiving medical treatment. Medical facilities were scarce in Ireland in the eighteenth century. There were none on the small island in County Leitrim where Carey was born, and he was not wealthy enough to afford a private physician, even if one had lived nearby. His only option for

---

[1] *The medical museum, or, a repository of cases, experiments, researches, and discoveries, collected at home and abroad by gentlemen of the faculty* (3 vols, London, 1763), i, 38–44.

[2] Roy Porter, *The greatest benefit to mankind: a medical history of humanity* (1st American ed., New York, 1998), pp. 267–8.

further treatment was to travel to Dublin to a voluntary hospital. Voluntary hospitals were a new phenomenon in the eighteenth century, and in Ireland the only hospitals outside Dublin were in Cork and Waterford, each of which was much further away from Carey's home in the north.[3] Voluntary hospitals were a significant part of the improvement programme. They combined religious directives on caring for the sick and poor with an Enlightenment agenda. Medical charity put forward a Protestant ethos, while addressing some of the myriad social problems affecting Ireland. In particular, they were thought to contribute to economic improvement by ensuring the health of the working poor and to social stability by reinforcing traditional social bonds.

Before the Reformation there were numerous hospitals in medieval Dublin, but they were primarily shelters or hospices for the sick and needy and were not centres of specialized medicine.[4] The suppression of religious houses by Henry VIII, beginning in 1537, changed all this, and for some time the growing population of Dublin now had little chance of receiving any kind of institutional medical care. As a result, from the mid-sixteenth through to the eighteenth century most Irish people continued to rely on traditional folk medicine.[5] Meanwhile, the wealthy had the option of receiving private medical treatment from physicians or surgeons. As for William Carey, in his home village he may have been able to receive medical advice and medicine from an apothecary, but it is unlikely that Carey would have had access to other medical professionals.[6] Even the residents of Dublin did not have many options for medical care. In 1672 Sir William Petty noted that Dublin had a hospital for 'sick, lame and old soldiers' that was not endowed, and a new hospital for poor children that 'was not yet fully erected or endowed'.[7] The children's hospital that Petty described was actually not primarily a hospital, in the modern conception of an institution to care for the sick. Rather, it was a school – the Hospital and Free School of Charles II, completed in 1674, more popularly known as the Blue Coat School or King's Hospital.[8] Neither of these institutions provided medical care to the community as a whole.

3 Geary, Medicine and charity in Ireland, p. 20.
4 Roy Porter, Blood and guts: a short history of medicine (1st American ed., New York, 2003), p. 136.
5 Eoin O'Brien, "'Of vagabonds, sturdy beggars and strolling women": the house of industry hospitals in the Georgian and Victorian eras' in Lorna Browne, Eoin O'Brien, and Kevil Malley (eds), The house of industry hospitals, 1772–1987: the Richmond, Whitworth and Hardwicke (St Laurence's Hospital) a closing memoir (Dublin, 1988), p. 2.
6 John Woodward, To do the sick no harm: a study of the British voluntary hospital system to 1875 (London, 1974), pp. 2–4.
7 Sir William Petty, Tracts; chiefly relating to Ireland. Containing: I. A treatise of taxes and contributions. II. Essays in political arithmetic. III. The political anatomy of Ireland (Dublin, 1769), p. 328.
8 Sir Frederick Richard Falkiner, The foundation of the hospital and free school of King Charles II., Oxmantown Dublin: commonly called the Blue Coat School: with notices of some of its governors, and

The need to found an institution that would help the sick and serve a broad segment of the population was clear. In 1676 Petty wrote of the need for hospitals both to encourage advancements in medical science and to facilitate the health and prosperity of the nation. He advocated the building of hospitals 'for the accommodation of sick people, Rich as well as Poor, so instituted and fitted as to encourage all sick persons to resort unto them'.[9] The first voluntary hospital in Dublin, the Charitable Infirmary, was opened in 1718 and initially accommodated only four patients.[10] Dublin was not alone among early modern cities in needing greater provision for the care of the sick poor, and the founding of voluntary hospitals in London began at roughly the same time. Medical charity served a practical as well as a philanthropic purpose. The conventional wisdom of the time divided the poor into two categories: the deserving and undeserving. The deserving poor had social and economic potential that was undeveloped because of their circumstances. The undeserving poor were thought to be lazy and unwilling to work and contribute to society.[11] The thousands of beggars crowding the streets of Dublin fell largely into the latter category. In 1766 the lord mayor of Dublin complained of the 'idle vagabonds and sturdy beggars' crowding the streets of the capital, with their clamorous children, 'pretending to be miserable'.[12] Jonathan Swift advocated forcing the beggars of the city to wear badges so as to distinguish between real objects of charity and the sturdy beggars and foreigners, by which Swift meant new arrivals from the countryside, living off the city's charity.[13] Even charitably inclined citizens had little patience for those whom they classified as the undeserving poor.

The sick, however, were a different matter. They generally fell into the category of deserving poor, along with most children and the infirm. While intervening in the lives of the undeserving poor was seen as a fruitless effort, it was not so with the deserving poor. Advocates of voluntary hospitals appealed not only to the Christian impulses of potential donors but also to practical concerns. In 1738 Josiah Hort, bishop of Kilmore and Ardagh, argued that the sick poor were among the most deserving objects in the city. 'I am sure no man can plead the uncertainty of distinguishing fit objects; at least if he lives in, or near this City; let him go to Mercer's Hospital, or to the Infirmary, let him survey the blind, lame, the maimed, and the crippled, who are provided with lodgings,

of contemporary events in Dublin from the foundation, 1668 to 1840, when its government by the city ceased (Dublin, 1906).

[9] Marquis of Lansdowne (ed.), The Petty Papers: some unpublished writings of Sir William Petty, edited from the Bowood papers (2 vols, New York, 1967), ii, 175.

[10] Geary, Medicine and charity in Ireland, p. 16.

[11] Ryan, 'Divisions of poverty', pp. 131–2.

[12] Gilbert, Calendar of ancient records of Dublin, xi, 523.

[13] Jonathan Swift, A proposal for giving badges to the beggars in all the parishes of Dublin (Dublin, 1737), pp. 5–7.

and diet, and dressings, and medicines, and are sent away whole and are found in great numbers.'[14] The labouring poor were an important part of the economic well-being of the country and a healthy labouring class was essential to a healthy mercantilist economy. In 1714 John Bellers argued that Great Britain lost £200 from the early death of any 'able, industrious Labourer' capable of having children. The building of hospitals to provide medical care for the poor was thus the most efficient way to ensure the physical and economic health of the nation.[15] While charity schools in Ireland were inspired by earlier developments in England, the voluntary hospital movement developed simultaneously in both nations and out of similar charitable impulses. Ireland's first voluntary hospital, the Charitable Infirmary, was founded in 1718, while the first English voluntary hospital was the Westminster Infirmary in London, founded in 1719. The voluntary hospital movement eventually spread throughout the British Atlantic World, with voluntary hospitals being established in most major cities of the emerging British Empire.[16]

Voluntary hospitals served to reinforce social deference and to induce gratitude towards wealthy benefactors on the part of the poor.[17] Medical charity was thus both 'social lubricant and social obligation', in that it combined paternalism with pragmatism.[18] As with other charitable activities, there was also a religious dimension to the movement. While Irish voluntary hospitals did not serve as tools of conversion in the same way as Incorporated Society schools, they did serve a Protestant agenda. Medical charity, like other philanthropic endeavours, represented the union of Enlightenment concern for social utility with a religious concern for salvation. The charters for the hospitals bear this out. The Lying-In Hospital was founded in 1745 to provide care for poor women about to give birth. Its charter not only emphasized the utility of the scheme in terms of such factors as preserving the lives of infants and thus increasing the population but also played on humanitarian impulses, noting that it helped in 'preserving the lives, and relieving the miseries of numberless Lying-in women'.[19] The charter also referenced Enlightenment-era antipathy towards traditional folk medicine, noting that the new Lying-In Hospital would help to overcome the negative consequences of ignorant country midwives.[20]

---

14 Josiah Hort, *Sixteen sermons by Josiah, lord bishop of Kilmore and Ardagh* (Dublin, 1738), p. 67.
15 John Bellers, *An essay towards the improvement of physik. In twelve proposals. By which the lives of many thousands of the rich, as well as of the poor, may be saved yearly* (London, 1714), p. 3.
16 Woodward, *To do the sick no harm*, pp. 176–8.
17 Porter, *The greatest benefit to mankind*, p. 298.
18 Geary, *Medicine and charity in Ireland*, p. 4.
19 *A copy of His Majesty's royal charter for incorporating the governors and guardians of the hospital for the relief of poor lying-in women, in Dublin: dated the second day of December, 1756* (Dublin, 1756), p. 4.
20 Ibid.

The Charitable Infirmary, as noted, was the first voluntary hospital to appear in Dublin, followed by Dr Steevens's Hospital. The will of Dr Richard Steevens, who died in 1710, left instructions for his sister Mrs Grizel Steevens to establish a hospital in Dublin for the 'maintenance and cure of the sick, and wounded, curable Poor of the Kingdom'.[21] Mrs Steevens decided to build a much larger hospital then her brother probably intended, and one much larger than his fortune could support. Using a combination of legacies, donations, and charitable subscriptions, she and the governors of the charity were able to open the hospital in 1733. It was capable of receiving up to 300 patients, making it considerably larger than the Charitable Infirmary.[22] Dr Steevens's Hospital, however, was established to care for the 'curable' poor, and there was still a need to expand medical charity in the city for other cases. The other hospitals were Mercer's Hospital (1734), the Incurables Hospital (1744), the Lying-In Hospital (1745), Meath Hospital (1753), Lock Hospital (1755), and St Patrick's Hospital (1757). Of these, the Charitable Infirmary, Dr Steevens, Mercer's, and Meath were general hospitals. The rest dealt only with specific cases. The Lock Hospital catered to venereal disease; the Lying-In Hospital was for maternity cases; the Incurables Hospital dealt only with terminal and incurable cases; and St Patrick's was a mental hospital.[23]

Mercer's Hospital, Dublin's third voluntary hospital, was founded in 1734, shortly after the opening of Steevens's Hospital. That year four men presented to the city of Dublin a plan for establishing another voluntary hospital in the city. Dean William Perceval, the minister of St Michan's parish, Dr William Jackson, the minister of St Johns, William Stephens, a physician, and William Dobbs, a surgeon, argued that the city had no public provision to care for lunatics and other poor people with illnesses that were 'of tedious and doubtful cure'.[24] Since they were asking for financial assistance from the city they felt it expedient to stress that their new hospital would fill a gap left by Dr Steevens's Hospital's emphasis on 'curable' cases. Since the Incurables Hospital would not be established for another ten years, and St Patrick's would not open for another twenty, the city did have need for a hospital that would serve those cases. It was well known by friends and acquaintances of Jonathan Swift for years before his death that he intended to leave most of his fortune to the establishment of a hospital for the mentally ill, and as early as 1735 the Dublin City Council had recommended possible building sites for the institution.[25] However, Swift did not die until 1745 and his hospital, St

21 *The present state of Doctor Steevens's hospital.*
22 Ibid.
23 Geary, *Medicine and charity in Ireland*, p. 18.
24 Gilbert, *Calendar of ancient records of Dublin*, viii, 135.
25 Ibid., viii, 182.

Patrick's, would not open until 1757.[26] For the most part, in the early eighteenth century individuals deemed insane were confined to prisons, and there was limited provision in the Dublin Workhouse for poor people who were classified as insane. As originally envisioned, Mercer's Hospital was intended to serve a useful social purpose, providing medical care for those poor who had no other options. Mercer's willingness to accept cases not considered readily curable was unusual among eighteenth-century voluntary hospitals, which generally focused on curable cases by providing food, rest, and convalescence to individuals.[27] Mercer's, on the other hand, stated its willingness to treat those who suffered from cancer, the king's evil (scrofula), leprosy, falling sickness (epilepsy), and lunacy.[28]

The story of Mercer's Hospital begins some years before 1734 with Mary Mercer, a benevolent spinster, who donated the building for the hospital. The site of Mercer's Hospital had some history as a medical establishment. In the Middle Ages it was the site of St Stephen's Hospital, an offshoot of St Stephen's Church and a sanctuary for lepers.[29] St Stephen's parish had been disestablished in the seventeenth century and the land had been incorporated into St Peter's parish.[30] By the beginning of the eighteenth century the site was vacant and the churchwardens of St Peter's approached Mary Mercer, a well-known philanthropist, about taking it over.[31] Mercer and her sister, Alice, were the only heirs of their father, George Mercer, a doctor, who had spent most of his career at Trinity College as a fellow, and later as vice-provost.[32] While George Mercer's death date and the exact size of his estate are unknown, Mary Mercer was left affluent and devoted her time to charity work. Her primary interest was providing charitable education to poor girls. She had earlier purchased houses on Abbey Street to serve as asylums for poor girls, but she wanted to expand. The churchwardens of St Peter's granted her a 999-year lease on the site of old St Stephen's hospital in 1724 and Mercer set out to establish a school.[33] By 1734, when she was approached by Perceval, Jackson, Stephens and Dobbs, she was elderly and ill. They were supported by the minister and churchwardens of St Peter's, and wished to convert her almshouse for girls into a hospital for the poor. Mercer signed over the deed of the house

---

26 Elizabeth Malcolm, *Swift's Hospital: a history of St Patrick's Hospital, Dublin, 1746–1989* (New York, 1989), p. 7.
27 Geary, *Medicine and charity in Ireland*, p. 23; Porter, *The greatest benefit to mankind*, p. 299.
28 Gilbert, *Calendar of ancient records of Dublin*, viii, 135.
29 Lyons, *The quality of mercer's*, p. 18.
30 The only remnant of the original parish today is St Stephen's Green.
31 Lyons, *The quality of mercer's*, p. 18; N.L.I. 17/5/1865.
32 N.L.I. 17/5/1865.
33 N.L.I. 17/5/1865.

and they almost immediately set about establishing the hospital and petitioned the Corporation of Dublin for aid in renovating the building to receive patients.[34]

Mercer was not particularly interested in medical charity. Her decision to sign over the almshouse was probably for practical reasons, dictated by her own failing health. Each of her houses for poor girls was entirely funded by Mercer herself and this one might well have not survived her passing. She never abandoned her life's work of educating poor girls and, when she died on 4 March 1735, she left the bulk of her fortune to the establishment of a charity school for girls, and nothing to the hospital that bore her name. This will was dated 1733, before she signed over the deed to create the hospital.[35] She also named William Jackson, one of the founders of Mercer's Hospital, as one of the executors. However, she did direct her executors to see to it that the rents collected from some of her lands were directed towards the 'cure and relief of such poor indigent sick persons as from time to time shall be found and be resident in the several following parishes in the city of Dublin – St Peter, St Bridget, St Luke and St Nicholas Without the Walls'.[36] That money was to be given to the ministers of the parishes to be distributed to those who they deemed 'proper objects' of charity. In 1740 the governors of Mercer's Hospital decided to apply to the ministers of those parishes, asking them to transfer to the Hospital the legacy left to the parishes by Mercer.[37] It is not recorded whether or not any of the ministers acceded to the request, but given the burden that care of the poor placed on Dublin parishes at the time, it is unlikely that they would have willingly surrendered any legacies specifically marked for that purpose.

Mercer's original deed had provided a firm establishment for the hospital, but it did not establish any clear line of succession to keep the hospital running for a long period of time. In 1748 the surviving original trustees and several new ones who had been elected since decided to seek incorporation for the hospital. This step was essential to the long-term survival of the organization. It was intended to ensure smooth succession between trustees and to enable them to more easily purchase land and receive legacies for the benefit of the hospital.[38] Securing incorporation involved passing a statute to that effect in parliament. In 1749 an 'Act for regulating the hospital founded by Mary Mercer, spinster' was passed by the Irish parliament. The Act, which was drawn up by the governors themselves, formally confirmed the current governors of the hospital and set up procedures for replacing governors on their decease. It did not place any maximum limits upon the number of governors the hospital could have. The governors had the

34 Lyons, *The quality of mercer's*, p. 22.
35 N.A.I. 999/836/1.
36 N.A.I. 999/836/2.
37 N.A.I. 2006/97.
38 N.A.I. 2006/97.

right to elect more as they saw fit, so long as those people were deemed likely 'to promote and encourage the charitable designs' of the hospital.[39] The Act is indicative of the close relationship between voluntary hospitals and the Irish parliament. The Act of Parliament did not substantially change the operation of the hospital, but it did codify and enshrine the governing procedures that had arisen during its fifteen years of operation.

Like other voluntary hospitals and charitable societies of the period, Mercer's was run by a combination of the Anglo-Irish social elite and Church of Ireland bishops and clergymen.[40] The trustees appointed in 1734, along with the first governors, illustrate the mixture of elite citizens appointed to oversee the hospital.[41] The forty-nine governors consisted of a number of Church of Ireland bishops, aristocrats, and members of the Anglo-Irish political elite. In general, such charitable boards contained two types of governors: those who were appointed *ex officio* and those who were elected.[42] The primate, lord chancellors, the speaker of the House of Commons, and the archbishops of Dublin and Tuam were all appointed by virtue of their office. It was common practice at the time to appoint such men to prominent offices as a way of seeking official validation, and examination of the minute books reveals that they played little active role in the day-to-day governance of the hospital. The trustees of Mercer's Hospital met once a month, and a committee of three trustees who lived in town met once a week to oversee hospital business. The hospital's minute books reveal that, on average, meetings were attended by between three and ten members, mostly elected governors. The credit for actually running Mercer's Hospital belongs to less famous elected governors, such as John Putland, who served as treasurer for many years, and the Reverend Samuel Hutchinson, dean of Dromore, who was secretary.[43]

John Putland was the very model of the active, improvement-minded, Irish Protestant of this era. In addition to his duties as treasurer for Mercer's

---

[39] *The statutes at large, passed in the parliaments held in Ireland: from the third year of Edward the Second* (21 vols, vii, Dublin, 1786), vii, 94.

[40] Geary, *Medicine and Charity in Ireland, 1718–1851*, p. 33.

[41] *The statutes at large, passed in the parliaments held in Ireland: from the third year of Edward the Second*, vii, 90–91; N.A.I. 2006/97. The trustees named were: the archbishops of Armagh, Hugh Boulter; the archbishop of Dublin, John Hoadley; the bishop of Kildare, Charles Cobb; Thomas How, the lord mayor of Dublin; Charles Burton and William Woodworth esqs, the high sheriffs of the city; Charles Whittingham, archdeacon of Dublin; Jonathan Swift, the dean of St Patrick's; William Jackson, minister of St John's; Dean Percival, the minister of St Michan's; doctors William Stephens and Francis LeHunt esqs; and, finally, surgeons Hannibal Hall, John Stone and William Dobbs esqs. The governors named were: the lord bishop of Cork, Jonathan Swift, Charles Whittingham, Dean Madden, Doctor William Stephens, Reverend Mr James King, Hannibal Hall, William Dobbs, and Mr John Stones.

[42] Geary, *Medicine and charity in Ireland*, p. 95.

[43] N.A.I. 2006/97.

Hospital, he also served as treasurer of the Royal Dublin Society and was both treasurer and a member of the Committee of Fifteen of the Incorporated Society. Putland was also a governor of Dr Steevens's Hospital, the Lying-In Hospital, and the Dublin Workhouse. Nor did he simply rack up membership in these organizations through subscriptions. He actively attended most meetings and dutifully donated annually. Like many Anglo-Irish of the period, he did not have particularly longstanding roots in the country. The Putland family probably arrived in the 1630s among a number of English migrants to the country. Upon their settling in Ireland the family fortunes rose rapidly. In 1649 George Putland, the great-great-grandfather of John, was named an honorary freeman of the city. George's son, Thomas, was also a freeman of the city and early in life was apparently a blacksmith. Thomas would later move away from such work and into banking and investing, and secured the future wealth of his family by buying large quantities of land confiscated from Catholics. The Putlands owned land in Dublin, but much of their income came from estates in Counties Cork, Wicklow, Kilkenny, and Queen's County. Thomas Putland and his son, Thomas junior, also worked as bankers and investors, though they were not necessarily well liked or well respected for this work, as both were implicated in financial scandals involving extortion and misappropriation.[44]

John Putland was the son of Thomas junior and his wife, the wealthy and well-connected Jane Rotton. Thomas junior died young, in 1721, aged only thirty-five, and John was raised under the influence of his stepfather Richard Helsham. Helsham came from a landed family in Kilkenny; he was educated at Trinity College Dublin, becoming a doctor of physic, a mathematician, and a professor of natural and experimental philosophy. He was a physician and personal friend to Jonathan Swift. John Putland's interest in voluntary hospitals seems to have come from his stepfather, who was a trustee and benefactor of Dr Steevens's Hospital. Like his stepfather, John Putland attended Trinity College, attaining his bachelor's degree in 1731 and a becoming Master of Divinity in 1734. Putland was never a minister, though he was a spiritual man. In addition to his involvement in charity organizations, he was also a member of the Spiritual Society, a Dublin-based religious society.[45] How John Putland made his living is unclear. He seems primarily to have lived off the family's land and investments; there is also some evidence that, like his father and grandfather, he was an investor. Jonathan Swift, who knew Putland through his stepfather,

---

[44] Liam Clare, 'The Putland family of Dublin and Bray' in *Dublin Historical Record*, 54 (2001), pp. 183–92.

[45] Little else is known about the Spiritual Society, though Putland was apparently held in high esteem by fellow members. *On Faction; a poem occasionally wrote by a member of the Spiritual Society; and inscribed to Mr. John Putland* (Dublin, 1753).

trusted him enough to invest £1,500 with him, money that he intended to go towards the future St Patrick's Hospital.[46]

Putland also invested in several theatres in the city of Dublin and was an active patron of the arts. During his lifetime his family obtained a new level of respectability. The desire for social approbation may, in part, have motivated the degree of Putland's social and charitable involvement. As the philosopher Bernard Mandeville argued in 1714, 'pride and vanity have built more hospitals then all the virtues together'.[47] Many benefactors of medical charity were motivated by philanthropic motives, but there were also practical benefits to providing medical care to the poor. It did help to protect the interests of the upper classes to which Putland belonged.[48] In addition to his duties with various voluntary societies, Putland was also a mason and served in several positions in public office. In the 1740s he was a magistrate and later high sheriff for the County of Dublin. He remained actively involved in voluntary societies until at least 1772, when ill-health forced him to retire. He died in 1773.[49]

Men like John Putland helped ensure the smooth operation of voluntary hospitals. More socially prominent but less actively involved governors also played an important role, even if they were absent from most meetings. On a practical level, all the governors could be counted on to donate money regularly. Their contacts were also useful. Mercer's Hospital relied on an annual cathedral service and musical performance to raise money, and the connections of many governors helped to make the Mercer's musical performance into an important social occasion. Well-known governors could be counted on to attend the performance and also to petition other prominent individuals, such as the lord lieutenant, to attend as well.[50]

When Mercer's first opened in 1734 it had only ten beds, and it quickly outgrew such modest accommodation. Within a few years the governors were able to expand to forty beds, and by 1738 a sizable addition had been built onto the original property.[51] The hospital originally used the same house that Mary Mercer had erected in 1724, but that house was not very large and was apparently 'inconvenient for the purposes of a hospital'.[52] In order to expand, they needed a new, larger building. The governors soon began work to raise

46 Clare, 'The Putland family of Dublin and Bray', pp. 183–92.
47 Bernard Mandeville, The fable of the bees, or private vices, publick benefits (2 vols, Indianapolis, 1924), i, 261.
48 Geary, Medicine and charity in Ireland, p. 102.
49 Clare, 'The Putland family of Dublin and Bray', pp. 183–92.
50 N.A.I. 2006/97.
51 John Warburton, History of the city of Dublin, from the earliest accounts to the present time (2 vols, London, 1818), ii, 717.
52 N.A.I. 2006/97.

funds for a new building, applying to the archbishop of Dublin as early as 1736 for land and funds to enlarge the building. The decision to incorporate in 1749 and the additional lands granted to them by the parish helped make this possible. By 1757 a new building had been completed, containing fifty-two beds, though it had the potential to hold as many as eighty beds. The governors of the hospital petitioned parliament for assistance in setting up these additional beds, the costs of which were estimated to be about £10 a year each. Since Mercer's was a charity hospital patients did not pay for the services they received, but benefactors could endow beds at voluntary hospitals, which gave them the privilege of recommending patients for admittance.[53] John Putland, for example, permanently endowed a bed at Steevens's hospital.[54] In 1738 Mrs Mary Coghill was granted the privilege of 'occasionally' recommending 'a distressed person to the hospital's care' in exchange for fulfilling the generous legacy left to the hospital by her deceased brother Dr Marmaduke Coghill. Other subscribers seemed to have donated primarily because they desired to have a bed to recommend patients for and they were willing to pay £10 a year for the privilege.[55]

In order to be admitted to Mercer's Hospital or any voluntary hospital, prospective patients first needed the recommendation of someone like Mrs Coghill or John Putland, a subscriber or benefactor, someone who had the privilege of recommending patients. Before recommending admittance, the subscriber would determine if the prospective patient was a suitable object of charity, if they were one of the 'deserving poor', which generally meant the working poor. The recommendation system is one of the ways in which voluntary hospitals reinforced the social order. Patients had to produce a certificate of poverty signed by a clergyman or respectable householder. In England voluntary hospitals were stricter about such requirements. In Ireland there was a greater willingness to admit paupers; medical charity was targeted towards the deserving poor, but the level of need in Ireland and the lack of an official mechanism for poor relief led to greater flexibility on such terms.[56] In some cases, patients might be admitted without having first secured a recommendation, but this was only in emergencies, such as in cases of injuries that required immediate treatment. Mercer's admitted accident victims 'indiscriminately', without any recommendation.[57]

Some hospitals required patients to make a deposit to defray the cost of the burial in the event of the patient's death, but there is no evidence that Mercer's

[53] N.A.I. 2006/97.
[54] Clare, 'The Putland family of Dublin and Bray', p. 190.
[55] N.A.I. 2006/97.
[56] Geary, Medicine and charity in Ireland, pp. 107–8.
[57] N.L.I. 17/5/1865.

had such a policy.[58] It did, however, have a policy of holding recommenders financially accountable for the cost of removing a patient should they turn out to be incurable.[59] Once admitted, patients were expected to be well-behaved, to follow the instructions of physicians, and to show a proper amount of deference and gratitude towards their benefactors for the services that were being provided for them.[60]

With regards to religion, the governors, medical officers, and the staff of voluntary hospitals were almost universally Protestant, but the patients were not. There is no evidence to suggest that voluntary hospitals in Ireland discriminated against the objects of charity on the basis of their religion; there was, however, discrimination based on other factors. The rules of Mercer's Hospital in 1768 stated that patients with infectious fevers, 'venereal disorders culpably contracted', lunatics, and Incurables could not be admitted.[61] This was a retreat from their earlier admittance policy, but by that point other hospitals existed to address each of these ailments specifically.

As with other voluntary hospitals of the period, Mercer's originally had no endowment and was maintained on the basis of the charitable subscriptions it raised each year. These financial limitations affected the size of the hospital and the number of people it could help at any given time. Funding was a constant concern. Charitable subscriptions were not a particularly stable financial base, since they depended on irregular and often inadequate donations.[62] This was a problem felt by other types of voluntary societies as well. The Incorporated Society routinely suffered from funding shortfalls and relied on regular grants from the Irish parliament to remain in operation. Voluntary hospitals did not always have that level of government support. In the 1750s, while Mercer's new building was being erected, the hospital was granted £500 from the king at the recommendation of parliament. In 1757, once the new building had been opened, they again requested parliamentary assistance in order to furnish it with more beds.[63]

Parliamentary grants, however, were not a large or regular source of funding for Mercer's. Other voluntary hospitals, such as the Lying-In Hospital, relied on them more routinely. Mercer's did at times receive grants from parliament, but only after its formal incorporation. In an act of 1765 establishing public infirmaries across Ireland, it was decided that Mercer's, along with the Charitable Infirmary and the Hospital for Incurables, should be granted £150 a year to be

58 Woodward, *To do the sick no harm*, pp. 38–9.
59 N.A.I. 2006/97.
60 Geary, *Medicine and charity in Ireland*, p. 103.
61 N.A.I. 2006/97.
62 Geary, *Medicine and charity in Ireland*, p. 33.
63 N.A.I. 2006/97.

split evenly between them.[64] Between 1753 and 1767 Mercer's received £500 in grants from parliament. However, this was very little in comparison with the help received by other voluntary hospitals. St Patrick's received £6,000 and the Lying-In Hospital £19,300. All told, between 1703 and 1771 hospitals received £44,251 in parliamentary grants. This was a considerable amount, but not in comparison to that given to other organizations. The Dublin Society received £64,000, the Incorporated Society £96,000, and the Linen Manufacture over £180,000 in that same period.[65] Each of these organizations was far larger than any single voluntary hospital, and they were also more successful at linking their aims with political utility. By the nineteenth century most of Mercer's revenue came from rents and income from land it owned and interest from securities. In 1823 Mercer's income, of approximately £900 per year, consisted of a £50 grant from parliament and £738 in revenue; the rest was annual subscriptions.[66]

By the nineteenth century the tradition of public support for charities in Ireland became a source of controversy. Declining subscriptions to voluntary hospitals and other charities were thought to be a result of parliamentary funding discouraging private philanthropy, but, just as the Incorporated Society saw its financial support from parliament decline and eventually end in the nineteenth century, the government also began to question the utility of regular grants to hospitals. Mercer's, however, was among those that was almost wholly supported by private funding, while by that point Steevens's Hospital, the Lying-In Hospital, Meath Hospital, and the Incurables Hospital relied on a combination of private charity and government grants.[67] Mercer's did apply for this type of support, however, but a visit by the Dublin Hospital Commission determined in 1855 that, despite the value of the service provided by Mercer's, it did not possess any features that should entitle them to government aid.[68] The reasons why Mercer's did not qualify are not clear but presumably it was because, to the government inspectors, Mercer's seemed redundant. Both the Lying-In and the Incurables Hospital served only certain cases that could not be treated elsewhere. Mercer's was a general hospital, like Steevens's and Meath, but it was smaller and its geographic location did not help it to distinguish itself.

Government grants were never a major source of income for Mercer's and, before its incorporation in 1750, the hospital did not have the property or securities that made up most of their income in the early nineteenth century.

[64] *The statutes at large passed in the parliaments held in Ireland* (21 vols, Dublin, 1769), ix, 382.

[65] Arthur Young, *A tour in Ireland; with general observations on the state of the kingdom* (London, 1780), pp. 62–3.

[66] John Warburton, *History of the city of Dublin*, ii, 719; *Reports of the committee of St Mary's parish on local taxation* (Dublin, 1823), p. 80.

[67] N.L.I. 7646.

[68] N.L.I. 7646.

Instead they relied on donations given either in person or placed anonymously in a poor box, and subscriptions. Most voluntary hospitals, like other charities, relied on an annual charity sermon to help raise funds. Charity sermons were an immensely popular form of philanthropic fundraising in the eighteenth century. They became important social occasions and attendance was considered obligatory among the prosperous classes of Dublin. Events such as charity sermons and Mercer's musical performances paired charity with conviviality. For subscribers these events allowed them to witness the results of their donations – for instance, charity schools frequently displayed the children well-behaved and in matching uniforms, as a way of aligning charity with consumer culture.[69] Attending these events also allowed the subscriber to establish a public presence, visually demonstrating their benevolence and their civic virtue.[70] Each charity chose a particular time of year for such appeals. Mercer's was usually in March; the event was well publicized in advance, and it was considered important to find a prominent and popular preacher to give the sermon.[71] While there was some degree of performance involved in charitable fundraising of this sort, most Dublin charities did not display the same level of performance as seen in contemporary London charities, which were critiqued at times for the combination of luxury and spectacle they used to advertise themselves, a charge that was not brought against Dublin's charities.[72] By the nineteenth century, charity sermons had become so commonplace that John Warburton argued that it was ineffective for the Lying-In Hospital to keep holding one.

> When the frequency of appeals of this kind are considered, and that they are made for parish schools and minor charities depending solely on such casual means for support, and moreover that, in general, these collections arise from the charitable dispositions of the same set of individuals nearly, who go from Sunday to Sunday from one charity sermon to another, it is hoped that the Governors and Guardians of the Lying-In Hospital will not appear remiss to the general interests of charity, in waving this form of appeal to the public for the support of an institution of such general utility.[73]

As far as Warburton was concerned, a well-supported and endowed institution such as the Lying-In Hospital did not need the approximately £150 a year it

---

[69] Sarah Lloyd, 'Pleasing spectacles and elegant dinners: conviviality, benevolence and charity anniversaries in eighteenth-century London' in *Journal of British Studies*, xli, no. 1 (2002), p. 27.

[70] Kelly and Powell, 'Introduction', p. 20.

[71] Karen Sonnelitter, '"To unite our temporal and eternal interests": sermons and the charity school movement in Ireland, 1689–1740' (M.A. thesis, Queen's University Belfast, 2006), pp. 16, 28.

[72] Lloyd, 'Pleasing spectacles and elegant dinners,' pp. 50–52.

[73] Warburton, *History of the city of Dublin*, p. 678.

was raising by charity sermons, since so much of its income by that point came from other sources.[74]

Warburton was correct in noting that the Lying-In Hospital, an extremely successful and popular institution, had numerous other avenues of support. Founded in 1745 by Dr Bartholomew Mosse, the Lying-In Hospital succeeded in winning public support and government grants. It received over £19,000 from parliament between 1753 and 1767, considerably more than Mercer's or any other Dublin voluntary hospital. Even before becoming chartered in 1756 the Lying-In Hospital, later known as the Rotunda because of the building it would eventually inhabit, was granted £6,000 from parliament for assistance in building its new location.[75] In addition to grants from parliament, the hospital also was granted the income from a tax placed on private sedan chairs in the city, indicating that it was regarded as an institution of great importance carrying out an important public duty.[76] This tax was shared with the Dublin Foundling Hospital and Workhouse, which was founded by order of the city and was funded primarily by a local property tax. The Incorporated Society was regarded as similarly important, and was granted the income of licensing fees for hawkers and peddlers. The Lying-In Hospital, which catered to poor pregnant women, hoped to reduce the mortality rates of both the women and their infants. Also contributing to the popularity of the hospital was the hope that by providing aid to poor women and their children it would reduce the rate of one of the more distressing social problems of the time, infanticide.[77] Despite such good intentions, neither the Lying-In Hospital nor the Foundling Hospital before it was able to prevent this practice, however. Rates of infanticide in Dublin remained about the same even after the new Rotunda building was completed.[78]

Mercer's Hospital did not lack for public support either, but it did not have the same broad appeal as an institution such as the Lying-In Hospital. In the crowded charity sermon market of eighteenth-century Dublin, the governors of Mercer's had to do something to set themselves apart. Towards that end they decided that instead of holding a simple yearly charity sermon they would instead hold an extravagant cathedral service marked by a musical performance, with ticket sales benefiting the hospital. The annual Mercer's musical performance became an important social event in Dublin society; the

[74] Ibid., p. 679.

[75] Ibid., p. 670.

[76] *A correct copy of the registry of private licensed sedan chairs, in the city of Dublin, as they appear on the collector's books, 25th March, 1786. Published pursuant to order of the governors of the foundling and lying-in hospitals* (Dublin, 1786).

[77] *A copy of His Majesty's royal charter for incorporating the governors and guardians of the hospital for the relief of poor lying-in women, in Dublin*, p. 4.

[78] James Kelly, 'Infanticide in eighteenth-century Ireland' in *Irish Economic and Social History*, 19 (1992), p. 6.

1736 performance, for example, was described as 'the grandest performance ever heard here'.[79] Throughout the eighteenth century, the proceeds of the performance were to serve as an important source of income for the hospital. In 1738 Mercer's governors considered holding a different type of performance, a play, for the benefit of the hospital, but nothing came of their enquiries.[80] Meanwhile, the annual musical performance generally consisted of a service at St Andrew's parish and a performance of spiritual music. In later years they would occasionally hold the performance in other locations, such as the Great Music Hall on Fishamble Street, where Handel's *Acis and Galatea* was performed in 1759. The musical performances were elaborate occasions. There was a captain's guard, stewards carrying gold and white rods were appointed from the nobility and the gentry, parliament and law courts were adjourned, and the political and social elite of the city were expected to attend. When held at St Andrew's parish there was also a sermon given by a prominent Church of Ireland bishop. Performances were given by the Dublin Philharmonic Society, with the choir of St Patrick's Cathedral.[81] The Mercer's musical performances demonstrate the close relationship between medical charity and the Church of Ireland. Mercer's, like other voluntary hospitals, relied on the support of the church for its fundraising, and the use of sermons and spiritual music to raise funds indicates the importance of religion to medical charities. They relied as much on religious tenets encouraging charity for support as they did on Enlightenment values.

Mercer's musical performances are historically significant not only in their use of entertainment to raise money for charity but also in some of the pieces performed. The composer George Frederic Handel, who visited Dublin between 1741 and 1742, was a particular supporter of Mercer's. In 1738 his *Te Deum Jubilate* and two coronation anthems were performed for the benefit of the hospital. In 1741 he volunteered a performance of 'his choicest music' for the benefit of Mercer's, the Charitable Infirmary, and the indebted prisoners of Marshalsea. It was the first public performance of his *Messiah*. Organizing the performance seems to have taken quite a bit of effort on the part of the Mercer's governors. Jonathan Swift, the dean of St Patrick's Cathedral, at one point banned his choir from taking part in a Handel performance; eventually he allowed them to perform only as long as the dean of Christ Church also allowed his choir to participate. Swift was an *ex officio* governor of Mercer's Hospital, but, owing to his own ill-health, played little active role in the hospital aside from allowing the St Patrick's choir to perform at these occasions.

---

[79] *Pue's Occurrences*, 10 April 1736.
[80] N.A.I. 2006/97.
[81] N.A.I. 2006/97.

In public notices it was mentioned that the money raised at such performances served as 'the principal support of this useful charity', and women were asked not to host any private assemblies or 'drums' that might compete with the Mercer's performance for attendance. Eventually the annual Mercer's performance began to suffer from a pattern of diminishing returns. In 1757 the governors did not hold a performance at all, 'in consideration of the many necessary calls and Collections for Charity in this City at this Time of Dearth', and also because their own new building was not yet open for the reception of patients.[82] Once they began the performances again the following year the governors began to worry over the decline in the revenue generated. In a 1759 advertisement publicizing the performance they noted that in the early years the performances brought in as much as £500 pounds and that lately they had brought in only about £100.[83] This decline might be attributed to the crowded landscape of Dublin charities, or might have occurred simply because the novelty of the musical performances had worn off. By 1818 the performances had become 'unproductive' and were abandoned.[84]

Musical performances were not the only avenue of funding available to Mercer's, as noted above. In addition to annual subscriptions and casual benefactions they also kept a poor box, which never yielded much revenue. The hospital received more significant funding from legacies left them, either in the form of money or property. Most of Mercer's income for any given year was made up of legacies and casual donations, rent from property they owned, and the interest on government debentures. In 1768 the hospital reported receiving only £82 3s. 6d. from subscriptions and £123 12s. 3d. from the musical performance at St Andrew's. These two combined did not come near to meeting their expenses for that year, which they listed as exceeding £1,100. This included the expenses for in- and out-patient services; in that year the hospital treated 312 people as in-patients and 6,636 as out-patients. In addition, there were provisions, maintenance and repairs to the building, and salaries for employees and servants. The physicians and surgeons who worked at the hospital did so free of charge. As treasurer for many years, John Putland was responsible for handling the Hospital's finances and he seems to have done well. Not only was he re-elected unanimously year after year, but despite declining income from the musical performance and declining subscriptions the hospital remained financially sound, thanks largely to his management.

The other occasional avenue of funding for Mercer's, and other voluntary hospitals, was the state lottery. In 1747 representatives from the Charitable

---

[82] N.A.I. 2006/97.
[83] N.A.I. 2006/97.
[84] Warburton, *History of the city of Dublin*, p. 719.

Infirmary approached the governors of Mercer's with the intention of holding a state lottery during the next year to benefit all the Dublin voluntary hospitals. The governors quickly agreed to participate. While lottery income was not a stable or regular source of support for Mercer's, it could be sizable. In 1768 the Committee of Exchange Lottery Scheme brought in £500.[85] Of all the Dublin voluntary hospitals, the Lying-In Hospital benefited the most from lotteries. The Lying-In Hospital's founder, Dr Bartholomew Mosse, was noted for his distinctive fundraising methods, including theatrical performances, concerts, and lotteries. Mosse was unique in Dublin's charity culture for the extent to which he managed to combine benevolence with conviviality and consumer culture. His reliance on public performance as a means of fundraising was probably inspired by the success he saw Mercer's having with its musical performances. In 1748 Mosse acquired a four-acre site in the north end of Dublin, near the newly fashionable areas of the city, to erect a new hospital. He began by laying out an elaborate pleasure garden along the lines of Vauxhall Gardens in London; in addition to the gardens, there was an orchestra platform, an indoor concert room, and a coffeehouse, all of which were intended to raise money towards the building of a new hospital on the same site.[86]

In 1753, while the new building for the Lying-In Hospital was being constructed, Dr Mosse concocted a scheme to raise £10,000 towards its completion by means of a Dutch Lottery. He had tried lottery schemes in the past, but without much success. One in 1752 that was to benefit several Dublin hospitals was ultimately forbidden by the Lords Justices.[87] On this occasion, lottery tickets were brought to England to be sold as well and, in order to encourage the selling of tickets, the lottery was well publicized for months in advance. Unfortunately for Mosse, private lotteries were illegal in England, and this particular lottery, which was organized by Mosse solely for the benefit of the Lying-In Hospital, was a private lottery. Several coffeehouse owners were convicted of selling the tickets and others were convicted of publicizing the scheme. The coffeehouse owners argued that they had assumed the scheme was legal by virtue of how well advertised it was. The publicists argued the same. Their punishment was the payment of fines ranging from £200 to £500 and one year's imprisonment, though they did petition to have their convictions overturned.[88] William Sharpe's report on the petition of Joseph Hazard, one of the publicists, seems to have agreed with this judgement. Sharpe argued that

---

[85] N.A.I. 2006/97.

[86] Alan Browne, 'Bartholomew Mosse, 1712–1759, founder and first master' in Alan Browne (ed.), Masters, midwives, and ladies-in-waiting: the Rotunda Hospital 1745–1995 (Dublin, 1995), p. 9.

[87] William Wilde, 'Illustrious physicians and surgeons in Ireland: Bartholomew Mosse, M.D. Surgeon' in Dublin Quarterly Journal of Medical Sciences, 2 (1846), pp. 573–4.

[88] T.N.A. T1/356/54–62.

Hazard and the others were 'unwittingly drawn into' the entire scheme, 'by the specious pretences published and propagated by Dr Mosse of Ireland (the principle contriver and promoter of this pernicious scheme)'.[89] Unfortunately, Hazard's conviction was upheld, and he was ordered to pay £500 and sentenced to a year in Newgate, leaving behind a wife and two young children with no ready means of supporting themselves.[90] Mosse's dedication towards his hospital, it can be seen, sometimes led him to poor decision-making. In 1754 he was arrested on the grounds of a debt of £200 – perhaps the fine of one of the shopkeepers convicted in the lottery scheme – and was imprisoned for a time in Beaumaris Castle in Anglesey, from which he managed to escape via a window. He spent three weeks hiding in mainland Wales before returning to Dublin, where he attempted to re-establish his reputation by publishing the receipts from the lotteries. He seems to have cleared his name from any accusation of misappropriating funds, but the experience convinced him that lotteries were not the best way to fund his hospital.[91]

Mercer's Hospital benefited only from legal state lotteries in Ireland, and only on rare occasions; scandals such as Mosse's had convinced the governors to be wary of such fundraising schemes. By the 1750s, with revenue from the musical performance and subscription rates declining, the importance of legacies and bequests became even clearer to them, so much so that in 1757 they paid a clerk in the Prerogative and Conciliary offices to inform them of any legacy left to the hospital which they had no notice of. This strategy seems to have worked to their advantage, since in 1758 they were awarded the estate of one Phillip Ramsey, who had died in 1752 and left his lands to the governors of the hospital. Legacies were so important to the governors that at times they had to threaten legal action to see that they were paid. In 1764 they threatened suit against an Edward Butler if he did not pay the £100 legacy left by William Boyton.[92]

Fundraising was the issue which dominated most meetings of the Mercer's Hospital governors, trustees and managers, but it was not their only concern. The actual operation of hospital proved challenging. Particularly in the early years of operation there were routine staff difficulties. In 1736 the house steward was fired for being unqualified, and when he failed to return hospital goods and accounts in his possession the governors had to threaten prosecution. Several years later there was a similar problem with a clerk, who was fired and later prosecuted for stealing hospital funds. There were also a number of problems with the nursing staff. Nurses in the eighteenth century had no formal medical training, and were

89 T.N.A. T1/357/79.
90 T. N.A. T1/356/61–62.
91 Browne, 'Bartholomew Mosse, 1712–1759', p. 10.
92 N.A.I. 2006/97.

essentially thought of as servants. Nursing was regarded as an unskilled profession, not suitable for respectable women, and as a result nurses were among the lowest paid of the hospital's employees.[93] They had a reputation for drunkenness, and moralists warned of the ill consequences that would befall patients, as well as hospitals, unless nurses were banned from drinking entirely.[94] One pamphleteer, Edward Foster, described nursing as a 'mean station' in the hospital, but still an important one. Foster stressed that ideally they should have experience caring for the sick and that they should be able to administer medications so as to save the apothecary from having to be present for this at all times.[95] As voluntary hospitals became more widespread in this period, some in the medical profession began to recognize the importance of training nurses. The English physician Robert Johnson published a manual in 1767 intended to instruct nurses on the basics of their profession. Johnson felt it essential that nurses should have basic knowledge of how to care for patients. He also felt that not all women were qualified to become nurses. 'Honesty and Fidelity' were the two most important qualities, but he also noted that 'sobriety is essential'. Aside from this, Johnson felt that nurses should be quick, efficient, and quiet in carrying out their duties.[96]

At Mercer's Hospital nurses were expected to ensure the cleanliness of wards and bedding, to wash clothes, linens, and bedding as often as they were directed, and to attend the sick, giving them assistance and nourishment. Nurses were also supposed to prevent damage to hospital furniture and prevent fires by preventing patients from having candles too near their beds. The governors' concern over fires dated from an incident in 1739 where a candle ignited nearby bedding and caused serious damage. For all these responsibilities nurses were paid £5 per year when the hospital first opened.[97] Nursing was a difficult job and one for which the hospital had trouble finding qualified women. One nurse, Alice McCann, was ordered to be discharged in 1736 as soon as a suitable replacement could be found. But McCann was still employed by the hospital in 1738, when she was finally fired for seducing the hospital's patients. Another nurse was dismissed in 1740 for stealing coal. In 1739 a nurse called Eleanor Ware ran off with another employee, James Dan, taking with them a large quantity of medicine and drugs as well as some of the hospital's linens. Afterwards, the governors decided that anyone employed as a nurse should be at least forty years old.[98]

93 Woodward, To do the sick no harm, p. 32.
94 An epistle to the fair-sex on the subject of drinking (London, 1744), pp. 46–7.
95 Edward Foster, An essay on hospitals. Or succinct directions for the situation, construction and administration of country hospitals (Dublin, 1768), pp. 67–8.
96 Robert Johnson, Some friendly cautions to the heads of families: containing ample directions to nurses who attend the sick, and women in child-bed (London, 1767), pp. viii–x.
97 N.A.I. 2006/97.
98 N.A.I. 2006/97.

Voluntary hospitals also served as training grounds for physicians and surgeons and contributed to the professionalization of both fields in this period. The Lying-In Hospital, for instance, was the first training hospital for midwifery in the British Isles. In general there were three classes of medical professionals in the eighteenth century. Physicians, who were considered learned professionals, used medicines and remedies; surgeons, who were skilled craftsmen, used operations to treat patients; and apothecaries, who were tradesmen, dispensed medication.[99] Physicians and surgeons together had founded Mercer's Hospital and they attended upon the patients there free of charge. At all times there were several on the governing board of the hospital and they played an important role in running the institution. At the time of its incorporation the board included six surgeons and one physician, who were permitted to appoint others so long as they served the hospital without payment.[100] Other hospitals did pay at least some of their medical professionals, who were appointed as members of staff. Apothecaries, on the other hand, were employees of the hospital. The apothecary on the staff at Mercer's was to be resident in the house constantly and to dispense medications as directed by physicians and surgeons. He was selected by the physicians and surgeons of the hospital.[101]

Many voluntary hospitals, including Mercer's, maintained close relationships with the Royal College of Physicians in Ireland and the Royal College of Surgeons in Ireland. By the nineteenth century, medical teaching in Ireland was generally hospital-based, a practice which first emerged in the eighteenth century. When the Dublin Society of Surgeons, later the Royal College of Surgeons, was established in 1780 its premises were deliberately placed near Mercer's Hospital.[102] Practical experience was increasingly considered an essential part of a medical education. Edward Foster, writing in 1768, noted that an ideal physician was one with experience, 'for to be able to know diseases, it is necessary to have before seen them'.[103] Surgeons were a class below physicians. They were to be well-educated, but their education was gained through apprenticeship with a qualified surgeon and not through a university education.[104] They were described by Foster as 'second' to physicians in terms of their utility to the hospital; physicians were in charge of patient care except when it came to surgical matters, but only in these cases were they expected to defer to the

---

[99] Geary, *Medicine and charity in Ireland*, p. 123.

[100] *The statutes at large, passed in the parliaments held in Ireland: from the third year of Edward the Second*, vii, 94.

[101] N.A.I. 2006/97.

[102] James Kelly, 'The emergence of scientific and institutional medical practice in Ireland, 1650–1800' in Greta Malcolm and Elizabeth Jones (eds), *Medicine, disease and the state in Ireland, 1650–1940* (Cork, 1999), p. 33.

[103] Foster, *An essay on hospitals*, p. 46.

[104] Ibid., pp. 48–62.

judgement of surgeons. Apothecaries were an equally important part of hospital operation, but were ranked below both physicians and surgeons, although they were also expected to be educated and to have served an apprenticeship. Apothecaries were experts on medicines and their preparation, but at least in hospitals they did not deal directly with patients; instead, they followed the instructions of physicians.[105]

Voluntary hospitals were generally regarded as excellent charities, but reports of conditions in hospitals varied widely. In 1784 Archibald Richardson, who was inspecting the Dublin hospitals, wrote to a friend describing Steevens's Hospital as 'a perfect brothel filled with prostitutes and servants infected with venereal complaints and no vacancy'.[106] Meanwhile, Robert Nelson in 1752 had described the same hospital as 'commodious' and 'the cleanest of any hospital of the kind in Europe'.[107] Nelson was writing much earlier and in a pamphlet intended to encourage the wealthy of Ireland to give to worthy charities, including voluntary hospitals. John Howard, the prison reformer who exposed poor conditions in the Incorporated Society schools, also toured the hospitals of Ireland. In 1789 he said of Steevens's Hospital that the wards 'are close and offensive' and that the windows were too frequently shut. He also seemed to agree with Richardson's interpretation of the hospital as 'a perfect brothel', hinting at the improprieties which could occur as a result of both the hospital's lax visitation policy, allowing men into women's wards and vice versa on any day of the week, and the privacy that was available because beds were 'enclosed with wood and curtains'.[108] Mercer's Hospital was spared from such insinuations by Howard; he noted that it 'was a few years since very dirty, offensive and unhealthy; but now it is one of the cleanest in Dublin'.[109] Howard's account of other Irish hospitals was generally mixed.

Mercer's Hospital worked not only on improving general conditions but also on improving the level of care it was able to provide. In 1737 the surgeons requested that a bagnio and fluxing room be set aside in the hospital. A bagnio was essentially a room for vapour baths, while a fluxing room was for purging, generally by bleeding. Eighteenth-century medicine assumed that most diseases could be cured by purging them from the body either through sweating, bleeding, or vomiting. We have seen that William Carey was given mercury to produce an excessive flow of saliva; this, along, with mercury plasters and sea bathing, were the only treatments the physicians at Mercer's could think of to treat the ossification of his muscles. When Elinor Proudfort was admitted to Mercer's

---

[105] Ibid., pp. 63–6.
[106] P.R.O.N.I. D207/20/49.
[107] Nelson, *An address to persons of quality and estate*, p. 68.
[108] Howard, *An account of the principal lazarettos in Europe*, p. 81.
[109] Ibid.

in 1762 with an abdominal tumour she, too, was bled, purged, blistered, and given a plaster, though, unlike in Carey's case, none of these had any positive effect.[110] Requests to set up a bagnio and fluxing room, as well as to expand the surgery, indicate that the physicians and surgeons who worked at Mercer's were interested in trying to provide high-quality medical care. However, since they were unpaid for their work at the hospital, they could not attend to the patients there constantly. Surgeons were in attendance every day from eight to ten in the morning, while physicians attended on Mondays and Fridays from twelve to two.[111] In general, the governors of the hospital, most of whom were not medical professionals, did not interfere with patient care, though they did routinely enquire about costs. In 1765 they requested that the physicians and surgeons hold a meeting to discuss the rising expense of running the hospital and attempt to come up with strategies to reduce them.[112]

Voluntary hospitals were able to operate thanks to cooperation between emerging medical science and Church of Ireland clergymen. While the hospitals themselves served patients regardless of religious affiliation, they were all managed by a combination of Anglo-Irish nobility and gentry and Church of Ireland clergy. Mercer's Hospital represents this union: it was established by cooperation between local clergymen and medical professionals and throughout its years of operation both laity and clergy worked together to keep it going. Like other eighteenth-century charities, voluntary hospitals served a dual purpose: they were simultaneously a selfless charitable act towards the poor of the city and a self-interested attempt on the part of the propertied classes to reinforce social ties of deference. Providing medical care to the poor was an 'improvement' project in both the traditional and the broader sense. Voluntary hospitals focused on providing medical care to the working poor, a service which would also bring economic benefits to the nation. They contributed to improvement by aiding in the health and well-being of a group that was essential for economic improvement. In a broader sense voluntary hospitals represented an example of what many more prosperous citizens saw as their duty towards the lower classes. Service towards the poor was not only a social but a religious obligation. The trustees, governors, physicians, and surgeons who gave so much of their time and money towards promoting voluntary hospital schemes did not act solely out of self-interest. They were also motivated by a genuine, and frequently spiritual, desire to aid the less fortunate in accordance with what they saw as their Christian duty.

---

[110] Kelly, 'The emergence of scientific and institutional medical practice in Ireland', p. 32.
[111] N.A.I. 2006/97.
[112] N.A.I. 2006/97.

4

Improvement as Philanthropy: The Royal Dublin Society

On 28 June 1731 fourteen gentlemen gathered in the rooms of the Philosophical Society of Trinity College and unanimously agreed to form a society for 'improving husbandry, manufacturing, and other useful arts'.[1] The Dublin Society, which upon receiving a royal charter in 1750 became the Royal Dublin Society, differed from other scientific organizations in its focus and methods. Earlier scientific societies primarily sought knowledge for its own sake. From its earliest inception, the Dublin Society sought concrete ways to improve Ireland economically by focusing on encouraging new methods of agriculture and manufacturing and by seeking to use Enlightenment values and new scientific ideas for practical applications. The Society's methods, operation, and ideology demonstrate that its improvement agenda was both practical and philanthropic.

The word 'improving' in the Society's statement of philosophy was a significant one. The Dublin Society participated in the broader agenda for improvement in the eighteenth century. In the seventeenth century English settlers had advocated improvement as a way of making Ireland more like England. This meant developing a system of English laws and government, an English-speaking and Protestant population, and English industries and agriculture.[2] The Dublin Society represented a large-scale attempt on the part of the eighteenth-century Anglo-Irish to put those ideas into practice. The Society's agenda was one of practical benevolence and its aims, which intended to produce security and prosperity, were implicitly philanthropic. Throughout the eighteenth century the Society was the 'principal agent of economic development in the country', working closely with the Irish government to foster progress in the economy and agriculture.[3] At the same time, the Anglo-Irish membership of the Dublin Society demonstrated an emerging sense of Irish patriotism. Members of the Dublin Society were genuinely concerned for the overall health of Ireland, and saw themselves in stark contrast to many others

[1]   R.D.S. Minute Books vol. 1.
[2]   T. C. Barnard, 'Gardening, diet and "improvement" in later seventeenth-century Ireland' in *Journal of Garden History*, 10, no. 1 (1990), p. 71.
[3]   James Livesey, 'The Dublin Society in eighteenth-century Irish political thought' in *The Historical Journal*, 47, no. 3 (2004), pp. 615–16.

in their class who sought merely to profit from Irish landholdings while living in England.

The Dublin Society was also an Irish adaptation of the broader concept of enlightened reform. Enlightened reform was an ideology that included initiatives for agrarian renewal, the encouragement of manufacturing and industry, and legal and governmental reform initiatives.[4] Strictly speaking, improvement, the stated goal of the Dublin Society, referred to the practice of rendering land and manufacturing more profitable. On a broader level, however, improvement was about a commitment to change. Improving culture 'bridged the material and spiritual spheres'.[5] Organizations such as the Incorporated Society and Mercer's Hospital represented an improvement agenda, even if they were not directly linked to agriculture or manufacturing. The Dublin Society was clearly committed to encouraging improvement in the traditional definition of the word, but it did not limit itself to that alone, advocating also a broader agenda for improvement that included clearly philanthropic projects such as poorhouses and education. Each of these endeavours was designed directly to strengthen Ireland economically and indirectly to reinforce the power of the national government and the estab-lished Church. As with the Incorporated Society and Mercer's Hospital, the Dublin Society represented a union between a spiritual and an Enlightenment agenda.

Credit for founding the Society belongs primarily to Thomas Prior. Prior devoted most of his life to encouraging industry among the Protestant population of Ireland and the foundation of the Dublin Society was the culmination of his endeavours. He was born in Queen's County in 1681. His grandfather, Captain Thomas Prior, had come to Ireland in 1636 with his regiment. Captain Prior settled in the area of Rathdowney in Queen's County, where he was granted about 800 acres of land that had been confiscated from a Catholic family.[6] Like John Putland, Thomas Prior was thus the descendant of New English settlers to Ireland, and within a few generations his family became part of the ruling class of Ireland. These basic characteristics are true of most of those associated with the voluntary societies of eighteenth-century Dublin. The founders of the Dublin Society, like those of Mercer's Hospital and the early members of the Incorporated Society, belonged to the Anglo-Irish elite and were primarily second- or third-generation residents of Ireland. The historians James Meenan and Desmond Clarke described these men as 'conscious of their duty to the

---

4   Gabriel B. Paquette, *Enlightenment, governance, and reform in Spain and its empire, 1759–1808* (New York, 2008), p. 11.
5   Borsay, 'The culture of improvement', p. 185.
6   Desmond Clarke, *Thomas Prior 1681–1751, founder of the Royal Dublin Society* (Dublin, 1951), p. 1.

country which gave them birth and sustenance'.[7] Most of these families owed their prosperity to the greater opportunities for land and advancement available in seventeenth-century Ireland.

Prior attended Trinity College and obtained his bachelor's degree in 1703. While at Trinity Prior, along with friends such as George Berkeley, John Madden, Edward Synge, and Samuel Molyneux, was a member of the Philosophical Society. All of these men would go on to be active in improvement movements and were members of the Dublin Society. While intelligent and a good student, Prior was described as being 'of a weak habit of body', which apparently led him to decline entering into any learned profession. He lived in England for a time and earned a Master's degree at Oxford University. Once he returned to Dublin, Prior began to work as an agent for landowners. The Rawdon family of County Down were his major employers and this connection helped both Prior and Sir John Rawdon develop their ideologies of improvement.[8] He obtained some land himself and, on the death of his brother, inherited his family's estate, which was the primary source of his income. It was not until the 1720s that 'he entirely turned his thoughts and studies to promote the real happiness of his country'.[9]

While never a member of parliament, Prior was active in the political controversies of the day. In the 1720s Ireland was suffering from a shortage of small coins, which had its most immediate impact on the poor, who relied on them. The British parliament sold the right to produce copper coins to an Englishman, William Wood, without consulting the Irish privy council. The incident provoked widespread condemnation from the Anglo-Irish and the Irish parliament. Jonathan Swift famously condemned the currency in his *Drapier Letters*, contending that the coins were of inferior quality. Several years after the controversy, in 1729, Prior published his first pamphlet, *Observations on coin in general with some proposals for regulating the value of coin in Ireland*. Prior's tract was not merely a manifesto that retroactively railed against Wood's halfpence; it was also a reasoned examination of the problems which gave rise to the controversy – namely, the continuing scarcity of small coins in the country. Prior addressed broader economic concerns, such as the shortage of silver and gold resulting from Ireland's depressed economy, the lack of equivalency between English and Irish money, and absentee landowners. While he advocated some corrections, such as establishing an Irish mint, he placed most of the blame on human behaviour – namely, absenteeism – which resulted in

---

7 Meenan and Clarke, 'The RDS 1731–1981', p. 1.

8 D. W. Hayton, 'A question of upbringing: Thomas Prior, Sir John Rawdon, 3rd Bt, and the mentality and ideology of "improvement"' in D. W. Hayton (ed.), *The Anglo-Irish experience, 1680–1730: religion, identity, and patriotism* (Woodbridge, 2012), p. 175.

9 Robert and John Cash Pool, *Views of the most remarkable public buildings and monuments in the city of Dublin* (Dublin, 1780), p. 102.

'the great and constant drains of money out of this kingdom, for the support of our gentlemen abroad'.[10]

Prior made the same argument later that year when he wrote *A list of absentees of Ireland and the yearly value of their estates and incomes spent abroad*. In this pamphlet he called to account the many landowners of Ireland who lived in England either entirely or predominantly. Prior saw no problem in attacking members of his own class, even close friends, for draining the resources of Ireland by living abroad, and would continue his attacks upon absenteeism for the rest of his life.[11] Indeed, his list of absentees continued to be published and updated well after his death in 1751. According to Prior, the evils of absenteeism were clear. More than £600,000 left the country each year to support the lifestyles of absentee landlords.[12] This enormous sum of money would be far better served if it were to remain in Ireland and be reinvested in the country. Chief among Ireland's economic problems, according to Prior, was a basic lack of capital. 'This want of money in the kingdom, throws a damp upon all Business; Manufacturers can't be set to work, Materials purchased, or Credit subsist; and people who are willing to support themselves by their Industry, are left to struggle with Poverty, for want of employment.'[13] Prior's assessment of absentees as individuals was harsh; he wrote of 'the vanity of those, who have thus wantonly abandon'd their Country'. In doing so, he sought to establish a social stigma against absenteeism. He argued that absenteeism represented a loss of trade, capital, and taxes to the nation and that the practice had to be discouraged by any means necessary. He suggested, for instance, the placing of a tax of 4s. in the pound on the estate of absentees.[14] At one point he stated 'there is no Way left to save us, but by obliging them to live at home, or making them pay for living abroad'.[15] Absenteeism was damaging to the Irish economy in other, less obvious ways as well. In general, the absentees were relatively poor landlords, interested only in drawing income from their tenants and estates and not in making practical investments to improve the long-term health of the land. Like all dedicated improvers of the period, Prior linked these immediate problems to underlying concerns about Ireland's political stability. Absenteeism and its accompanying economic problems would only bring about the 'ruin' of Ireland.

Both *Observations on coin* and *A list of absentees* were initially published

---

[10] Thomas Prior, *Observations on coin in general. With some proposals for regulating the value of coin in Ireland. By the author of the list of the absentees of Ireland* (London, 1730), pp. 162–4.

[11] Clarke, *Thomas Prior 1681–1751*, p. 22.

[12] Thomas Prior, *A list of the absentees of Ireland, and the yearly value of their estates and incomes spent abroad. With observations on the present state and condition of that kingdom* (Dublin, 1729), p. 20.

[13] Ibid., p. 19.

[14] Ibid., p. 33.

[15] Ibid., p. 23.

anonymously. However, Prior was not content to limit himself to publishing pamphlets. By 1731, it was clear to him that something more concrete and practical had to be done to correct the problems that were plaguing Ireland. This desire to take concrete steps to improve the economy and society of the country was what set the Dublin Society apart from earlier organizations. While at Trinity College Prior had been a member of one of these organizations, the Dublin Philosophical Society, which had been founded in 1683 by William Molyneux. Modelled on the Royal Society in London, it was meant to encourage the pursuit of knowledge in general while placing special emphasis on new scientific ideas. It was a relatively small group, primarily comprising friends of Molyneux, and did not meet regularly; by 1709 it had ceased meeting altogether.[16] While the Philosophical Society certainly played an important role in encouraging new scientific ideas in Ireland, it also lacked any clear agenda. Proposals for improving agricultural production in Ireland were made, but there was no means to encourage their implementation.[17] This was a failing that the Dublin Society would attempt to correct.

The thirteen men who joined Prior in founding the Dublin Society shared many similarities with him. All were of Anglo-Irish stock, most with roots in the country dating back only a generation or two. They were also generally wealthy and influential, and many of them were involved in other reform movements. Six were members of parliament, two were clergymen, and three were physicians. Two of the founding members, Dr William Stephens and Dr Francis LeHunte, were active in the voluntary hospital movement. LeHunte was a trustee of Mercer's Hospital and also provided his services to Steevens's Hospital. Stephens, too, was a trustee of Mercer's and also worked at Steevens's, where he eventually became a governor.[18] The Dublin Society from its inception also had a strong clerical element. Two more of its founding members, Reverend Dr John Whitcombe and Reverend Dr John Madden, were Anglican clergymen. Other important Anglican churchmen joined the Society in its early years, including Edward Synge, bishop of Clonfert; Robert Clayton, bishop of Killala; Theophilius Bolton, archbishop of Cashel; and Josiah Hort, bishop of Kilmore.[19] Overlapping membership and strong Church of Ireland involvement indicates a strong connection between the Dublin Society and voluntary charitable societies.

After establishing the Society, the members next turned themselves to its

[16] K. Theodore Hoppen, 'The Dublin Philosophical Society and the new learning in Ireland' in *Irish Historical Studies*, XIV, no. 54 (1964), pp. 99–108; Hoppen, *The common scientist in the seventeenth century*.

[17] J. V. Luce, *Dublin societies before the R.D.S.* (Dublin, 1981), p. 3.

[18] Fergus Mulligan, *The founders of the Royal Dublin Society* (Dublin, 2005).

[19] Henry Berry, *A history of the Royal Dublin Society* (London, 1915), p. 30.

governance. Officers had to be chosen and, like other voluntary societies of the time, the Dublin Society was careful to appoint prominent figures to important offices. The president was the lord lieutenant, at the time Lionel Sackville, duke of Dorset. There were seven vice-presidents and, while each of them was elected, as opposed to being appointed *ex officio*, the Society did elect such prominent figures as Hugh Boulter, the primate, James FitzGerald, duke of Leinster, and Charles Butler, earl of Arran. The presence of these prominent men on the governing board indicates that the Society and its programmes were endorsed by those who held important positions in the nation's political landscape. Prior served as the Society's secretary of foreign affairs,[20] working to develop contacts with other progressive organizations and improvers abroad, to gather knowledge from places such as Holland and England, and to determine how it might be utilized in Ireland. The Dublin Society considered itself a part of an international community of Enlightened reformers. Prior, however, did not limit himself to this role alone. Officials such as the lord lieutenant and the lord primate might have held important formal positions within the Society, but that does not mean that they were actually actively involved in the Society. In December 1731 the new society was presented by the primate to the lord lieutenant, who agreed to serve as president and signed his name to the subscription book, but aside from paying the annual subscription fee required of all members neither man actually attended meetings or participated in society business. In the early years, Prior more than anyone else seems to have played the role of leader of the Society, and until his death in 1751 the Society did very little without his involvement.[21]

The membership of the Dublin Society quickly expanded beyond the original fourteen. The rules regarding new members were simple. Men had first to be chosen by at least seven current members and then had to pay an annual subscription of 30s.[22] Membership expanded rapidly, fuelled by the initial excitement many felt for its agenda. As with other organizations for 'improvement', such as the Incorporated Society and Mercer's Hospital, the Dublin Society actively sought out members from the social elite in the hopes of boosting its prestige. A number of temporal and spiritual lords joined immediately and others would join in subsequent years. However, as with Mercer's Hospital and the Incorporated Society, their actual level of involvement varied significantly. Most did not attend meetings regularly, with the exception of Francis Hutchinson, bishop of Down and Connor, who was an active improver

---

[20] *By-laws and ordinances of the Dublin Society. For the good government of the corporation* (Dublin, 1769), pp. 3–5; R.D.S. Minute Books vol. 1.

[21] R.D.S. Minute Books vol. 1; Clarke, *Thomas Prior 1681–1751*, p. 28.

[22] R.D.S. Minute Books vol. 1; *The Royal Charter of the Dublin Society. To which are added, the Society's by-laws and ordinances, for the good government of the corporation* (Dublin, 1766), p. 16.

and attended meetings as often as he was able.[23] As with Mercer's Hospital, the most active members of the Society were from the class below the nobility, men such as Thomas Prior and, later, John Putland, who devoted a great deal of time, energy, and money to the Dublin Society and its endeavours. Clergymen also played an active role in the Society, including several bishops. However, with the exception of Hutchinson, most of these clergy tended to be parish ministers. This does not mean that the nobility and episcopacy were necessarily uninterested in improvement or charity. The fact that they joined these organizations and regularly subscribed funds to them indicates some degree of support. Many lords and high-ranking clergy had greater calls on their time, however, and frequently did not reside year-round in Dublin. Mid-ranking clergymen who were based in Dublin not only had more time than most bishops but were also physically able to attend meetings, unlike bishops who lived in distant dioceses. The Dublin Society, like other improvement organizations, derived most of its active membership, and most of its energy for reform, from urban professionals and others who resided permanently in Dublin.[24] Total membership expanded rapidly, and by 1734 there were 267 members.[25] There was significant overlap with other voluntary societies: members of the Incorporated Society and governors or trustees of Mercer's Hospital were almost guaranteed to also be members of the Dublin Society. Membership in the Dublin Society, more so even than other organizations, became almost socially obligatory for Anglo-Irishmen of significant economic means. Women were not permitted to become members, though they could be awarded honorary membership. The first woman to be so recognized was Lady Arbella Denny, in 1766.

It was clear to many, even outside the Dublin Society, that Ireland in the early eighteenth century was in poor economic shape. One commentator noted in 1741 that 'The kingdom has for a considerable time been gradually, but not by slow degrees, wasting in its riches, strength, and power.'[26] Another commentator, writing in 1737, noted that 'It will hardly be denied, that this Kingdom is at present in a declining Way. Money is certainly scarce and Credit weak … Indeed, all ranks and orders of men among us, are more or less sensible of our poverty.'[27] Most agreed that this poverty had several causes. While Prior associated it with absenteeism, other commentators looked at more direct causes, but it was generally agreed that Ireland was not as agriculturally developed as it should be. The nation was not producing enough to support itself, meaning

---

23 Barnard, A new anatomy of Ireland, p. 33.
24 Ibid., pp. 100–01.
25 Berry, A history of the Royal Dublin Society, p. 27.
26 Samuel Pierson, A dissertation on the inlargement of tillage, the erecting of public granaries, and the regulating, employing, and supporting the poor in this kingdom (Dublin, 1741), p. 5.
27 Some thoughts on the tillage of Ireland: humbly dedicated to the parliament (London, 1737), pp. 5–6.

that foodstuffs such as corn or wheat had to be regularly imported. As with absenteeism, this importation was a drain on capital in a country that did not have much to spare. An anonymous pamphleteer estimated in 1737 the total value of coin in circulation Ireland to be only about £500,000. This was a situation that contributed to the shortages of specie noted by Prior in his earlier pamphlets. The lack of capital in Ireland also meant there was little money to invest in manufacturing, which further hampered the nation's economy. In this environment the Dublin Society, like the Incorporated Society and Mercer's Hospital, sought to address the evils and dangers of rampant poverty in Ireland.

From the beginning the Dublin Society's primary interest was in promoting improved agricultural methods. Particularly in its early years, the bulk of its publications focused on that goal. In September 1731, shortly after its founding, the Society chose to print and distribute an edition of Jethro Tull's *Horse-hoeing husbandry*.[28] The earliest papers to be presented at Dublin Society meetings all concerned agriculture: one dealt with new methods of draining marsh land, another dealt with the cultivation of hops.[29] The agricultural aims of the Society were always varied, but one of its routine critiques regarding Irish agriculture was the amount of land that lay unused. Central to its goal of improving the state of agriculture in the country, therefore, was increasing the amount of land under cultivation. It asserted that Ireland was troubled by 'vast tracts of land' that were not being properly utilized.[30] Bogs were a major part of this problem, as Henry Brooke noted in an essay presented to the Society. Brooke estimated that perhaps as much as a quarter of Ireland was bog, making the land less valuable and disrupting commerce and communication between areas. According to Brooke, Ireland's bogs were 'worse than useless'; they were, in fact, 'the greatest Nuisance that the kingdom contains'.[31] Innovative methods for reclaiming bog land were a constant endeavour of the Society. Tracts such as Brooke's indicate another facet of the improvement movement: at its core this movement was focused on Anglicizing Ireland. In order to improve the nation the Incorporated Society focused on raising Irish children with English language, religion, and manners. The Dublin Society, meanwhile, felt that economic improvement could be achieved only by fundamentally altering Ireland's geographical features to make them more like those of England.

Bringing more land under cultivation seemed like a quick fix for Ireland's economic problems. However, it was not only the economy of Ireland that was in danger. Ireland was prone to demographic crises in the seventeenth

[28] R.D.S. Minute Books vol. 1.
[29] R.D.S. Minute Books vol. 1.
[30] *The Royal Charter of the Dublin Society*, p. 1.
[31] Henry Brooke, *A brief essay on the nature of bogs, and the method of reclaiming them. Humbly addressed to the Dublin Society* (Dublin, 1772), pp. 1, 14.

and eighteenth centuries. Crop failures caused famines every few years, which contributed to a range of social problems troubling both the country and the city of Dublin. Prior was resident in Ireland for the relatively minor famines of the 1720s, and as a land agent and landowner was certainly aware of the devastating impact crop failures could have on the population. The same could also be said of the other founders of the Society, all of whom were landowners. The necessity of their agenda became clear on a wider scale between 1739 and 1741 when a severe famine hit the country as a result of abnormal weather conditions causing widespread crop failure. In addition, conditions abroad prevented the country from being able to import enough food to make up the shortfall. The over-reliance on imported foodstuffs that had been warned against in 1737 had particularly disastrous results during this period, which constituted the most severe famine of the eighteenth century. To many, the solution seemed to be increased cultivation. If Ireland was producing more food and storing the surplus in public granaries, then such severe famines could be prevented. Prior advocated this solution in 1741, as the famine was coming to a close. He also noted that Ireland suffered from either a scarcity of corn or an overabundance of it, where low prices discouraged further cultivation. This interpretation differed from that of other commentators, such as the author of the 1737 pamphlet. Prior did, however, agree with the general consensus that government-owned public granaries, which would purchase the surplus, were essential to preventing future famines and would encourage farmers to continue corn cultivation by always ensuring them a market.[32]

Tillage could be improved by a variety of methods. Some advocated increasing land under cultivation at the expense of land used for animal pasture.[33] The Dublin Society never explicitly discouraged animal husbandry; its charter reiterated the statement from its first meeting about 'improving husbandry', but it interpreted husbandry primarily as crop cultivation and devoted little energy to the raising of animals.[34] The Society did not believe that the sole problem with Irish agriculture was the amount of land being cultivated for food. Instead, its agenda demonstrates the belief that the problem was also how land already under cultivation was being utilized. The Society sought instead to encourage the growing of new crops and the use of new methods that would increase yields.

Particularly popular with the Society, and a pet project of Prior's, was the growing of hops and flax. Though neither of these was an important foodstuff, both were essential to other important industries. The Dublin Society did not

---

32 Thomas Prior, A proposal to prevent the price of corn from rising too high, or falling too low, by the means of granaries. By Thomas Prior, Esq (Dublin, 1741), pp. 1–7.
33 Some thoughts on the tillage of Ireland.
34 The Royal Charter of the Dublin Society, p. 2.

believe that making Ireland agriculturally self-sufficient was enough, in and of itself, to solve the country's economic problems. The Society frequently acknowledged that Ireland suffered economically in part because of its unequal relationship with England. The second pamphlet published by the Society shortly after its founding dealt with the growing of hops, an undertaking advocated by Prior in his *List of absentees*. Prior's argument was that Ireland wasted money importing large quantities of hops each year while the southern part of the island was perfectly suited for growing them, the only problem being the lack of trees to make hop-poles.[35] Learning more about hop cultivation was important enough to the Society that in 1733 one member was sent to England for six weeks to observe and learn more about managing the plant.[36] The pamphlet specifically noted a 1711 stature that prohibited Ireland from importing hops from anywhere except England, ensuring a high price for English hop-sellers. It argued that if Ireland grew its own hops it would not only benefit farmers but also help to correct the country's trade deficit.[37]

The Dublin Society also worked to encourage the cultivation of flax and, along with it, the growth of the linen manufacture. With the suppression of the woollen industry, Ireland's economy depended on the success of the linen manufacture, and so its encouragement was dear to the hearts of many improvers. In 1732 linen composed one-third of all Irish exports and had enjoyed considerable growth since the beginning of the century, but many felt that there was room for still more growth. For the most part, the cultivation of flax and the manufacture of linen were situated in the north of Ireland, where they were eagerly embraced by the majority Protestant population that lived there. Advocates of increased cultivation in general and of flax in particular pointed to the north of Ireland as a beacon of relative prosperity. The anonymous tillage pamphleteer of 1737 described

Our common People, in the Northern Parts, are not much to be boasted of, for their Wealth or Manner of Living; and yet, they are greatly superior to those of the Pasture countries: Indeed the Poverty of the latter is scarcely to be parallel's in any other nation. Their cloathing is Rags; their Houses Hovels, fitter for Swine than human Creatures; and the Scantiness of Nastiness of their Food are hardly to be conceived. It is astonishing to see such a Difference in the People of so small a Kingdom. We find among our common People, in those Parts where Tillage abounds, warm houses, clean and decent Apparel, wholesome Food, Manufactures, Industry, and the Protestant Religion: Among those of the Pasture Countries, there is nothing to be found but Misery and Poverty, Rudeness and Barbarity, Sloth, Idleness, and Popish Ignorance.[38]

---

[35] Prior, *A list of the absentees of Ireland*, pp. 75–6.

[36] R.D.S. Minute Books vols 1–3.

[37] *Instructions for planting and managing hops, and for raising hop-poles. Drawn up and published by order of the Dublin Society* (London, 1733).

[38] *Some thoughts on the tillage of Ireland*, p. 23.

Not explicitly stated was the fact that those prosperous Protestant farmers of the north were primarily the descendants of Scottish settlers who had arrived during the Plantation of Ulster. Such commentators saw the expansion of the linen manufacture as associated with the expansion of Protestantism.[39]

The Dublin Society was not explicitly anti-Catholic, but some of its rhetoric is similar to that of anti-Catholic writers – namely, that Ulster, with its large concentration of Protestant settlers, was more prosperous because of its willingness to adopt English crops and methods, while the southern counties of Ireland were less so because their majority of native Catholic inhabitants clung stubbornly to old ways. In his 1732 treatise for the Dublin Society on this subject Lionel Slator noted that while the province of Ulster in fact contained the worst land in the country it was, thanks to the cultivation of flax and the manufacture of linen, perhaps the most prosperous region. The cultivation of flax had the ancillary benefit of providing employment in linen-making. Slator noted that an acre of flax yielded employment to six people annually.[40] The growth of the linen industry was considered essential to Ireland's economic well-being; Ireland might become self-sufficient if it grew its own hops and corn, but, as Thomas Prior noted in 1749, it would not become truly wealthy unless it also became an exporting nation. 'The Home-Consumption of Manufactures and of the Produce of Land, do not bring Wealth into a Country, it is the Exportation of them alone, that has that Effect.'[41]

Ireland was at that time importing flax and then processing it into linen, some of which was sold abroad and some of which remained in Ireland. If Ireland produced more of its own flax it would increase profit margins for the linen that was produced and manufacturers might be able to produce even more linen, which could be sold to foreign markets.[42] For the most part, Ireland traded with Great Britain. In some cases, such as the ban on importing hops from Europe, Ireland was legally prohibited from trading with other countries. In other cases, little effort was made to expand the range of trading partners. As a result, most of Ireland's linen exports went directly to Great Britain. Irish commentators assumed that England, which was importing linen from elsewhere as well, would be more than willing to buy great quantities of Irish linen if it were available at a lower price than from other countries. Slator even theorized, somewhat idealistically perhaps, that Ireland might be able to expand

---

[39] Ibid., p. 20.
[40] Lionel Slator, *The advantages, which may arise to the people of Ireland by raising of flax and flax-seed, considered. Together with instructions for sowing and saving the seed, drawn up and published by the direction of the Dublin Society* (Dublin, 1732), pp. 4–5.
[41] Thomas Prior, *An essay to encourage and extend the linen-manufacture in Ireland, by premiums and other means* (Dublin, 1749), p. 4.
[42] Ibid., pp. 4–5.

its trading partners thanks to an increase in linen, and potentially export cloth to countries such as Spain, Portugal, and the West Indies, a hope which did not materialize.[43] With the suppression of the woollen industry, linen was encouraged by organizations such as the Dublin Society as the most effective means to bring about prosperity in Ireland. In a letter to Prior, the County Cork landowner and member of parliament Sir Richard Cox expressed what came to be the widely held view about the futility of resisting the suppression of wool. He argued that it would be foolish for the Anglo-Irish not to 'submit as early as possible to power which they cannot conquer'; they relied on the power of England for their own protection, so it would be pointless to resist over some 'airy fancy of natural right'.[44]

Slator's pamphlet, like other Dublin Society pamphlets on similar topics, provided detailed instructions on the best-known methods for cultivating flax. The Society published similar instructional pamphlets on reclaiming bog land, growing hops, growing saffron, keeping bees, and tanning leather. Disseminating information through such instructional booklets was the earliest method that the Society adopted for encouraging improvements in husbandry and manufacture. However, the Society soon realized that simply providing instructions was not enough to encourage the adoption of new crops or methods. In 1740 it adopted the use of premiums to further encourage the adoption of its ideas and methods. These were the brainchild of Dr Samuel Madden, who became a member of the Society in 1733. In fact, premiums were so much associated with Madden, who personally funded many of them, that he became known as 'Premium Madden'. He first proposed the idea in a 1731 pamphlet, *Proposal for the general encouragement of learning in Dublin College*.[45] Madden's original proposal revolved around providing rewards each quarter to the students of Trinity College who distinguished themselves in 'Industry, Regularity, and Scholarship'.[46] That basic concept was easily transferred to the work of the Dublin Society.

In 1739 Madden wrote an anonymous letter to the Society advising it on how to improve its funds. Madden, like Prior, was a fervent improver. He was a descendant of William Molyneux and had inherited considerable property on his father's death in 1703. After his education at Trinity College he was ordained a minister in the Church of Ireland and granted a living in County

---

[43] Slator, *The advantages, which may arise to the people of Ireland by raising of flax and flax-seed*, p. 4.
[44] Sir Richard Cox, *A letter from Sir Richard Cox, bart. To Thomas Prior, esq; shewing, from experience, a sure method to establish the linen-manufacture; and the beneficial effects, it will immediately produce* (Dublin, 1749), p. 9.
[45] Berry, *A history of the Royal Dublin Society*, pp. 52–3.
[46] *Some remarks occasion'd by the Reverend Mr. Madden's Scheme, and objections rais'd against it* (Dublin 1732), p. 13.

Fermanagh. He seems to have left the care of his parish primarily in the hands of a curate and the care of his household in the hands of his wife while he devoted himself to philanthropy and writing. Like Prior, he believed firmly in the responsibilities of landowning Irish Protestants towards the country which was responsible for their wealth. In 1738 he published his *Reflections and resolutions proper for the gentlemen of Ireland,* in which he agreed with many of the premises of Prior's writings, particularly those in the *List of absentees.* Like Prior, Madden criticized those noblemen and gentlemen of Ireland who 'riot and blaze abroad, while some thousands of their fellow Citizens are starving for want of their help at home'.[47] He argued that actions must be taken to rescue Ireland from complete ruin and praised Prior, describing him as 'as worthy and as useful a member of his country as I know in it'.[48] He also mentioned his premiums idea, which, he theorized, could be used to encourage some of those reforms that are essential for Ireland's well-being. 'What vast importance Premiums may be to any nation, and to ours above all others, if we could apply them in a proper Manner to the many useful purposes and designs, which want most to be established among us.'[49]

Madden made clear that he saw the Dublin Society as an ideal means of organizing and distributing such awards. In a 1739 letter to the Society he contended that the Dublin Society was not fulfilling its potential and that it ought to do more than publish educational treatises. Madden's letter did not simply propose the use of premiums: he also advocated a general broadening of the Society's activities. This proposal came at a difficult time for the Dublin Society, as, following the initial founding, there had been a decline in enthusiasm for the Society. In October 1739 a committee was organized to draw up resolutions for the Society's better governance, which addressed first the problem of its own membership; in recent years members had been withdrawing as they had failed or refused to pay their subscription fees. As a result, the Society's finances were in considerable disarray and it had barely enough funds to cover ordinary operating costs, let alone conduct the experiments on which it prided itself.[50] It certainly did not have the funds on hand for the experimental farms or premiums that Madden proposed.[51] To address these difficulties the committee proposed limiting membership and establishing an annual deadline for subscription fees. The Society had been struggling with collecting

---

47 Samuel Madden, *Reflections and resolutions proper for the gentlemen of Ireland, as to their conduct for the service of their country, as landlords, as masters of families* (Dublin, 1738), p. 7.
48 Ibid., p. 30.
49 Ibid., pp. 234–5.
50 R.D.S. Minute Books vols 1–3.
51 Samuel Madden, *A letter to the Dublin Society on the improving of their fund; and the manufactures, tillage, etc. in Ireland* (Dublin, 1739).

its fees since as early as 1733, but by 1739 the level of non-payment had reached a crisis. Members were to be informed of the amount they owed and, if they did not pay by a set time, were to be excluded from the Society.[52] The committee seemed to believe that part of the problem lay with the members, who did not have the 'proper spirit' of enthusiasm for the Dublin Society's work. It proposed establishing a series of subcommittees to direct the Society's activities: for correspondence, experiments, publication, and accounts.[53] Whether it was the reorganization or the adoption of Madden's premiums, this period saw the young Dublin Society reinvigorated. Regular attendance at meetings began to grow as more members became active participants in the Society's many varied interests.

Madden may have published his letter anonymously, but at least within the Dublin Society he was known to be the author. In December 1739 the Society noted that it had received Madden's 'generous' plan from the hands of Thomas Prior, and determined to consider it more closely at the next board meeting. Madden's letter had its own ideas for reforming the Society. He proposed increasing its funds by increasing membership, applying to the wealthy for contributions, and becoming formally incorporated.[54] Madden did not content himself with simply proposing these changes; he took an active role in raising funds to make it possible for the Society to fund more experiments. He himself pledged £150 annually during his life towards funding premiums and devoted himself to raising even more money from a variety of subscribers.[55] The Society responded favourably to Madden's plans, despite the financial straits it was in. In February 1740 it agreed to advertise that it would award premiums to persons who made improvements in 'any useful arts of Manufacture'. By that point, Madden had been able to raise £900 per year in subscriptions to support his plan.[56]

Premiums were given out for a variety of achievements, but Madden and the Society were particularly interested in encouraging manufactures, especially of items that Ireland had to import: earthenware, gunpowder, paper, hardware and cutlery, sugar, salt, and, in times of shortage, corn. Premiums were awarded for experiments in agriculture and the best invention in any of the manual or liberal arts. The Society did not immediately adopt all Madden's proposals. Instead, it asked for advice from gentlemen conversant with the fields of husbandry and manufactures as to which activities ought to be encouraged by the Society's premiums. Eventually, it decided to award its first premiums for the growing of hops and flax and the production of cider, earthenware, thread, malt

---

52 R.D.S. Minute Books vols 1–3.
53 R.D.S. Minute Books vols 1–3.
54 Madden, *A letter to the Dublin Society*, pp. 10–22.
55 R.D.S. Minute Books vols 1–3.
56 R.D.S. Minute Books vols 1–3.

liquor, and lace.[57] Premiums were an enormous success for the Society, so much so that they were gradually expanded to include almost anything that might be of use to the community as a whole. They were eventually granted for a variety of agricultural achievements: the reclamation of bog land, the production of honey, sowing the most wheat, parsnips, turnips, hops, or mustard. They were also used to encourage other projects supported by the Dublin Society. One premium went to whoever employed the greatest number of children in any manufacture; another was granted for the writing of a natural history of any county in the kingdom.[58] The Society used premiums to encourage almost any industry or art that it thought would benefit Ireland. In 1752 it gave two guineas to a Joseph Mason as an encouragement for his industry: he had taught his children to make feathered hats and bugle baskets.[59] The range of premiums offered illustrates how the Society had expanded beyond its initial concern with agriculture.

Though the primary interest of both Prior and the Dublin Society was in improving agriculture and manufacturing, they did not limit their endeavours to that alone. The Society awarded premiums for artistic achievements in its earliest round of premiums, and also opened a drawing school in the 1740s, appointing a master for drawing human heads and figures, a master of ornament drawing, and a master of architecture drawing. The latter two were paid a salary of £60 a year, the former £100 a year. All three saw students, who were chosen at the discretion of the Society, several days a week and were expected to exhibit regularly the work of their students to the Society to ensure that satisfactory progress was being made. Classes in each were scheduled at different times, presumably so that some students could work with more than one master if they qualified.[60]

The Society awarded premiums to several women for encouraging children in the production of bone lace or knit stockings at various charity schools.[61] It also provided support to women involved in manufacturing. In 1769 Elizabeth Madden, the widow of Church of Ireland clergyman Reverend John Madden, petitioned the Society for assistance in setting up a thread manufacture in County Londonderry, where she resided with her thirteen children. The Society eventually agreed that the manufacture of thread was a valuable use of its funds and voted her assistance of £100 to establish a mill and purchase implements,

57 R.D.S. Minute Books vols 1–3.
58 Premiums offered by the Dublin Society, in the year 1766, for the encouragement of agriculture, manufactures, and useful arts, in Ireland (Dublin, 1766).
59 R.D.S. Minute Books vols 5–7.
60 R.D.S. Minute Books vol. 9.
61 R.D.S. Minute Books vol. 10.

giving the money to Reverend Benjamin Domvile, a member, to purchase the mill and implements on Madden's behalf.[62]

While the Dublin Society did not have the overt religious aims of the Incorporated Society, it was established and run by Irish Protestants. The forwarding of a Protestant agenda was not an explicit aim, but was implicit in some of its actions, such as the decisions to grant premiums to discharged soldiers or sailors who took leases for small farms in the predominantly Catholic regions of Leinster, Munster, or Connaught.[63] By the time that that grant was established in 1766, the Society had been formally chartered and had received significant support for its premiums and other endeavours from the Irish parliament. Premiums, therefore, had a variety of uses, but the general idea behind them was 'to raise a spirit of emulation, and to engage a number of persons to endeavour to outdo one another in the same work'.[64] Prior felt that premiums encouraged the 'spirit of industry and improvement' through positive means.

There were also premiums for honey production, which is not surprising given the Society's long-term interest in bees. As early as 1733 the Society was publishing instructional pamphlets on raising and managing bees and arguing for the 'great profit that arises from this branch of husbandry'. *Instructions for managing bees*, like other Dublin Society pamphlets, served two purposes. It was primarily an instructional pamphlet: the bulk of the work consisted of basic information about the subject, including a detailed description of the different types of bees to be found in each hive, their life cycle, their appearance, and their purpose within the hive. The same basic form was used for pamphlets on hops, or flax, or any other topic. Furthermore, all pamphlets contained practical advice on how the subject was to be best cultivated or cared for. Aside from this, each pamphlet also played a secondary, persuasive role. It was not enough to inform readers about the subject; they also had to argue for the importance of the subject and the numerous benefits that could arise from cultivation. *Instructions for managing bees* concluded with a detailed discussion of the profits of raising bees, namely honey and wax, and their many uses. Dublin Society pamphlets presented each of these endeavours, whether it was raising bees or cultivating flax, as a patriotic necessity and not simply as an economic opportunity.

Madden's other proposal to benefit the Society was that it seek a royal charter. This suggestion was not initially followed through, as some members feared that becoming chartered might lead the Society to be politicized.[65] Those concerns notwithstanding, the benefits of incorporation were numerous. Members began

---

[62] R.D.S. Minute Books vol. 10.

[63] *Premiums offered by the Dublin Society, in the Year 1766*, p. 18.

[64] Prior, *An essay to encourage and extend the linen-manufacture in Ireland*, p. 10.

[65] Berry, *A history of the Royal Dublin Society*, p. 75.

to pursue it in 1749 and, on 2 April 1750, were formally chartered by the king. Incorporation by royal charter, which the Dublin Society and the Incorporated Society received, was slightly different than incorporation by the Irish parliament, which Mercer's Hospital enjoyed, but the benefits were the same. The Dublin Society had evidence of official approval before its charter. In 1746 George II granted it £500 annually to use in whatever manner it saw fit. The royal charter formally signified official approval. More practically, it allowed it to purchase land and stabilize its finances. The royal charter also explained, clearly and succinctly, the intended benefits of the Dublin Society: it raised a 'spirit of industry and emulation' and produced many improvements in agriculture and manufactures. Furthermore, 'many further improvements are still wanted which would have a natural tendency to civilize the natives, render them well affected to his majesty's government and more capable of contributing to the increase of the revenue and to the support of the established of this kingdom'.[66] A fact not explicitly stated, but which all contemporary readers would have known, is that those natives who were presently not civilized or well affected towards his majesty's government were Catholic. While the Dublin Society had no explicit proselytizing agenda, it was hoped that its activities would help to 'civilize' the native population, and the conventional wisdom of the period saw civilization and Protestantism as going hand in hand. Incorporation also saw an increase in parliamentary financial support for the Dublin Society. The Irish parliament came to see funding the Dublin Society as an ideal way to encourage economic development, and the two worked cooperatively together on a number of issues. Initially at least, with the exception of the £500 granted by the king, public grants to the Society were irregular. That situation lasted until 1761, when it received a grant of £12,000, and after that it received regular grants from parliament in the amounts of several thousand pounds to both continue its premiums and also to support either agriculture or manufacturing.[67]

A year after receiving its royal charter, the Dublin Society was struck by a major blow when its founder and most active member, Thomas Prior, died after a long illness. He attended his last meeting in June 1751 and died on 21 October 1751. Prior's devotion to his country and his cause was well known. Philip Stanhope, Lord Chesterfield, described him as 'one of the few in Ireland who always think of the public without any mixture of private interest'.[68] The *Dublin Journal* said that he 'never declined the most difficult tasks where the interest of the public was concerned. No man more ready to perform every good and charitable act than he was.'[69] To commemorate him, the Dublin Society

66   P.R.O.N.I. T3019/1465.
67   Berry, *A history of the Royal Dublin Society*, pp. 209–10.
68   P.R.O.N.I. T3228/1/26.
69   *Faulkner's Dublin Journal*, 23 October 1751.

agreed at its next meeting to begin raising funds for a monument to be placed in Christ Church Cathedral. The monument, designed by John Van Nost, was completed in 1756.[70] The loss of Prior's energy and enthusiasm was certainly felt by the Dublin Society, but by that point it was a well-established and formally chartered organization with a large and active membership.

From the beginning, the Dublin Society maintained a good relationship with the state. Several of its founders were members of parliament and the lord lieutenant was officially its president. Its chartering in 1750 further cemented its close relationship with the Irish state. James Livesey termed the Society an 'instrument of governance' and there is a strong basis for this assertion.[71] After its incorporation the Society received large sums of money from parliament to help fund its many different projects. The Dublin Society was a vehicle for a certain type of constructive Anglo-Irish patriotism, although that is certainly not all it was.[72] For the most part, before this time the Society had funded itself through a combination of membership dues and charitable subscriptions. Premiums were particularly expensive for the Society, which routinely requested parliamentary assistance in maintaining the programme. However, judging by the minute books, it did not have the same, often severe, financial concerns which afflicted the Incorporated Society or Mercer's Hospital.

As befits a scientific society, the Dublin Society did not limit itself to publicizing or encouraging, but also undertook many experiments on its own initiative. Premiums and publications were not enough to satisfy its aims and, in 1764, the Society appointed an Englishman, John Wynne Baker, to conduct a variety of agricultural experiments. Baker first came to the attention of the Society with his pamphlet *Some hints for the better improvement of husbandry*, addressed to it in 1762. That treatise impressed the Society enough to grant Baker £100 to defray his expenses, as he experimented in the cultivation of cabbage, turnips, barley, and wheat.[73] The Society did not give Baker free rein, however. A committee of several members was appointed to routinely keep track of his progress and experiments and report back to the Society.[74] Baker did well by the Society for several years, before falling out of favour in 1769.[75]

---

[70] R.D.S. Minute Books vol. 4.

[71] Livesey, 'The Dublin Society in eighteenth-century Irish political thought', p. 615.

[72] Barnard, 'The Dublin Society and other improving societies', p. 87.

[73] John Wynn Baker, *Experiments in agriculture, made under the direction of the right honourable and honourable Dublin Society, in the year 1764* (Dublin, 1765), pp. 5–6.

[74] R.D.S. Minute Books vol. 9.

[75] John Wynn Baker, *To his excellency, the right honourable, Lord Visc. Townshend, lieutenant general, and general governor of Ireland, president, his grace, the duke of Leinster, his grace, the right reverend archbishop of Armagh, vice-presidents. And to the rest of the lords composing the Dublin Society, the following remonstrance is most humbly addressed by John Wynn Baker* (Dublin, 1769).

During the period of his work with the Society, Baker was also responsible for writing on its behalf a plan for instructing children in new agricultural methods. The idea behind this scheme was simple, and was similar to the principles that informed the Incorporated Society: namely, that it was easier to teach proper agricultural methods to children than to adults, just as it was easier to convert children to Protestantism. Agriculture in Ireland suffered because of a lack of skilled labourers, and many adult farmers were too attached to old, inefficient customs to adopt the new ideas being put forth by the Dublin Society. 'Whilst we attempt to instruct Men, whose imaginary knowledge, renders them above being taught, we can never hope to disperse about the Kingdom, such as are worthy of being called Workmen.'[76] There was no overt religious aim alongside this idea. Young boys were to be apprenticed to skilled farmers; the first of these students would work with Baker himself. Baker, and the others, would each be given a yearly sum to support and clothe the boys. The children themselves were to be taken from orphanages so that 'they had no Home to fly to', thus neatly avoiding one of the problems of the Incorporated Society, which frequently had to contend with parents who changed their minds or children who attempted to return home.[77] The education was to take place between the ages of ten and fourteen, and boys would be taught to read and write. The children selected for this opportunity were to be chosen on the basis of their morals, temperament, and disposition. They were to be housed in a small barracks, where a woman was employed to do household labour for them. All the boys selected were to be Protestants, and they were to attend church weekly. This would not be a problem, as any child raised in a public orphanage in Ireland in the period was instructed in the Anglican faith.[78] This particular scheme of the Society did not amount to anything, and the Society's discussion of Baker's proposals does not survive. Baker was apparently instructed to take on a few apprentices himself to test the programme, but aside from that nothing was done.[79] In many ways, the proposed scheme would have competed with the work of the Incorporated Society, which claimed to teach proper agricultural methods to children at some of its schools. Financing such an endeavour would thus have been difficult when the Incorporated Society already existed and seemed to serve the same purpose.

From its inception the Dublin Society was always concerned with the problem of poverty, and most of its activities hoped to ameliorate Irish poverty by working to create employment. While many charities dealt with the consequences of poverty the Dublin Society, like other improvement

---

[76] John Wynn Baker, *A plan for instructing youths in the knowledge of husbandry, published at the request of the Dublin Society* (Dublin, 1765), p. 6.

[77] Ibid., p. 7.

[78] Ibid., pp. 1–15.

[79] R.D.S. Minute Books vol. 9.

organizations, hoped to address the causes. However, by the 1760s it was clear that its improvement schemes were not having the large-scale impact that it had envisaged, so it began to consider other ways of tackling poverty. In 1766 the Society published a plan for erecting poorhouses in every county in Ireland. The problem of rural poverty in Ireland was a severe one and while, during the famine of 1741, the residents of Dublin were able to rely upon an emergency feeding programme underwritten by the archbishop of Armagh and managed through the Dublin Workhouse,[80] those who lived in rural areas had no such opportunity, which led to large-scale vagrancy.[81]

This proposal by the Dublin Society was careful to note that while some provision was made for poor children by the Incorporated Society, its own scheme focused on adults. It proposed a hospital for the aged and disabled poor, an infirmary for the sick, and a house of correction for vagrant beggars. Those poor who were capable of working were to be employed in linen or wool production, depending on the region, in making fishing nets, or in knitting stockings. The author of the proposal, a prominent clergyman named Richard Woodward, later the bishop of Cloyne and most famous for writing *The present state of the church of Ireland* in 1787, saw women as playing an important role in the oversight and governance of his hypothetical poorhouses. Under his plan, all who subscribed at least twenty guineas to their local poorhouses were to become governors for life, and women who subscribed the same amount were granted the same privilege. While women could become governors, Woodward seemed to feel that they might not like to actually attend board meetings and so female governors were to be granted the privilege of voting by proxy if they chose. To ensure the success of these poorhouses effective oversight was necessary, and so Woodward proposed that each house have six appointed visitors, three men and three women, who were to visit every week and inspect in detail the conditions as well as hear complaints against the masters or matrons.[82]

In Woodward's scheme every pauper residing in the county would be entitled to be admitted to a poorhouse and every beggar would be liable to be sent to it. Paupers were to be given special badges showing that they were among the industrious poor. Vagrants were to be punished with hard labour for one week upon admittance. They were to be marked with gunpowder with a letter V on the back of their right arm. This allowed the mark to be concealed by their clothes once they were released, should they return to 'honest labour'. It also made identifying them easier if they ever returned to the house. Vagrants who

[80] Dickson, *Arctic Ireland*, pp. 35–6.
[81] Geary, "'The whole country was in motion'", p. 121.
[82] Richard Woodward, *A scheme for establishing county poor-houses, in the kingdom of Ireland. Published by order of the Dublin Society* (Dublin, 1766), p. 9.

returned were to be whipped and set to hard labour for even longer, until the fourth time they returned, when they would be transferred to a common jail.[83]

The Society tried to argue that this plan would incur minimal expense. After the initial outlay of about £900 for building and furnishing the house there would be no need for a permanent fund. Maintaining the residents and paying the few employees would cost only about £550 a year. That sum, it was thought, could be raised through a combination of voluntary subscriptions, the income from some taxes appropriated for the charity, and possibly a tax on absentee landowners. The taxes chosen to benefit the poorhouses were selected very specifically. They were morality taxes, such as the proposed tax on sporting dogs. Woodward, defending this, noted that this tax was incurred voluntarily and that it primarily taxed the rich, 'who ought to contribute cheerfully to the poor, or on those whose time should be employed more profitably to their families and country'.[84] He argued that the 'frivolousness of the amusements' made them ideal to be taxed to support such an important endeavour. 'By suppressing an idle extravagance, or by raising money, for a valuable Purpose', they were tackling multiple social ills at once.[85] It was also hoped that parliament in its wisdom would consent to provide additional funds to the poorhouse as needed. The proposed tax on absentees demonstrates the continued influence of Thomas Prior and his ideas on the Dublin Society's members even fifteen years after his death. Woodward argued that absentees 'who at present contribute nothing to Government for the Protection of their Property' had a responsibility to in some way provide for the poor of their areas.[86] The Dublin Society did not manage to enact this plan itself, but its influence can be clearly seen in an Act of Parliament of 1772 which created Corporations for Poor Relief across the country.[87]

The 1760s also saw the Society engage in attempts to revive the declining silk manufacture. Parliament tasked it with this responsibility and the Society decided to use parliamentary funds to open a silk warehouse that would give premiums to silks made in Ireland. The warehouse, which opened in February 1765, was strictly for the retail sale of silk. It was for some time a great success and the encouragement of Irish silk manufacture was in keeping with the Society's general idea that Ireland should be as self-sufficient as possible. The warehouse was so successful, in fact, that in the 1780s the Society was able to withdraw from involvement. However, by the 1790s the manufacturers

---

83 Ibid., pp. 1–10.
84 Ibid., p. 14.
85 Ibid., p. 14.
86 Ibid., p. 15.
87 Corporation for the Relief of the Poor in the City of Dublin, *An account of the proceedings, and state of the fund of the corporation instituted for the relief of the poor* (Dublin, 1774).

of silk begged it to return as patrons of the warehouse and a committee of the Society reported in 1795 that the silk manufacture in the city was in a state of decline. By this time, silk manufacturers could no longer maintain the expense of the warehouse and formally asked the Society to take it on itself and maintain it for retail purposes.[88] The Society had never completely removed itself from running retail warehouses, and had in fact been running the Irish woollen warehouse since 1772 in the same manner as the original silk warehouse.[89] The silk warehouse was significant, though, as one of the Society's only endeavours to permit active involvement from women. The purchasing power of wealthy women was essential to the initial success of the silk warehouse and the Society soon determined that women ought to be involved on other levels as well. It was decided that the best way to stimulate the manufacture of silk was to appoint a group of fifteen prominent ladies from the customers of the warehouse, among them Lady Arbella Denny, to serve as patronesses. Patronesses were appointed to visit the warehouse regularly and make recommendations based on what they saw. The idea was that, as women represented the primary customer base for the warehouse, appointing them to positions of some authority would help to encourage both the warehouse and the manufacture.[90] In this respect the silk warehouse was an exception; in general, the Dublin Society felt that its interests in agriculture and manufacturing fell outside the domestic sphere, where women's input was at times sought by voluntary societies.

By the 1780s and 1790s enthusiasm for the Dublin Society had waned among its members. The Society remained active and still awarded premiums, but fewer members were actively attending meetings than in its heyday in the middle of the century. Nonetheless, the Dublin Society could easily be termed the most successful of the voluntary societies. Not only does it still survive, but many of the institutions it helped to found, including the National Library and the Botanic Gardens, are also still in existence. However, the Society's success in improving Ireland's economy and manufacturing is difficult to measure. It is unique among the voluntary societies discussed here in that it did not represent the co-opting of an English idea into the Irish milieu; while it was in some ways modelled on the Royal Academy it was a uniquely Irish institution which inspired similar organizations elsewhere in Europe. As an organization it was highly active, and operated on a larger and more varied scale than the other voluntary societies discussed here. While the members of the Incorporated Society and Mercer's Hospital all worked towards a single goal, the Dublin

[88] R.D.S. Minute Books vol. 15.
[89] R.D.S. Minute Books vol. 12.
[90] R.D.S. Minute Books vols 9 and 11.

Society supported a variety of enterprises and had only a vague aim to direct it. At its core, the Dublin Society, like the other voluntary societies, was directed by a desire to stabilize Ireland socially and economically. It attempted to transform the energy of the Enlightenment into practical results to benefit an ailing country both economically and socially.

5

'The Benevolent Sympathies of the Female Heart': Women, Improvement, and the Work of Lady Arbella Denny

On the morning of 18 March 1792 Mrs Meliore Adlercron of Dawson Street, Dublin, wrote in her book of household accounts, as indeed she did almost every day. This entry, though, was considerably different from most. Instead of her usual dry recitations of household expenses she wrote sadly regarding the death of a dear female friend. She referred to her friend as a 'saint' and recounted the friend's last visit, wherein she had laid her hands on the heads of Adlercron's children, blessing them. Adlercron felt that her friend was fortunate to be 'translated from this world of woe and wickedness to the unspeakable delights of bliss of an eternal one which is prepared for the spirits of the just made perfect'. There was no question in Adlercron's mind that her friend would be admitted to paradise. She was cordial and kind; 'her manners endeared her to all, the strength of her understanding the goodness of her heart of the multitude of virtues with which it was fraught made her the admiration of the age she lived may all those I love strive to imitate her lovely example'. Adlercron's only regret was that her own 'great imperfections' made it unlikely she would see her again in the 'next world'.[1]

The woman of whom Adlercron wrote so highly, who seemed to embody every imaginable virtue, was Lady Arbella Denny, who had died that day at the age of eighty-five. Adlercron was not unique in her reverence for Denny, who genuinely did have the 'admiration of the age'.[2] The reason that Denny was the object of so much appreciation was her extraordinary devotion to charity work. She spent years of her life working to improve conditions at the Dublin Foundling Hospital and went on to help found the Dublin Magdalene Asylum for Penitent Women, but did not limit herself to these projects. She was also interested in the broader improvement of Ireland. She became an honorary member of the Royal Dublin Society and was a patroness of the Irish silk warehouse.[3] Her charity work united the principles of both philanthropy and improvement.

---

[1] N.L.I. MS 4481.
[2] Ibid.
[3] B. B. Butler, 'Lady Arabella Denny, 1707–92' in *Dublin Historical Record*, 9 (1947).

A woman celebrated for her philanthropy is not unusual by nineteenth- or twentieth-century standards. But in eighteenth-century Ireland Denny was a unique figure. Her charitable career is illustrative of the limited roles permitted to women in eighteenth-century philanthropy. Just as the nature of philanthropy was changing in this period, so was the role of women in charity. The era saw the rise of a new way of thinking about and executing philanthropy. Public philanthropy came to be dominated by voluntary societies, funded by the same joint-stock method that financed many business ventures. Charitable societies were frequently managed in the same way as businesses. The Incorporated Society, Mercer's Hospital, and the Dublin Society, as well as many other smaller organizations, were founded by, and run by, men. For perhaps the first time philanthropy became male-dominated, and just as women were excluded from participation in joint-stock corporations, they were also largely excluded from joint-stock charities.[4] This is not to say that women stopped participating in philanthropy, merely that they rarely received public recognition. In eighteenth-century Ireland very few women were well known for their charity work. Mary Mercer, who was primarily remembered for the hospital that was named after her, and Lady Arbella Denny were exceptions.

Women's involvement in eighteenth-century philanthropy has received relatively little attention from historians. It was not until the 1800s that charity once again came to be widely regarded as a female activity, and scholars of the nineteenth century have noted the importance of women and philanthropy in that era. A great deal of significant historical research has been done on female philanthropy in the Victorian era in Ireland, England, and the United States.[5] The general consensus is that charity work was regarded as a natural and acceptable extension of the female sphere of influence, although there were still limits placed on women's involvement. However, in the nineteenth century women's involvement in philanthropy became so pervasive that it was at times an object of concern and mockery.[6] By participating in philanthropic activity, Victorian women were not only addressing the social ills of the day but also reinforcing their class identity,[7] although in fact involvement in benevolent

---

4 D. W. Elliott, *The angel out of the house: philanthropy and gender in nineteenth-century England* (Charlottesville, 2002), p. 23.

5 Maria Luddy, *Women and philanthropy in nineteenth-century Ireland* (Cambridge, 1995); Elliott, *Angel out of the house*; G. J. Barker-Benfield, *The culture of sensibility: sex and society in eighteenth-century Britain* (Chicago, 1992); F. K. Prochaska, *Women and philanthropy in nineteenth-century England* (Oxford,1980); Lori D. Ginzberg, *Women and the work of benevolence: morality, politics, and class in the nineteenth-century United States* (New Haven, 1990).

6 Eliott, *Angel out of the house*, pp. 2–3; Leonore Davidoff and Catherine Hall, *Family fortunes: men and women of the English middle class, 1780–1850* (Chicago, 1987), pp. 430–31.

7 Ginzberg, *Women and the work of benevolence*, pp. 1–11; Elliott, *Angel out of the house*, p. 4.

organizations served to liberate middle- and upper-class women from their confined domestic spheres.[8]

Women's participation in philanthropy, though, was a well-established tradition prior to the nineteenth century. The conflation of femininity with charity and sentimentality did not happen overnight. Even in the Middle Ages, it was regarded as one of the roles of the wives of landowners to set aside money and food for the poor.[9] Such activities reinforced the bonds of social deference between classes and were an accepted part of a female head of household's duties. In addition, there was the long tradition of female religious orders and their involvement in charity. England and Ireland had not had convents since the dissolution of the monasteries in the sixteenth century, but in the eighteenth and nineteenth centuries there was a revival of interest among Protestants in the idea of a group of women cohabitating and devoting themselves to charity. Sarah Scott's English novel *Millennium hall*, published in1762, is one example.[10] In seventeenth-century France devout lay women had become involved in organized charity through organizations such as confraternities. Early modern Italy had similar examples of organized female charity.[11] Meanwhile, Catholic women in Ireland were also involved in charity work, but in a less structured way. The weaknesses of Catholic ecclesiastical structures in the penal era gave Catholic laywomen a greater degree of latitude in managing their own charities in the early part of the eighteenth century.[12]

For the most part, scholars agree that the institutionalization of charity work which took place in eighteenth-century Britain and Ireland worked to exclude women from active involvement. The prevailing narrative stresses that women remained involved in philanthropic activity. In some cases, their involvement was actively sought by organizers. However, women were still not permitted to hold official positions in any of the voluntary societies that came to dominate charity work in the eighteenth century. Even in the nineteenth century, they were kept in subordinate positions in philanthropic organizations. Running a benevolent organization was seen as akin to running a family and, as in the domestic sphere, men were needed to provide direction while women provided the 'heart'.[13] 'The benevolent sympathies of the female heart' were credited with

---

8   Barker-Benfield, *The culture of sensibility*, p. 225; Davidoff and Hall, *Family fortunes*, pp. 431–2.
9   Elliott, *Angel out of the house*, p. 25.
10 Sarah Scott, *Hall, and the country adjacent* (London, 1762).
11 Susan E. Dinan, *Women and poor relief in seventeenth-century france: the early history of the daughters of charity* (Aldershot, 2006); Barbara B. Diefendorf, *From penitence to charity: pious women and the Catholic Reformation in Paris* (New York, 2004); Monica Chojnacka, 'Charity and community in early modern Venice: the Casa Delle Zitelle' in *Renaissance Quarterly*, 51, no. 1 (1998).
12 Raughter, 'A discreet benevolence'.
13 Prochaska, *Women and philanthropy*, p. 17.

helping to found many benevolent organizations in early nineteenth-century Dublin,[14] but 'benevolent sympathies' alone were not considered sufficient to run an organization. When voluntary societies first began to appear in Ireland, the only role available to middle- and upper-class women was as donors. The subscription lists for Dublin charities bear out that a number of women did subscribe to various voluntary societies. The roles permitted to women gradually expanded, but all were subordinate. Women were not permitted to hold positions on the boards that governed charities; in most cases, they were not even considered members of the voluntary societies and held no influence over direction or policy. The organized philanthropy which characterized the eighteenth century was not about sympathy, with its feminine connotations, but practical improvement, and that improvement was to be directed by men.

This chapter will hope to demonstrate that, despite these restrictions, women still found ways to be actively involved in charity throughout the eighteenth century. Traditional private benevolence continued on a local level. Women were able to find ways to participate in voluntary societies, so that, by the end of the eighteenth century, Irish women could be celebrated for their benevolence.[15] The philanthropic career of Lady Arbella Denny and the operating structure of the Dublin Magdalene Society illustrate how women were able to participate in and even direct certain endeavours. The Dublin Magdalene Asylum, which Denny founded, is one example of a voluntary society that did not exclude women from positions of authority. While corporate philanthropy worked to exclude women from most positions of authority, charitably inclined women such as Arbella Denny were still able to carve out spheres of influence for themselves in this age of improvement. They did so by focusing on charity geared towards poor women and children, both of which were considered natural, and acceptable, objects of female sympathy.

In their early years voluntary societies might not have permitted women to participate in an official capacity, but they did come to recognize that there were arenas in which female participation was needed. Women's participation in charity was welcome, just not in an executive capacity. The eighteenth century had wrought changes in understandings of charity and sympathy which opened the door for more male participation, but these qualities were still regarded as occurring more naturally in women.[16] The focus on improvement, with its more practical and emotionally distant connotations, was a way of masculinizing charity work. While male-dominated institutional structures came to control

---

14 Warburton, *History of the city of Dublin*, ii, 770.
15 Raughter, 'A natural tenderness: the ideal & the reality of eighteenth-century female philanthropy' in Maryann Valiulis and Mary O'Dowd (eds), *Women & Irish history: essays in honour of Margaret Maccurtain* (Dublin, 1997), p. 71.
16 Elliott, *Angel out of the house*, p. 22.

most philanthropy in the period, it was never the case that women's participation in charity was regarded as inappropriate. It is more likely that women
were not regarded as truly capable of participating in the new organizational
structures; however, the contemporary perception that women were naturally
inclined towards charity meant that they were never excluded entirely.[17]
Between 1730 and 1760 this involvement was primarily limited to donations,
as noted, but from 1760 onward their roles gradually began to expand as new
organizations such as the Magdalene Society appeared and existing organizations actively solicited the participation of women.

The Incorporated Society and the Dublin Society both prevented women
from becoming full members, but by the 1760s each was actively seeking
women's involvement in certain arenas. By the 1760s many improvers had
come to recognize the value of a feminine perspective, but only in fields that
seemed to fall within women's allotted sphere: namely, anything concerned
with women and children.[18] The Dublin Society itself did not deem women's
participation particularly valuable, since its emphasis was on agriculture and
manufacturing, not considered part of the feminine sphere. There were certain
exceptions, most notably Lady Arbella Denny, who was made an honorary
member of the society. The growing acceptance of active female participation in the activities of voluntary societies was in response to the particular
challenges facing each organization. The Incorporated Society had begun to
receive negative reports of conditions at their schools, a problem which would
continue to plague them and gradually became public. A shortage of visitors
at the local level, as well the particular needs of schools with female pupils,
meant that there was an immediate need for concerned visitors to schools
in general and women visitors in particular. Since the Incorporated Society
catered to children, who were considered natural objects of women's sympathy,
the involvement of women was, to a degree, welcomed. The Dublin Society had
also begun to accept women's involvement in this period; in 1765 it opened the
Irish silk warehouse where it saw that the involvement of women was essential
to success.

The growing acceptance of women's participation in voluntary societies was
motivated in part by necessity, but another explanation for this is the work
of Lady Arbella herself. Richard Woodward, in his poorhouse proposal to the
Dublin Society, justified the involvement of women as visitors and governors
by noting that 'the propriety of associating Ladies in this Department is
obvious. But if any Proof were necessary, the Dublin Work-House affords an
extraordinary instance of the effect of it in a Lady, who does Honour to her

17 Ibid., pp. 22–3.
18 Ibid., p. 25.

Sex.'[19] Woodward was referring to Denny, who had begun visiting the Dublin Workhouse and Foundling Hospital in 1759 and became famous for her tireless efforts to improve that institution.

Lady Arbella was born Lady Arbella Fitzmaurice in 1707. The Fitzmaurices were, and continued to be, a prominent family in the Anglo-Irish nobility. Arbella was the second daughter of Thomas Fitzmaurice, the twenty-first lord of Kerry, and later created the first earl of Kerry. Her mother Anne was the daughter of Sir William Petty, from another prominent Anglo-Irish family.[20] The Fitzmaurices had a longer history in Ireland than most, their title dating back to Henry II. Denny lived most of her childhood far from Dublin at her father's home, Lixnaw Castle in Tralee, County Kerry. In 1727 she married Colonel Arthur Denny, who died in 1742 of an apoplexy. Since they had no children, his estates remained within his family and Lady Arbella returned for a time to her father's home. She would never remarry and it seems that her marriage to Colonel Denny was not a particularly happy one.[21]

Lady Arbella's nephew, William Petty-Fitzmaurice, marquess of Lansdowne and for a time prime minister of Great Britain, was quite close to his aunt and wrote admiringly of her in his autobiography. According to Lansdowne, Colonel Denny was from a neighbouring family, one that was also descended from one of the oldest English families in Ireland. He described Colonel Denny as 'a very good sort of man' but also 'uninformed and ignorant'. The particular unhappiness in the marriage for Lady Arbella came from her brother-in-law Sir Thomas Denny, 'a coward, a savage, and a fool who set himself to make her life unhappy'. The exact nature of this abuse is not explicitly stated, but it led Lady Arbella to thoughts of suicide. She was apparently in enough fear for her personal safety that she learned to fire a pistol, and demonstrated her newfound marksmanship to her brother-in-law, threatening to shoot him if he did not alter his behaviour towards her. Fortunately, this seems to have had the desired effect. The experience apparently left her soured on the institution of marriage. While her husband was not guilty of any particular cruelty, Denny did not feel that she could safely confide his brother's actions to him. After his death in 1742 she was left a reasonably affluent widow, as she had inherited some income from her husband and had additional income from her father. At only thirty-five years old she was still an eligible match, but remarrying held no appeal for her. According to her nephew, she vowed never 'to become a slave again'.[22] Widowed, young, and with an income, she moved to the Dublin area in

19 Woodward, A scheme for establishing county poor-houses, p. 9.
20 Butler, 'Lady Arabella Denny, 1707–92', p. 1.
21 Fitzmaurice, Life of William, earl of Shelburne, i, 12–13; Butler, 'Lady Arabella Denny, 1707–92', pp. 1–2.
22 Fitzmaurice, Life of William, earl of Shelburne, i, pp. 12–13.

1748, eventually settling in Blackrock, a little south of the city of Dublin.[23] She travelled frequently and undertook a prolonged tour of the continent in 1751.[24] In 1759 she began her charity work in earnest when she visited the Dublin Foundling Hospital with a group of ladies. Of the party, only Denny persisted in working to reform that troubled institution.[25]

By 1759 the Dublin Foundling Hospital was notorious for its poor conditions, its high death rate, and institutional corruption. Denny was horrified by what she saw and set out to reform and improve operations at the hospital. The Foundling Hospital was unique among Dublin charities in that it was not established at the behest of a voluntary society, but by the Corporation of Dublin, which funded it primarily through taxation. It did have a Board of Governors, first appointed after the founding of the institution. Perhaps because it had not been founded on their own impetus, the governors were generally uninterested in the Foundling Hospital, preferring their other endeavours. This situation made it possible for Denny to become the patroness of the Hospital. Denny's involvement in the Foundling Hospital, and her later founding of the Magdalene Asylum, was considered acceptable behaviour, for which she was highly lauded because of her gender and not in spite of it.

Her friend Meliore Adlercron was not alone in regarding Denny as a 'saint'. Even before her death in 1792, she was described in terms so admiring they often seem excessive. She was so wonderful a woman that she compensated for the failings of her entire gender. One writer described her as 'a woman above all praise!' and noted in rhyme that, 'Were the sex deaf to fair discretion's call,/ One Denny makes a full amends for all'.[26] This description is from 1787, by which point she was well-known for her devotion to charity. Even earlier in her life, she had been described in glowing terms that imply that she transcended the failings of not only her gender but also her social class. Reverend William Henry termed her 'the Protectress of the Orphans' and noted that she helped to 'maintain the Cause of pure Christianity, even in the midst of a thoughtless Generation'. He felt that she restored 'religion to be fashionable, among Persons of high rank'.[27] Edward Bayly spoke of her possessing 'that perfect Esteem and Veneration, which Birth and Titles only cannot inspire'.[28] The most common appellation for her, in addition to her customary title of 'Right Honourable',

[23] N.A.I. Pembroke/ 96/46/1/2/7/48; 96/46/1/2/7/50; 97/46/1/2/7/51.

[24] Butler, 'Lady Arabella Denny, 1707–92', p. 2.

[25] Ibid., pp. 6–7.

[26] Richard Lewis, *The Dublin guide: or, a description of the city of Dublin, and the most remarkable places within fifteen miles* (Dublin, 1787), pp. 50–51.

[27] William Henry, *The cries of the orphans: a sermon preached in the parish church of St Michael, on Sunday April 27th for the support of the orphans in the foundling hospital* (Dublin, 1760), p. 2.

[28] Edward Bayly, *A sermon preached on the opening of the chapel of the Magdalene asylum for female penitents* (Dublin, 1768), p. 4.

was simply 'excellent'. Henry's praise came from a charity sermon given on behalf of the Foundling Hospital and dedicated to Denny. Edward Bayly, in his 1768 sermon on behalf of the Magdalene Asylum, noted the tendency for such dedications to be excessively laudatory, but saw his as an exception since it was dedicated to Denny. 'If Dedications must necessarily be filled with extravagant Praises, valued by None but such as do not merit them, This is not One. No, Madam; I would have the World judge freely of You; I would have them judge, not from my Words, but from your Works.'[29] Few male improvers were the objects of so many glowing tributes, which indicate the widespread social acceptance of Denny's many good works. Women's participation in charity was considered natural and acceptable, but Denny did not merely participate in charities, she organized and directed them, an undertaking that in this period was more associated with men.

Such sentiments were to be expected within the context of sermons dedicated to her and given to benefit the charities that she championed. Denny, however, was held in such high esteem that she was praised in works with no connections to her charities. Richard Lewis' *The Dublin Guide*, primarily a description of notable buildings and sites in the city, described Denny as 'above all praise'. Her reputation did not suffer after her death. Her nephew, the marquess of Lansdowne, deeply admired his aunt, although he had little affection for anyone else in his family. He described his grandfather, Lady Arbella's father, as 'the most severe character ... obstinate and inflexible', noting later that 'he governed his own family as he did the country. In consequence his children did not love him, but dreaded him.' He has a few compliments for his grandmother and his parents, but on the whole Fitzmaurice regarded one of his greatest accomplishments as rising above his family, with their 'uncultivated, undisciplined manners and that vulgarity which make all Irish society so justly odious all over Europe'.[30]

The exception was his aunt Arbella, 'to whose virtues, talents, temper, taste, true religion and goodness of every kind, it is impossible for me to do sufficient justice'.[31] Arbella, according to her nephew, was responsible for teaching him to read and write and to articulate his thoughts. 'She was the only example I had before me of the two qualities of mind which most adorn and dignify life – amiability and independence.'[32] He made little mention of her charity work, except to note that, following the death of her husband, she devoted herself to charity work and was a great 'example to her sex'.[33] Fitzmaurice was writing in

---

[29] Ibid.

[30] Fitzmaurice, *Life of William, earl of Shelburne*, pp. 1–11.

[31] Ibid., pp. 11–12.

[32] Ibid., p. 12.

[33] Ibid., p. 13.

the nineteenth century, by which point women's involvement in charity work was widely accepted. To nineteenth-century commentators her involvement in philanthropy was not inherently noteworthy, but she remained a figure to be admired. For example, William Wodsworth's account of the history of the Dublin Foundling Hospital describes her time as patroness as a golden age in the history of a troubled institution. On a personal level, she was a 'noble, energetic, and good woman' lacking in any religious bigotry whose hard work in good management and financial generosity helped the once astronomical death rate to drop to a mere 25 per cent.[34]

Denny's involvement in the Foundling Hospital came on the heels of a 1758 parliamentary investigation that documented both numerous abuses within the hospital and its mortality rate of about 89 per cent. On the whole the people of Dublin were shocked by this revelation, but Denny alone was sufficiently moved to become actively involved in reforming the Foundling Hospital. She engaged nurses to care for the young children. She clearly organized duties for them and implemented a system of rewards for nurses who did good work. To make sure the infants were fed regularly she purchased a large grandfather clock that was set to go off every twenty minutes to ensure that they were fed.[35] A uniform was adopted for children at the hospital, and they were regularly marched to the courtyard of Dublin Castle in neat blue suits and dresses with red collars and cuffs to be inspected by the lord lieutenant.[36] Denny was credited with saving thousands of lives and with ensuring that the children were healthy and properly clothed and instructed. In recognition of her achievements at the Foundling Hospital she was formally thanked by parliament and awarded the freedom of the City of Dublin in 1765.[37]

She was also a devoted improver and maintained close relationships with other voluntary societies. She recommended children for admission into the Incorporated Society and, in turn, the Incorporated Society looked to her experiences at the workhouse for guidance when it came to the children's diet or the treatment of diseases among them.[38] Denny maintained an even closer relationship with the Dublin Society. In 1765 she was appointed as one of the first patronesses of the silk warehouse, and in 1766 was named an honorary member of the society. She was the first woman to be awarded this honour; as a woman she was not eligible for full membership, but the extension of honorary

---

[34] William Dudley Wodsworth, A brief history of the ancient foundling hospital of Dublin, from the year 1702 (Dublin, 1876), pp. 34–6.
[35] Morning Herald and Daily Advertiser, 11 September 1781.
[36] Robins, The lost children, pp. 24–6.
[37] British Evening Post, 22 July 1765; Debates relative to the affairs of Ireland, in the years 1763 and 1764 (2 vols, London, 1766), ii, 735.
[38] T.C.D. 5237, 5239.

membership demonstrates that the Dublin Society's leadership held Denny in high esteem.[39] She was granted several premiums by the society to encourage the production of bone lace, a skilled manufacture encouraged by the Dublin Society, and in which Denny had been instructing the Foundling Hospital children.[40] She also had the children instructed in glove-making and, in 1769, while on a visit to London, presented a pair made by the children to Queen Charlotte.[41] The idea behind these endeavours was essentially the same one behind the Incorporated Society: to teach the foundling children a skilled trade. This was deemed essential to their becoming successful citizens as adults. Denny was particularly interested in encouraging the manufacture of lace, and saw to it that penitents in the Magdalene Asylum received similar instruction.

Aside from the Foundling Hospital, the other great charitable venture of Denny's life was the Magdalene Asylum. Her reasons for founding another benevolent organization, at a point in which she was still deeply involved in the Foundling Hospital, are not entirely clear. However, her work at the Foundling Hospital had certainly made her aware of the difficult plight of the women who had borne many of those foundlings and been forced to give them up.[42] Denny's involvement in the Magdalene Asylum was encouraged by other charitable women, who sought the validation that her fame would provide. The project began in 1766, but opening was delayed owing to difficulties finding a suitable location to house the asylum.[43] Finally, in 1767 the Magdalene Asylum of Dublin opened on Lower Leeson Street.[44] The idea for the Magdalene Asylum did not originate in Ireland; Denny and her cohort were inspired by the London Magdalene charity, which had opened in 1758. The London charity, and later the Dublin house, were designed to promote the rehabilitation of penitent prostitutes. The London Magdalene charity was managed in much the same way as most other contemporary charity organizations. It had a patroness, the queen, whose involvement was largely ceremonial. It was run primarily by a president, initially Francis Conway, earl of Hertford, four vice-presidents, a treasurer, general court, and a general committee of twenty-one governors. Anyone who subscribed twenty guineas was eligible to be a governor for life of the charity, regardless of gender. However, while women could be governors they did not hold other posts. The General Court consisted of ten governors, and the committee of twenty-one governors that oversaw much of the operation of the charity was composed entirely of men, as were the other official positions.

39 R.D.S. Minute Books vol. 9.
40 R.D.S. Minute Books vol. 10.
41 *Lloyd's Evening Post*, 19 April 1769.
42 Butler, 'Lady Arabella Denny, 1707–92', p. 9.
43 N.A.I. 97/46/1/2/6/73.
44 Butler, 'Lady Arabella Denny, 1707–92', p. 9.

The asylum did have two female employees, the matron and assistant matron, who resided at the asylum and strictly supervised the activities of the penitents.[45]

The exact origins of the Dublin Magdalene Asylum are unclear, but presumably the impetus came from the earl of Hertford and his wife, Isabella Conway, in England. They were respectively named president and patroness for life. Hertford was an important courtier and close confidant of the king. Inspired by the success of the establishment in London, they sought to establish a similar institution in Dublin while Hertford was serving as lord lieutenant of Ireland from 1765 to 1766.[46] They recruited Lady Arbella, who was already well known for her charity work. Lewis' guide to the city praised the Asylum for providing such an important service not just to the penitents but to the citizens of the city as well. 'An institution of this kind was greatly wanted for Dublin, where our sight was constantly struck with objects disgraceful to human nature; with wretched strumpets, tricked out in tawdry apparel, or covered with tattered weeds; and were our ears were continually assaulted with vociferations that would startle deafness, and appal blasphemy.'[47] Lady Arbella, named vice-patroness, took a far more active role in the Dublin Magdalene Asylum then either of the Hertfords, who did not spend any time in Ireland after 1766.[48] The Dublin Asylum was run on a different model from the London one. Instead of the normal governing officers and boards, consisting entirely of male governors, the government of the Dublin Asylum was split into two departments segregated along general lines. This unique set-up was said to be required by 'the nature of the charity', though the London asylum, which had the same purpose, did not have the same type of governance.[49]

The feminine side of the charity's organization consisted of the patroness and vice-patroness, plus any woman who donated enough money to become a governess. The governesses elected a committee of fifteen women annually, who were termed visitors. The visitors, the patroness, and the vice-patroness were the only people allowed unrestricted access to the penitents. The patroness of the asylum was the countess of Hertford, who was named patroness for life. She in turn appointed Denny vice-patroness for life. They oversaw their activities and made decisions with regard to the diet, dress, employment, and discipline of

[45] William Dodd, An account of the rise, progress, and present state of the Magdalen charity, to which are added, the Rev. Mr. Dodd's sermon, preached before the president, vice-presidents, and governors (London, 1761), pp. 210, 28.

[46] William C. Lowe, 'Conway, Francis Seymour-, first marquess of Hertford (1718–1794)' in Lawrence Goldman (ed.), Oxford Dictionary of National Biography (online ed., Oxford, <http://www.oxforddnb.com/view/article/6121>) Accessed 14 July 2010.

[47] Lewis, The Dublin guide, p. 51.

[48] Lowe, 'Conway, Francis Seymour-, first marquess of Hertford (1718–1794)'.

[49] Bayly, A sermon preached on the opening of the chapel of the Magdalene asylum for female penitents, p. 1.

the residents of the house. The patroness and vice-patroness were also charged with appointing the secretary, hiring all domestic servants, and admitting all penitents. The men among the administration were termed guardians. The earl of Hertford was president; there were thirteen vice-presidents drawn primarily from the aristocracy and the upper ranks of the Church of Ireland episcopate; and a treasurer, two physicians, two surgeons and an apothecary. Other guardians qualified based on monetary donations. They met four times a year and received reports on conditions in the house and the treasury of the society. The guardians were also charged with appointing the medical officers, the treasurer, and the chaplain. The chaplain was subject to the approval of the patroness and vice-patroness, but the treasurer was appointed by them alone.[50]

The reasons for this unique method of government were practical. The residents of the Magdalene Asylum were to be entirely removed from the society which might tempt them into sin again. They were especially to be kept apart from men until their reformation was complete. At the London Asylum the penitents were strictly observed by matrons who resided there, but there were also resident in the house a steward, porter, and messenger, none of whom were supposed to have any contact with the residents. The steward was to reside at the house 'to protect the Magdalen Asylum from insults from abroad', but he was still strictly segregated from female residents and was to dine alone.[51] Medical professionals were permitted to attend on the residents, but only with the strict supervision of a matron. Governors were permitted to see the women only with the express written permission of a chairman, and even then only under the supervision of a matron.[52] At the Dublin Magdalene Asylum contact was regulated just as strictly. The only people allowed to see the penitents without the permission of the patroness or vice-patroness were the fifteen elected visitors. Men, even guardians, required written permission from the patroness or vice-patroness to meet penitents, but such contact was strictly regulated and never unsupervised. Even in cases of sudden illness or accidents physicians were permitted contact with the Magdalenes only in the presence of the matron. The chaplain of the asylum was not permitted private contact with them; he was to interact with them only in the nearby chapel, and even then a matron was to present at all times.[53]

The time allotted by each asylum for reformation varied. The London Asylum permitted women to remain for up to three years, but they could

[50] Ibid., pp. 3–6.
[51] *Rules and regulations for the asylum of penitent females: with an account of receipts and disbursements* (Dublin, 1796), p. 8.
[52] Dodd, *An account of the rise, progress, and present state of the Magdalen charity*, pp. 220–25.
[53] Bayly, *A sermon preached on the opening of the chapel of the Magdalene asylum for female penitents*, pp. 2–3.

be released earlier if it was into the care of parents or friends, or to a house-keeper who would employ them.[54] The Dublin Asylum permitted women only eighteen months for their rehabilitation; however, they could remain longer with special permission from a patroness. The time-frame was later expanded to a maximum of two years. The rules stated that women would not be dismissed from the asylum 'until safe and decent retreats shall be provided for them'.[55] Both Magdalene Asylums stressed that once they became penitents women left behind their previous sins and identities. To ensure anonymity women were known only by numbers, which coincided with their admission to the charity. They were also not to be criticized for their pasts: 'reproaches for the irregularities of their past lives are strictly forbidden, and also all enquiry into their names or families, except such as the parties shall consent to'.[56] This forgiveness did not mean that their past conduct was forgotten. The daily lives and activities of penitents were strictly super-vised. They were not permitted contact with anyone on the outside, except for certain members of the charity, and their days were carefully structured. Bad behaviour was seen as a symptom of insincere repentance and could be grounds for dismissal.

Because of their focus on prostitutes Magdalene Asylums were an unusual charity for the time, and the governors of the asylums felt it necessary to police the behaviour of inmates strictly. Most eighteenth-century charities drew a clear line between the deserving and the undeserving poor and focused their efforts on the deserving. Magdalene asylums had to contend with the social stigma of providing charity to prostitutes, not generally considered among the deserving poor. Voluntary hospitals primarily offered their services to the working poor, who had the recommendation of a donor or governor, and charity schools focused on children, who were automatically considered deserving by virtue of their youth. The asylums in London and in Dublin devoted a great deal of energy to challenging the assumption that prostitutes were unworthy of philanthropy and portrayed the girls they helped as worthy objects of charity. They also stressed, as most charities did, the good social effects that came from their work. It was argued that rescuing women from prostitution had economic benefits because they were taught a trade while the number of prostitutes, who were a drain on the resources of the nation, was decreased.[57] Similar arguments

---

[54] Dodd, *An account of the rise, progress, and present state of the Magdalen charity*, p. 226.
[55] Bayly, *A sermon preached on the opening of the chapel of the Magdalene asylum for female penitents*, p. 2; *Rules and regulations for the asylum of penitent females: with an account of receipts and disburse-ments*, p. 2.
[56] Ibid., p. 8.
[57] Jonas Hanway, *A plan for establishing a charity-house, or charity-houses, for the reception of repenting prostitutes. To be called the Magdalen charity* (London, 1758), pp. ix–x.

were frequently used by other charities to promote the tangible practical benefits of their activities. Magdalene Asylums, like other charities, were meant to serve the interests of the state as well as of society. Other charities, such as hospitals or schools, also made frequent references to how deserving their charitable objects were, but rarely had to justify this to the same extent. It was taken for granted that children or distressed widows, or the working poor, were worthy objects of charity.

The supporters of the Magdalene Asylums faced the rhetorical challenge of portraying prostitutes not as idle sinners but as blameless victims. As a result they were not called prostitutes but Magdalenes, and Magdalenes could be redeemed. Magdalenes were described as virtuous but naïve young women seduced by worldly men and abandoned with no other way to support themselves. Most came from decent, though not prosperous, families, but lacked education or experience before their unfortunate seduction. 'When women of education, who are supposed to be the guardians of their own honour, trespass, it is the greater shame; but the poor and ignorant are less guarded against such formidable seducers.'[58] They are blameless for their original fall from grace because they were 'young' or 'deluded'; 'no girl can help being young or handsome, nor are youth and beauty things that the possessors are much inclined to conceal'. A woman's virtue had to be protected and women could not do this themselves. Many penitents were fatherless and so lacked anyone to guard their virtue from seducers. They could not be at fault because 'men are endowed, not only with superior faculties, but with all the advantages which education and fortune afford, if they will prostitute their honour to gratify their appetite, many will become their prey'.[59]

These portrayals were reinforced by the publications of various accounts of the lives of penitents after the founding of the society. Most of these descriptions reinforced the ideas put forth by Jonas Hanway in his justification of the Magdalene Asylum. One young woman was the daughter of a 'gentleman in the army' who lived alone with her mother. She had a genteel education but the family was impoverished. She was taken advantage of by an old family friend, drawn into 'criminal intimacy' with him, and then abandoned with child. Eventually, she turned to prostitution to support herself, before dying at twenty-six years old.[60] That penitent, unable to enter the Magdalene Asylum, died tragically young. In many of its own publications the Asylum preferred to stick to success stories, such as the account of the first woman to enter the London asylum. Written by the woman herself in the form of letters to a patron, she

---

58 Ibid., p. xiv.
59 Ibid., p. xiii.
60 *The Magdalen: Or, dying penitent, exemplified in the death of F.S. who died April 1763, aged twenty-six years* (Dublin, 1789), pp. 2–9.

describes herself as the daughter or a poor clergyman in west England, living in genteel poverty with a sick mother and one older sister. Her mother died when she was fourteen, and a year later her father died. Leaving her essentially on her own at the age of fifteen, 'my appearance, indeed, was womanly. I had been bred up in religious principles, but at that age they were not deeply grounded, nor so fixed as to stand against the temptations of the world, into which I was now thrown.'[61] Orphaned, she became a lady's maid and was seduced by her employer's son, thus setting her on a downward spiral from which she was later rescued by the Magdalene Charity.

Accounts such as this were meant to change the popular conception of prostitutes, to make them into worthy objects of charity who were not responsible, at least not wholly, for their situation. One compilation of such accounts justified this by writing:

> Tho' the profession of a prostitute is the most despicable and hateful that imagination can form; yet the individuals are frequently worthy objects of compassion; and I am willing to believe, that if people did but reflect on the various stratagems used at first to corrupt them, while poverty often, and still oftener vanity, is on the side of the corruptor, they would smooth the stern brow of rigid virtue, and turn the contemptuous frown into tears of pity.[62]

Such narratives had to walk a fine line between making the women largely blameless, while having them admit some degree of culpability and express sincere regret for their choices. Primary blame for their situation was placed on their seducers. Supporters of the charity were quick to point out the social hypocrisy of condemning their victims to poverty and disease while the man responsible 'obtains no other appellation by such villainy, than that of a man of gallantry'.[63] Most of these stories originated in England and referred to residents at the Magdalene charity there, but were published in Dublin in the years before and after the establishment of the Dublin Magdalene Asylum.

Denny was clearly aware of the challenges her new charity faced and stressed that Magdalenes would be held to a high standard of behaviour. As vice-patroness she initiated a standard speech that was given to all incoming penitents even after her death. In it, she welcomed sincerely all new women and assured them that the asylum was designed as 'A shelter from shame, from reproach, from disease, from want, from the base society that has either drawn you into vice, or prevailed on you to continue in it. To the utmost

---

61 William Dodd, The Magdalen, or, history of the first penitent prostitute received into that charitable asylum. With anecdotes of other penitents (London, 1799), pp. 13–14.

62 The histories of some of the penitents in the Magdalen-House, as supposed to be related by themselves (2 vols, Dublin, 1760), i, p. iv.

63 Ibid., i, p. ix.

hazard of your eternal happiness. A shelter that will afford you time to reflect, how grievously you have offended that gracious Author of all good.'[64] Prayer and repentance were meant to take up a good deal of the resident's time. They prayed three times a day, asking God to 'Renew in us whatsoever have been decayed by the fraud and malice of the devil, or by our own carnal will and frailness.'[65] Penitents were meant to spend their time in solemn contemplation of their past mistakes. Within the confines of the asylum women had to admit responsibility for their own failings in order to gain admittance to the charity. Prayer and contemplation were not their only occupations, for they were also to spend much of the day at labour. The idea was to keep the residents occupied and encourage an honest skill by which they might be able to support themselves at the end of their term. The London asylum chiefly kept the women at work spinning wool or flax, winding silk, making shirts or gloves, and embroidering. They could also be set to making lace, knitting hose, and making garters or carpets.[66] Vocational training was an important part of the Magdalene charities in both London and Dublin, and was deemed essential to prevent the penitents from returning to their former lives. Lady Arbella used the Magdalene Asylum to promote her own pet production causes, and many penitents were taught to produce lace, just as the children at the foundling hospital had been.[67] The Magdalenes' labour was not only a spiritual benefit to them, but also of some financial benefit to the charity, since the needlework done by penitents was sold and the proceeds put towards the operating costs of the asylum. In 1776 this work amounted to just over £81.[68]

While at the asylum, penitents were clothed at the expense of the society in simple uniforms of light grey. Figure 5.1 illustrates a standard uniform. They were expected at all times to be neat and plain in their dress and appearance.[69] Their own clothes and personal items were taken from them at the time of their admission and were returned to them when they left. Many women entered with very little in the way of clothes and in such cases were often permitted to keep their uniform when leaving the asylum, even if they had been expelled or dismissed for bad behaviour.[70]

---

[64] *Rules and regulations for the asylum of penitent females: with an account of receipts and disbursements*, p. 10.

[65] Ibid., p. 9.

[66] Dodd, *An account of the rise, progress, and present state of the Magdalen charity*, p. 223.

[67] R.C.B.L. 551–1–1.

[68] Matthew West, *Charity the seal of Christian perfection, a sermon preached before his excellency, the lord lieutenant, and the vice-patroness, governesses, and guardians of the asylum for penitent women* (Dublin, 1777), pp. 25–6.

[69] Dodd, *An account of the rise, progress, and present state of the Magdalen charity*, p. 221.

[70] R.C.B.L. 551–1–1.

Figure 5.1. Standard uniform for a Magdalene, from *An Account of the Rise, Progress, and Present State of the Magdalen Charity* (London, 1761).

Magdalene Asylums offered food, shelter, clothing, education, and vocational training to many unhappy women forced into prostitution. These same benefits also attracted women who were not penitent prostitutes. Because of this and their own limited resources, the governors in London and governesses in Dublin had to closely monitor admissions. Entrance to the asylum was granted only with written permission of the patroness or vice-patroness, upon the recommendation of a clergyman.[71] The London asylum granted admission following a petition from the woman and her passing a medical examination.[72] Admission to both asylums had to be closely monitored because of limited space. Both preferred to admit young women unhardened by their profession who could, theoretically, be more easily rehabilitated. In theory, both asylums were founded for penitent prostitutes, but the London asylum certainly expanded beyond that purview and the Dublin one may have as well. By the 1780s a significant number of women admitted to the London charity fell into the category of women who had been 'seduced' but had not yet turned to prostitution. Their admission into the asylum was a preventative measure.[73] The expansion was

---

[71] Bayly, *A sermon preached on the opening of the chapel of the Magdalene asylum for female penitents*, p. 2.
[72] Dodd, *An account of the rise, progress, and present state of the Magdalen charity*, pp. 219–20.
[73] Peter N. Stearns, 'Prostitution and charity: the Magdalen hospital, a case study' in *Journal of Social History*, 17, no. 4 (1984), p. 619.

a logical one, since seduced or even raped women were frequently cast out by family, friends, or employers. The prostitution narratives put out by the society stressed that most penitents had begun as respectable women who had been seduced and then turned to prostitution out of financial necessity. By 1786 the London Asylum had established separate provisions for 'seduced' women, who were housed separately from the former prostitutes.[74]

The Dublin Asylum was far more reluctant to expand their admissions policy and, while there are isolated admissions of women who were not prostitutes, their inclusion was never a general policy. The Dublin Asylum's admissions book gives only limited information about women who entered and does not generally give ages or circumstances prior to entrance. The Asylum is described at times as a 'refuge for fallen women', a broad description that could include the seduced. John Warburton, writing in 1818, described the asylum as catering to 'unfortunate females abandoned by their seducers, and rejected by their friends, who were willing to prefer a life of penitence and virtue to one of guilt, infamy, and prostitution'.[75] However, particularly during Denny's tenure, the Asylum was very strict in its admittance policy.[76] *The London Morning Chronicle* reported a story of a fourteen-year-old girl who applied to Denny for admission. She was refused after being questioned by Denny and discovered not to be a prostitute at all. A few days later she returned:

'Poor child! (said Lady Arabella) I told you before you were not qualified'. 'True, my Lady (answered the poor girl, dropping an humble curtsey, and displaying a conscious blush) but I have been qualified since'. She was admitted to the Asylum, and got that bread to eat, which her virtue could not provide her.[77]

The admissions book also records the admittance of one Sarah Lucas in 1777, who, according to a letter attached by the clergyman who recommended her, was pushed into prostitution by her profligate parents.[78] Lucas had definitely been a prostitute, but some others were not. In 1775 one Mary Anne Kelly left the hospital early owing to ill health and because it was discovered that she was not an object for the charity.[79] This could mean that Kelly was not genuinely repentant for her past life, or that she had nothing in her past life for which she needed to be penitent. Elinor Caugh, in 1785, was dismissed from the asylum after it was discovered that she had pretended to be a penitent prostitute so

[74] Ibid.

[75] Warburton, *History of the city of Dublin*, ii, 771.

[76] Denny was active in the asylum until the last years of her life. Through 1790 she routinely made notes in an increasingly shaky hand that followed up on former Magdalenes.

[77] *Morning Chronicle and London Advertiser*, 31 December 1781.

[78] R.C.B.L. 551-1-1.

[79] R.C.B.L. 551-1-1.

as to seek shelter in the asylum and learn needlework and reading, both of which she did learn.[80] While the Dublin Asylum probably did expand in the nineteenth century to admit other 'fallen' women, there is no evidence that in the eighteenth century they made provisions to house such women separately or admitted them regularly. This is not surprising, given that the Dublin Asylum was considerably smaller than its London counterpart. We have only one example of a known non-prostitute being admitted to the Dublin asylum in the eighteenth century. Maria Nugent was permitted to reside in the asylum for five years from 1783 to 1788. When she left for New York in 1788, the asylum collected over £19 to aid her on her journey. These special steps were taken because Nugent had never been a prostitute, but was instead deceived and seduced by a man who married her even though he was already married.[81]

As with the London Asylum, the Dublin Asylum preferred to admit young women. Between 1767 and 1795 388 women went through the asylum. Age information is provided for only 134 women and was not recorded until 1782. Of these 134 women the average age was just over nineteen years old. One woman as old as thirty-two was admitted and two girls as young as twelve entered between 1782 and 1795. Children younger than fourteen and women older than twenty-six were the exception, and most penitents were between fifteen and twenty-five years old.[82] The Dublin Asylum also had to contend with religious differences while maintaining close ties with the Church of Ireland, as it was open to women of all denominations. Penitents were usually recommended by a Church of Ireland minister, and there was an Anglican chapel built next to the asylum with an Anglican chaplain to oversee the spiritual health of penitents. However, the Asylum did not force conversion on penitents. The religion of incoming penitents was not regularly recorded until the 1780s, but in the 130 cases where it was recorded the majority (81) of incoming penitents professed to being Protestant, as opposed to 46 Catholics, two Presbyterians, and one woman who was 'bred up a Quaker'.[83] Figure 5.2 illustrates the religious affiliations of the penitents. While resident in the Asylum women were expected to pray regularly and attend Anglican church services at the attached chapel. This probably encouraged some penitents to convert, but it was not a requirement. By the second half of the eighteenth century the anti-Catholic sentiment which inspired the Incorporated Society had softened. Sarah Fayle entered the asylum at the age of thirty-one, having been 'bred' a Quaker. She left in 1792 after serving the regular eighteen-month term and was permitted to return to other Quakers. Several Catholics were also permitted to return to

[80] R.C.B.L. 551-1-2.
[81] R.C.B.L. 551-1-2.
[82] R.C.B.L. 551-1-1.
[83] R.C.B.L. 551-1-1.

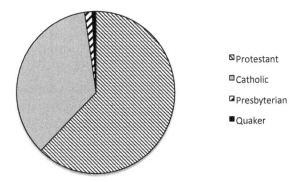

Figure 5.2. Religious affiliations of Magdalenes, 1767–1795.

their relatives after serving their regular terms. Of the two known Presbyterians who entered the Asylum, one returned to her parents, the other emigrated to Boston. It was more common for penitents, regardless of religion, not to return to their families. Many went into service, while others emigrated.[84]

Penitents were expected at the end of their term only to be 'reconciled to your God'.[85] The asylum granted an annuity of three pounds to women who successfully completed their terms, which was later amended so that women received the full three pounds only after demonstrating good behaviour for a year on the outside. This annuity was granted regardless of religion, either upon entering or leaving. This policy is in keeping with the description of Denny as being deeply religious but 'free from sectarian religious bigotry'.[86] The primary aim of the Magdalene Asylum was not religious conversion, but behavioural conversion. Effective behavioural conversion was also difficult to achieve, particularly when nothing was done to address the social forces that had compelled most of the women into prostitution in the first place. Of the 388 women who entered the asylum between 1767 and 1795 the vast majority, 224, completed the eighteen-month term with little problem and were dismissed regularly from the hospital. Some were returned to family or friends, many went into service, and others emigrated to America. However, while they might have been well behaved during their eighteen months in the asylum, there were significant concerns among those involved in the charity that they would not be able to maintain this good behaviour once they were returned to the temptations of the outside world. Upon leaving the asylum the women were warned: 'you will find the world you are returning to, the very same as when you were

---

[84] R.C.B.L. 551–1-1.

[85] *Rules and regulations for the asylum of penitent females: with an account of receipts and disbursements*, p. 14.

[86] Wodsworth, *A brief history of the ancient foundling hospital of Dublin, from the year 1702*, p. 34.

rescued from it; you will find that same levity, the same dissipation, the same vanity, the same follies, the same vices; in a word, the same temptations of all kinds, to shame and ruin'.[87] The asylum policy was to reward those women who were well behaved during their term with a three-guinea bounty upon their leaving. In 1777 Denny chose to amend this rule, noting that 'on some persons being guilty of misbehaviour after their leaving the asylum with a good character I have found it expedient to refuse two guineas of the bounty money till the magdalen produces a certificate that may be depended on that she has behaved well for twelve months after she has left the asylum'.[88] In 1785 Denny had to amend the rules yet again. She now declared that she would require Magdalenes to prove two years' good behaviour before they were rewarded with the full bounty. This change was deemed necessary after Denny felt that she had been deceived by one Magdalene, Ann Brereton, 'who behaved well till her year was expired which entitled her to the bounty which I had promised her from the Magdalene charity, and then relapsed into vice'.[89]

Relapsing into vice was considered a sign that a Magdalene was not sincere in her conversion, and so was blamed on the personal failings of the woman. The sincerity of conversions was a routine source of concern for those who ran the charity. The Magdalene Asylum provided food, clothing, education, and job training, making it an ideal place of refuge for many poor women, even those who were not penitent prostitutes. Because of limited resources, admission to the asylum was carefully regulated, but at least two women who had never been prostitutes did manage to gain admittance. Even if all the Magdalenes admitted were prostitutes, there was no real way to be certain that their repentance was sincere. The tendency was to associate any and all bad behaviour both during and after time spent at the asylum with insincerity. Of the women who did not complete at least a full eighteen-month term, 57 were dismissed or expelled, usually for bad behaviour of some sort or because they were found to be 'unfit' objects for the charity. An 'unfit' object was a fairly broad term, but generally speaking it seems to have referred to women who did not follow the rules of the house. Open bad behaviour by Magdalenes led to expulsion: for instance, one woman was expelled for striking the matron, another for talking to gentlemen in a neighbouring garden, yet another for stealing fruit from a neighbour's trees. Dismissal generally resulted from less blatant rule-breaking – infringements such as being disrespectful or ungovernable. The two terms were not interchangeable, though, and many women who were dismissed early from the charity did so with the permission of the house to attend to family emergencies, to seek positions in

---

[87] *Rules and regulations for the asylum of penitent females: with an account of receipts and disbursements*, p.14.
[88] R.C.B.L. 551–1–1.
[89] R.C.B.L. 551–1–2.

service, because they could not bear the confinement, and occasionally to marry. Upon dismissal, women gave back the clothes issued to them during their stay at the asylum and had their own personal items returned, though few had come in with very much in the way of personal items. In some cases of extreme poverty women were allowed to leave with clothes they had acquired while in the asylum.

Confinement in the Magdalene Asylum was entirely voluntary and the penitents seem to have been free to leave early if they so wished, though some, for whatever reason, elected to escape from the asylum. Being caught trying to escape generally resulted in immediate expulsion, but, perhaps in order to keep their clothes or other items, some who wished to leave did so illicitly. Between 1767 and 1795 38 women escaped from the asylum. The most common method seems to have been by eloping over the garden wall. However, since the eighteenth-century Magdalene Asylum was not an institution of confinement escape was not terribly difficult: at least one woman simply left through the street door.[90]

It is difficult to judge the success of the conversions that many Magdalenes underwent. The majority of those admitted did complete their eighteen-month term regularly, but follow-up data on them is incomplete. Lady Arbella's decision to delay awarding the full bounty provides some clues, and certainly implies that some women, after leaving the Asylum, fell back into their old lifestyle. However, the decision to require two years' good behaviour meant that many women did not follow up at all, even if they were well-behaved. Whatever her initial motivations for becoming involved in the charity, Denny remained extraordinarily committed to it and interested in the penitents until almost the end of her life. The records for many penitents are filled with her personal observations on them and their chances for repentance, and in some cases follow-up information after their leaving. Arbella Denny remained closely involved in the activities of the Magdalene Asylum until as late as 1790, when her handwritten, though increasingly shaky, personal notes and impressions on the penitents ceased to appear in the admissions books. Between 1767 and 1773 sixty-five women were admitted to the asylum; of those, twenty-two had left and were supporting themselves by honest employment, seven had married, three were dismissed almost immediately, two died in the house, sixteen were still resident in the asylum, and thirteen had relapsed.[91] By 1777 there had been 118 women admitted to the asylum; sixty-one were thought to have been successfully reformed, sixteen had relapsed and an additional twenty-one had either been dismissed, had escaped, or could not be located.[92] Figure 5.3 below illustrates the exiting circumstances of penitents between 1767 and 1795.

90 R.C.B.L. 551–1-1; 551–1-2.
91 R.C.B.L. 551–14–1.
92 West, *Charity the seal of Christian perfection, a sermon preached before his excellency, the lord lieutenant, and the vice-patroness, governesses, and guardians of the asylum for penitent women*, p. 33.

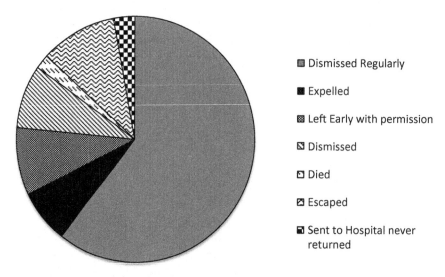

Figure 5.3. Exiting circumstances of Magdalenes, 1767–1795.

Because the Magdalene Society focused on women as the objects of charity, it was acceptable for women to take a more active role in governing the charity as well. The asylum did possess a board of male governors, but there is little indication that they were consulted about the running of the charity. They received reports as to the state of the house and the funds, but played little to no active role in the work. The instruction and admission of inmates, the running of the house, and most of the fundraising were all done by the lay women involved in the charity. The guardians of the Dublin Magdalene Asylum met infrequently, with only a few guardians present; they primarily heard accounts of the charity and listened to reports from Denny on the state of the house. They also audited the funds and expenditures of the house, but were not involved in its day-to-day operation.[93] The Dublin Asylum was unique in the level of authority it allowed women philanthropists, but it still believed that the business and financial interests of the charity were best handled by men, despite the fact that the funding for the Asylum came primarily from women. Women subscribers and benefactors to the charity significantly outnumbered men. In 1770 there were thirty-five female subscribers to only twenty-two male. Benefactors – anyone who had contributed support to the society – were similarly skewed, with ninety-two women to fifty men.[94]

Magdalene Asylums proved popular and useful charities. Perhaps because of the opportunities they afforded to philanthropic women, several more

---

[93] R.C.B.L. 551-2-1.

[94] Edward Bayly, *A sermon preached on the opening of the new chapel of the Magdalen asylum, in Leeson-Street, Dublin* (Dublin, 1770), pp. 57–62.

were established in the late eighteenth century, and the number of foundations increased considerably during the following century, in which many new
asylums were run by orders of nuns. In the twentieth century the nature of these
asylums changed. Magdalene Asylums became Magdalene Laundries, where
'fallen women' were confined indefinitely and forced to work and do penance
for their sins, either real or perceived. However, the sad later history of these
institutions should not detract from their earlier contributions.

Eighteenth-century Magdalene Asylums provided a valuable service to many
lower-class women. They were also an avenue allowing greater participation
for philanthropically inclined upper-class women. The success of Denny's work
at the Foundling Hospital, along with the success of the Magdalene Asylum,
made women's participation in the new structures of philanthropy more socially
acceptable and opened the doors for later generations of charitable women.
Lady Arbella Denny died in 1792 and was eulogized in the same glowing terms
used to describe her while alive. She was one of the most admired philanthropists of eighteenth-century Ireland. The widespread acclaim that she received
even during her lifetime indicates that it was possible for women to be involved
in and even direct eighteenth-century philanthropy. Women were excluded
from the initial enthusiasm for the joint-stock model of charitable societies,
and the emphasis on charity as improvement seemed to preclude the traditional definition which saw charity as sympathetic and feminine. Women were
definitely denied participation in the highly visible roles on most governing
boards, but with time many organizations were forced to loosen their restrictions and permit, or even encourage, greater female participation in certain
initiatives. Despite the limitations placed on Protestant women's charity by
the rise of corporate philanthropy, women were still able to make a substantial
contribution to the improvement agenda.

6

National and Local Government and Improvement

In 1854 a Dublin barrister by the name of John Vereker wrote a letter to Edward Grogan, a member of parliament, passionately defending the continuing practice in Ireland of providing public grants to hospitals and charities in the city of Dublin. Vereker's letter came at a time of controversy over this custom. After the Act of Union in 1801 the Irish parliament ceased to exist entirely, and by the mid-nineteenth century the parliament of the United Kingdom sought to curtail the awarding of government grants to charities in Dublin. Public grants for private charity was not the practice anywhere else in the empire. Furthermore, many argued that government support for hospitals and charities discouraged private donations. An 1842 report on the charitable institutions of Dublin concluded that 'public grants injudiciously bestowed, have a tendency to check private benevolence'. Vereker contested this conclusion and the decision to halt public grants. He argued that Dublin's charities served the entire nation, since it was common for people from the provinces to come to Dublin for medical care, but they were only able to raise funds in the Dublin area. He contended that government grants did nothing to hinder private charity. Dublin and its citizens 'extends more upon these charitable objects in proportion to the wealth of her inhabitants, than any other city in the empire'; yet, despite the generosity of its citizens, Dublin's hospitals relied on government grants to remain in operation. Vereker felt that most people preferred donating to educational charities, which were religiously affiliated, than to voluntary hospitals, which were non-sectarian. Aside from these arguments, Vereker defended the basic principle of government assistance for charity. He argued that 'a government grant increases public confidence in an institution, and makes people more willing to subscribe, as they know the hospital may be compelled at any time to present parliament with a proper return. A government grant is a public sanction of an institution, and a guarantee for its proper supervision.'[1] The case made by Vereker and others like him was successful; the Westminster parliament eventually chose to continue providing public grants to charity hospitals. However, it did severely limit which institutions were awarded support and imposed greater public oversight over those institutions that were

---

[1] N.L.I. MS 7646.

publicly funded. The decision was made to appoint a board of superintendents to oversee the Dublin hospitals and to continue funding those bodies which provided vital and necessary services.[2]

This nineteenth-century controversy came about because of what had become an established practice in Ireland in the eighteenth century: public support and provisions for organizations devoted to reform and improvement. Ireland as a country, and Dublin as a city, faced enormous and growing social problems in the eighteenth century, many of which stemmed from poverty. Both local government, such as the corporation of Dublin, and the national government, through the Irish parliament, were forced to take a dynamic and interventionist stance in dealing with these issues. Many historians take for granted that governments which actively intervene in the health and well-being of their citizens are a result of the creation of modern welfare states in the late nineteenth and early twentieth centuries,[3] but the eighteenth-century Irish state took an unusually energetic stance in supporting and funding charities and reform organizations designed to improve the nation and its people. The eighteenth-century culture of improvement was to an unprecedented extent made possible by government funding. Philanthropy and improvement was a concern not just of private individuals or independent voluntary societies but of the state.

Parliamentary historians have long noted that the eighteenth-century Irish parliament was willing to supply public money, raised through taxation, to particular causes associated with improvement through grants, appropriations, and bounties. Unlike the British parliament, which did not commonly issue such grants, the Irish parliament made them regularly.[4] While this practice would cause problems for the United Kingdom's parliament after the Act of Union in 1801, it became increasingly popular throughout the eighteenth century for the Irish parliament to issue grants for practical improvement projects, such as the building of canals and other improvements to the nation's infrastructure, and to charities such as hospitals and schools. Much of the money was wasted on ill-thought-out schemes or in support of well-established industries that did not require subsidies.[5] However, despite instances of misman-agement, these funds became essential to the operation of many philanthropic

[2]   Ibid.

[3]   Joseph Melling, 'Welfare capitalism and the origins of welfare states: British industry, workplace welfare and social reform, c. 1870–1914' in *Social History*, 17, no. 3 (1992), pp. 453–78; Peter Flora and Jens Alber, 'Modernization, democratization and the development of welfare states in western Europe' in Peter Flora and Arnold Heidenheimer (eds), *The development of welfare states in Europe and America* (New Brunswick, NJ, 1998), pp. 37–80.

[4]   D. W. Hayton, 'The long apprenticeship' in D. W. Hayton (ed.), *The Irish parliament in the eighteenth century: the long apprenticeship* (Edinburgh, 2001), p. 428.

[5]   Eoin Magennis, 'Coal, corn and canals: parliament and the dispersal of public moneys

organizations. Government funding was a response to a popular demand that state and local authorities address social problems. By involving themselves in improvement, the Irish parliament and the corporation of Dublin hoped both to develop stability and prosperity in Ireland and to secure their own positions.

Ireland's parliament had the same basic structure as Great Britain's. It consisted of both a House of Lords and a House of Commons. There were twenty-two lords spiritual in the Irish house and a varying number of temporal lords. Many Irish bishops in the eighteenth century were English. As for the temporal lords, not all who held Irish titles were active members of the House of Lords. Catholic nobles were prohibited from taking their seats. There were also a number of Englishman with Irish titles who had little connection with Ireland and did not travel to Dublin. Of the Irish peers who did attend regularly, many were dependent upon government patronage. By the late eighteenth century the temporal members of the House of Lords were of greater significance, as the House began to consist of more and more important Irish politicians who had won promotion to the peerage.[6]

Ireland's House of Commons had 300 members: two from each county, two from each of 117 boroughs, and two from Trinity College. As in England, the county franchise was 40s. freeholders. Their numbers varied widely in each county, however. Some counties had fewer than 1,000 electors, while most had between 3,000 and 4,000. The qualification as a voter in boroughs was more complicated, generally consisting of those who were considered members of either a corporation borough or a freeman borough. Boroughs had much smaller electorates, though size varied. Ireland had about a dozen 'potwalloping' boroughs and six manor boroughs. In these the resident householders and freeholders had the right to vote. At least one of these boroughs, Knocktopher in 1783, had only one qualified elector. Throughout the century parliament regularly adjusted the electoral machine, attempting to perfect the definition of who precisely was eligible to vote.[7] Irish electorates were small and bribery and corruption were both concerns. Catholics were prohibited both from holding seats in the House of Commons and from voting in parliamentary elections after 1727.[8] Protestant dissenters also faced some legal disabilities in Ireland until 1780. They were barred from municipal corporations but were permitted to vote in freeman and residential boroughs and to hold office in parliament, though

---

1695–1772' in David Hayton (ed.), *The Irish parliament in the eighteenth century: the long apprenticeship* (Edinburgh, 2001), pp. 71–86.

[6] J. L. McCracken, 'The political structure 1714–1760' in T. W. Moody and W. E. Vaughan (eds), *A new history of Ireland: vol. 4: eighteenth-century Ireland 1691–1800* (Oxford, 1986), pp. 71–2.

[7] Edith Mary Johnston-Liik, *History of the Irish parliament, 1692–1800: commons, constituencies and statutes* (6 vols, Belfast, 2002), ii, 125.

[8] Ibid., ii, 124, 126.

relatively few did. Parliament met roughly every two years, but elections were infrequent throughout the century, with some parliaments lasting for decades.[9] The first and only parliament of George I lasted from 1715 until 1727. The same was the case for George II; his only parliament lasted from 1727 until 1760.[10] Structurally speaking, Ireland's government both nationally and locally was similar to Great Britain's. However, there were significant differences; the Irish parliament was subservient to the British parliament and it never developed the same level of political authority as the eighteenth-century British parliament.[11] This did begin to change in 1782, when Poynings' Law was amended to provide a greater degree of legislative independence to the Irish parliament.[12]

Equally and perhaps more important in the daily lives of most Dubliners was the local corporation. Incorporated as a county in 1548, Dublin was governed by a lord mayor, twenty-four aldermen, two sheriffs, and a common council of 144 members. Those 144 were split between forty-eight sheriff's peers and ninety-six representatives of guilds. The mayor and aldermen met weekly and managed the daily business of the city. The Board of Alderman and the Common Council met four times a year to discuss municipal by-laws and to make appointments. Dublin's municipal institutions were essentially the same as those of other Anglo-Norman towns. Essential to the city's political life were the guilds, which served a variety of functions, but also maintained close relationships with the municipal corporation. Guilds were a means for tradesmen and women to obtain the 'freedom' of the city or the rights of citizenship. As with national government, local government was controlled by conformist Protestants. By the late seventeenth century, Catholics were no longer eligible for the freedom of the city and guilds were dominated by Protestants. Technically, women were eligible to achieve freedom through guilds, but by the eighteenth century this practice seems to have ceased.[13] There were some exceptions; for example, Lady Arbella Denny was awarded the freedom of the city through a special grant, in 1765, for her work at the Dublin Foundling Hospital.[14]

All levels of government were dominated by the Anglo-Irish elite. It is not surprising, then, that their interest in improvement began to overlap with their

9 Ibid., pp. 72–5.

10 Johnston-Liik, *History of the Irish parliament*, ii, 399–400.

11 D. W. Hayton and James Kelly, 'The Irish parliament in European context: a representative institution in a composite state' in James Kelly, David Hayton and John Bergin (eds), *The eighteenth-century composite state: representative institutions in Ireland and Europe, 1689–1800* (New York, 2010), p. 9.

12 Kelly, *Poynings' Law*, p. 315.

13 McCracken, 'The political structure 1714–1760', pp. 80–83; Jacqueline R. Hill, *From patriots to unionists: Dublin civic politics and Irish Protestant patriotism 1660–1840* (Oxford, 1997), pp. 24–35, 42–4.

14 Robins, *The lost children*, p. 25.

role in government. Parliament became seen as a potential tool for encouraging economic and social improvement.[15] An interest in improvement was one factor encouraging the granting of public money to support economic development and social reform. There was also another reason to favour the practice; some members of parliament wished to prevent the accumulation of surplus funds. In the eighteenth century the Irish parliament developed the practice of funding itself through short-term taxation, which required them to meet every two years to pass another tax. Unlike in Great Britain, there was no obligation upon the crown to summon Ireland's parliament regularly as long as the funds existed to pay the government's expenses.

The Irish state also became considerably more expensive to run thanks in part to the enlarged army that was permanently stationed there after William's victories. A 1699 Act of the English parliament authorized the continued maintenance of a standing army of 12,000 men in Ireland, a force that remained throughout the eighteenth century. The size and location of this force suited interests in both Ireland and England. The Irish Protestant elite were pleased to have the protection the army afforded them from both internal revolt and external invasion. Meanwhile, it suited the British parliament to have a sizeable force stationed nearby both to protect Ireland and their interests there and because they could not have maintained such a force in England, given the English people's traditional distrust of standing armies. This sizeable army, while primarily composed of English soldiers, was supported financially by the Irish.[16] Irish Protestants may have been pleased to have a large army stationed in the country, but its maintenance was a continual expense on the Irish exchequer.[17] The necessity of funding the army was one factor that allowed the Irish parliament to begin to meet more often and more regularly than it ever had in the past. By passing only short-term taxes, Irish members of parliament ensured that they met regularly throughout the century.[18] This same system also explains why the Irish parliament did not wish to accumulate surpluses in revenue, since these might be used by the lord lieutenant to avoid recalling parliament, or eventually remitted to England.[19] The widespread enthusiasm for improvement,

---

[15] Andrew Sneddon, 'Legislating for economic development: Irish fisheries as a case study in the limitations of "improvement"' in James Kelly, David Hayton, and John Bergin (eds), *The eighteenth-century composite state: representative institutions in Ireland and Europe, 1689–1800* (Basingstoke, 2010), p. 137.

[16] Irish Protestants could be officers in some cavalry regiments, but the rest of the army was recruited entirely from Great Britain. McCracken, 'The political structure 1714–1760', p. 82.

[17] McCracken, 'The political structure 1714–1760', pp. 82–3.

[18] C. I. McGrath, 'Parliamentary additional supply: the development and use of regular short-term taxation in the Irish parliament, 1692–1716' in David Hayton (ed.), *The Irish parliament in the eighteenth century: the long apprenticeship* (Edinburgh, 2001), pp. 27–54.

[19] Hayton, 'The long apprenticeship', p. 14.

both social and economic, helped to direct how parliament chose to disperse such funds. Improvement was not motivated solely by enthusiasm or because it was in fashion; it was also designed to address genuine social problems.

Parliament's use of public money to fund improvement has been criticized for several reasons. Many schemes were ill thought out, funds were most frequently awarded to friends or relatives of members of parliament, and the practice as a whole may have actually harmed the economy.[20] Many contemporaries were sceptical of the practice as well. Arthur Young, on his tour of Ireland in the 1770s, noted that funds were frequently voted by members of parliament to 'very scandalous private jobs'. But there were also many useful, excellent projects that were undertaken for the benefit of the kingdom and, as the funds were spent within the kingdom, the practice on the whole was 'far from being any great national evil'.[21] Young felt that most money voted for these improvement projects was misused because the public works projects it was meant to fund frequently went unfinished. He considered Ireland fortunate in having a 'great portion of public treasures annually voted for public purposes', but noted that those funds were 'abominably misapplied'.[22] John Hely-Hutchinson, the provost of Trinity College and a powerful member of parliament, felt that the grants were necessary because Ireland lacked sufficient private capital to fund such endeavours, so it fell to parliament to advance the money 'for the benefit of the public'.[23]

Young included in his list of funds spent on public works not only grants made to economic development initiatives but also funds for hospitals, schools, and workhouses. He concluded that between 1753 and 1767 over £700,000 had been granted for various public projects. The majority went to projects of the Navigation Board, to develop canals and waterways for inland navigation. There were also considerable grants made for building harbours and bridges, and for widening the streets in Dublin. Between 1703 and 1771 parliament issued £379,388 in grants to fund navigations, docks, and collieries. It awarded an additional £180,546 in grants to the linen manufacture, as well as £64,000 to the Dublin Society, which also focused on economic development. It seems clear that parliament placed a premium on economic development, but few of these projects were able to produce favourable returns. Many were badly managed and the actual money misspent, as Young alleged and most historians agree. Still, it is significant that the Irish parliament intervened to such

20 Magennis, 'Coal, corn and canals: parliament and the dispersal of public moneys 1695–1772'; Sneddon, 'Legislating for economic development'.
21 Arthur Young, *Arthur Young's tour in Ireland 1776–1779*, ed. Arthur Hutton (2 vols, London, 1892), ii, 123.
22 Ibid., ii, 130.
23 John Hely-Hutchinson, *The commercial restraints of Ireland considered* (Dublin, 1779), p. 54.

a degree in the economic development of the nation. It also involved itself in other improvement projects, such as those addressing specific social issues. Parliament granted £32,800 to hospitals between 1753 and 1767, £96,000 to the Incorporated Society from 1733 to 1771, and over £140,000 to workhouses in Dublin and Cork.[24] These appropriations were not motivated solely by political motives or official corruption. Behind them lay the idea that the government was responsible for addressing the economic and social issues that beset Ireland. The major categories of government appropriations were thus commercial and agricultural initiatives, but charities, hospitals, and schools received significant support.[25]

Both local and national government attempted to take an active role in addressing social problems. One example is the Dublin Workhouse and Foundling Hospital. The wars and famines of the seventeenth century had produced a number of social problems for the city of Dublin, including vagrancy in the form of large numbers of poor peasants coming in from the countryside. To address this problem, the corporation of Dublin, aided by an Act of Parliament in 1703, began to search for a suitable site to erect a workhouse. They eventually settled on a plot near St James Street, which was convenient to a water supply so that the site might serve the dual purpose of saving and improving the city's water supply while also confining the large number of indigent vagabonds and beggars in the city.[26] To support the Workhouse, the city was granted the revenue from licences for hackney coaches and sedan chairs operating within the city.[27] The Workhouse Corporation was also granted land and the revenue from a tax placed on houses in the city.[28] The Workhouse introduced into Ireland the principle that taxation be used to address the problem of poverty.[29]

As originally established, the Dublin Workhouse focused on addressing the problem of the adult poor: the so-called 'idle vagabonds' and 'sturdy beggars' whose numbers were rising and who were considered a nuisance by the more prosperous residents of Dublin.[30] The idea behind the Workhouse was simple enough. The poor were to be confined there, removing them from the streets. They were to be fed and clothed and put to work.[31] Begging was a significant problem on the streets of Dublin. For many, it presented a real nuisance.

---

[24] Young, *Arthur Young's tour in Ireland*, ii, 124–5.

[25] T. J. Kiernan, *History of the financial administration of Ireland to 1817* (London, 1930), pp. 165–79.

[26] Gilbert, *Calendar of ancient records of Dublin*, vi, 282.

[27] Ibid., vi, 307.

[28] D.C.L. Robinson Mss-MS 31.

[29] Robins, *The lost children*, p. 8.

[30] Gilbert, *Calendar of ancient records of Dublin*, xi, 523–4.

[31] Wodsworth, *A brief history of the ancient foundling hospital of Dublin*, p. 3.

Begging children irritated the well-heeled citizens of the city, crying by their doors at all hours of the night asking for relief.[32] Jonathan Swift complained that Dublin was 'infested' with 'strollers, foreigners, and sturdy beggars'.[33] While the Workhouse was originally intended, as noted, to address primarily the problem of adult beggars, children over the age of six were admitted to the Workhouse, given some degree of education and apprenticed out by sixteen.[34] Children were a large portion of the begging population and were far more likely to be caught and end up in the Workhouse; in fact, healthy adults were an almost non-existent minority of Workhouse inmates. In 1725, 50 per cent of the 222 inmates were children between the ages of five and sixteen. The average age of inmates was approximately thirty. However, this number was skewed by the presence of a number of inmates classified as 'superannuates', all of whom were over sixty (the oldest resident was ninety). Adults between the ages of seventeen and fifty constituted 22 per cent of the population, but were also overwhelmingly infirm in some way. Children were by far the healthiest age group. Most adults in the Workhouse were there because of extreme old age, mental illness, or physical infirmity.[35] In 1725 there were no charity hospitals that could provide care for the poor who were mentally ill or had incurable diseases, so many ended up in the Dublin Workhouse.

Before the Workhouse was constructed the indigent were the responsibility of their home parish, and collecting money to help support the poor was the responsibility of churchwardens in the city's parishes.[36] Indigent children below the age of six were also the responsibility of the parish in which they resided. Abandoned children were the responsibility of the parish in which they were found. Inmates in the Workhouse were classified according to the parish in which they resided prior to entrance. The establishment of the Workhouse eased some of the financial burden placed upon Dublin parishes, but not all of it. Unwanted children were a serious problem in eighteenth-century Ireland and infanticide a major social concern.[37] At the beginning of the eighteenth century, the House of Commons passed several bills designed to prevent illegitimate children from being murdered and another designed to oblige their parents to support them.[38] A 1707 law stated that any woman who was found to have drowned or buried her child was to be put to death. Furthermore, any woman found to be covering up the death of an illegitimate child was to be put

---

32 Gilbert, ed., *Calendar of ancient records of Dublin*, 11: 90; Robins, *The lost children*, p. 11.
33 Swift, *A proposal for giving badges to the beggars in all the parishes of Dublin*, pp. 5–6.
34 Robins, *The lost children*, p. 12.
35 Marsh's Library: Workhouse Materials, z3.1.1.
36 Ibid.
37 Kelly, 'Infanticide in eighteenth-century Ireland'.
38 *Journals of the House of Commons of the Kingdom of Ireland* (31 vols, Dublin, 1782–1794), iii, 308, 418.

to death unless she could prove, with at least one witness, that the child had been born dead.[39] In the case of abandoned children, responsibility traditionally fell on the parish, as was confirmed by law in 1727. Parishes were to appoint overseers to supervise the care of these children until they were old enough to be sent to the Workhouse, a practice seemingly already in place, given that in 1725 there were twenty-two children between the ages of five and seven in the Workhouse.[40] Since Dublin's parishes were already strapped for funds it was agreed that the funds for maintaining abandoned children were to come from cesses, a tax on householders in the parish that local vestries were empowered to levy. All householders in the parish were subject to the cess, though only Protestants could become members of the vestries imposing them. Restrictions such as this made cesses particularly unpopular with Catholic householders and it proved difficult to collect the funds.[41] A similar principle was used to fund the Dublin Workhouse. The corporation of Dublin operated on a financial model different from that of the Irish parliament: instead of awarding large grants to fund social reform projects such as the Workhouse, it awarded the revenue from new taxes to the initiative.

To ease the financial strain of supporting unwanted children, some Dublin churchwardens resorted to taking infants found in their parish and, in the dead of night, moving them to a neighbouring parish, thus placing the burden for their support somewhere else. This practice, although it resulted in the death of a number of infants, became so widespread that in 1729 the House of Lords launched an investigation. They heard testimony from Elizabeth Hyland, who was employed as a nurse by the parish of St John, that the churchwarden of St John's, Charles Fisher, had directed her to transport a number of children to a neighbouring parish. She further testified that to keep the children quiet during transport they were drugged by someone, presumably Fisher, with diacodium, an opiate syrup, made from poppy heads. Hyland noted that during her time as a nurse for St John's parish she was entrusted with twenty-seven foundling children. Of those, two were taken by their mothers, seven died in her custody, and the rest were transported to other parishes, and their fate was unknown. This practice was widespread throughout the city, and the Lords heard testimony that at least one of the children transported by Hyland was believed to have been transported to the parish by someone from the parish of St Luke's. The parish of St Mary's employed a woman known simply as a 'lifter'. Joan Newenham was paid about £4 a year to lift children out of St Mary's

---

[39] 'An act to prevent the destroying and murdering of bastard children' in *Acts and Statutes Made in a Parliament Begun at Dublin the Twenty First Day of September, Anno Dom. 1703* (Dublin, 1728), p. 807.

[40] Marsh's Library: MS z3.1.1, workhouse papers.

[41] Robins, *The lost children*, p. 14.

and carry them into another parish. The House of Lords concluded that their findings should be made public and that Charles Fisher should be prosecuted.[42] There was a public outcry when it was made widely known that 'in the midst of a great, populous, and plentiful city, [infants] perished through Want, or had its Miseries shortened by being devoured by Dogs or Swine, or trodden to Death'.[43]

Partly in response to the scandal caused by the Lords' investigation, the decision was made in 1730 to admit to the Workhouse all foundling children regardless of age. The Workhouse was divided into separate departments: one operated largely as it had done before, housing vagabonds and beggars of all ages, a number of whom were under sixteen, while a separate department was created to cater for young children. The governors of the Workhouse were empowered to levy an additional tax to help fund the maintenance of all children under the age of six now housed separately.[44] In effect, from this point on, the Workhouse focused almost entirely on the care of abandoned children of all ages.[45] A revolving basket was placed at the entrance to the Foundling Hospital in which children could be placed. When a bell was rung, a porter inside the Hospital would rotate the basket and collect the infant who had been dropped off anonymously. It was widely hoped that steps such as this would curb the rate of infanticide in Ireland. Unfortunately, these good intentions did not have the desired effect. There was no discernible drop in the rate of infanticide in Dublin after the Foundling Hospital was opened. In fact, it rose higher than ever in the 1750s and 1760s, indicating that infanticide was motivated by a number of social factors, not all of which the existence of a foundling hospital addressed.[46]

Still, the existence of the Foundling Hospital provided a necessary refuge for a number of poor unmarried women with little ability to care for an infant. One such woman, Bridget Kearney, travelled 100 miles on foot to place her new-born child safely in the Hospital's revolving basket. Several years later, with her circumstances much improved, she petitioned to have the child restored to her.[47] Some interpreted the Hospital as encouraging bad behaviour in certain situations. William Wodsworth, in his history of the Foundling Hospital, wrote that 'Seduction, villainy, cruelty, and vice were fostered and encouraged by the existence of the Institution, and by the knowledge, or belief, that the obligations of parentage could be got rid of by the reception, and

[42] *Journals of the House of Lords of the Kingdom of Ireland* (8 vols, Dublin, 1779–1800), iii, 115–16.
[43] Henry, *The cries of the orphans*, p. 10.
[44] D.C.L. Robinson Mss-MS 31.
[45] *Journals of the House of Lords of the Kingdom of Ireland*, iii, 424.
[46] Kelly, 'Infanticide in eighteenth-century Ireland', pp. 5–6.
[47] Wodsworth, *A brief history of the ancient foundling hospital of Dublin*, p. 13.

nursing out, of the children.'[48] Wodsworth placed greater blame upon men, who he described as seducers, than upon the 'injured, distracted' mothers, and made special note of the anguish of mothers whose love for their 'offspring never dies'; they could at least rely on the Foundling Hospital as a haven of last resort for their children.[49] Wodsworth's nineteenth-century portrayal is a noted contrast with many early eighteenth-century discussions, which showed little sympathy for the 'lewd women' who found themselves with illegitimate children.[50] Wodsworth, however, was reacting to a number of stories from the Hospital's records of women who were seduced and abandoned by their employers or other gentlemen. One young Catholic woman seduced by her employer, a wealthy Protestant, had her child forcibly taken away by him and sent to the Foundling Hospital. She later petitioned to have the child returned to her.[51]

While it could not solve the many social problems afflicting eighteenth-century Ireland, the Foundling Hospital did provide a valuable service. However, that did not prevent it from being beset by problems. Funding was always a major issue for the Hospital, as the tax revenue granted to fund the institution proved insufficient to support the large number of unwanted children. The Foundling Hospital operated on the same site as the Workhouse, although it had a separate building and was meant to operate from a separate fund; however, after it became apparent to the governors that their revenues were insufficient they were forced to begin transferring money from the Workhouse's funds to help keep the Hospital in operation.[52]

The Foundling Hospital was legally obliged to take in all children under the age of five who were presented to it or who were found abandoned in the parishes of Dublin and the surrounding liberties. As it was the only institution of its kind in the country, some women from outside the Dublin area, such as Bridget Kearney, travelled to Dublin to abandon their children there. The governors, unsurprisingly, thus concluded that, while the Hospital was being supported by tax revenue from Dublin only, it was providing a service to the entire nation. The sheer number of children who required support was proving onerous. In the first year of operation the Hospital admitted 260, and by 1740 they were taking in approximately 700 annually.[53]

Not all these children lived in the Hospital itself. The standard practice was to put those under the age of two out to nurse with local women until they were eight years old, when they were brought to the Workhouse to be educated.

---

[48] Ibid., p. 12.
[49] Ibid., pp. 12, 10.
[50] 'An act to prevent the destroying and murdering of bastard children', p. 807.
[51] Wodsworth, A brief history of the ancient foundling hospital of Dublin, pp. 15–16.
[52] D.C.L. Robinson Mss-MS 31.
[53] Ibid.

Each was marked with a badge placed on the necks and a brand impressed on one arm to prevent fraud. The nurses were paid about £2 a year in advance, and given two yards of flannel for the children. They were ordered to appear at the Hospital each year with the child to collect their pay, which was so attractive to poor women that some left their children exposed in the hopes of being hired to be their nurses. In response to these abuses, the governors of the Hospitals tried for a time to raise all children in the house itself, but quickly switched back to the original system.[54] Another flaw with the nursing system was that, since nurses were paid in advance, some were tempted to take the money and murder the children. In 1737 the bodies of thirteen Foundling Hospital children were discovered in a sand pit. Investigators could not satisfactorily determine whether the children were murdered before being thrown into the pit or whether they died of exposure afterwards. The House of Lords came to feel that this practice might be even more widespread. They concluded that 'much greater numbers have, from time to time, been destroyed by the savage cruelty of nurses, that are, or probably ever will be discovered'.[55] 'Marks of violence' were found on some of the children's bodies, but others were too mangled and decayed for an assessment to be made.[56] The entire affair suggests that there was little oversight once children were sent out to nurse. Elizabeth Quayle, the out-matron responsible for supervising the children put out to nurse, was blamed for negligence. The children's nurses were believed to be responsible and those who had not fled the city were arrested. A few claimed that they had handed the children over to other women without the knowledge of Quayle, and they were not responsible for tossing them into the pit. In response to the tragedy, the practice of paying nurses in advance was discontinued. Henceforth nurses were paid at the end of the year and only after presenting the child for inspection.[57]

Even without foul play there was an enormously high death rate among foundling children. Between March 1730, when they first began receiving children, and March 1737, when the House of Lords concluded its investigation, the Foundling Hospital received 4,025 children. Of those, 3,236 had died, a death rate of just over 80 per cent.[58] The Hospital's death rate remained extremely high for most of the eighteenth century, as revealed by a series of parliamentary investigations. Figure 6.1 illustrates the findings of these investigations and shows the steadily increasing number of admissions to the Hospital, along with the steadily increasing death rate. The sharp drop

---

54 *Journals of the House of Lords of the Kingdom of Ireland*, iii, 429.
55 Ibid.
56 Ibid.
57 Ibid., iii, 430–31.
58 Ibid., iii, 429.

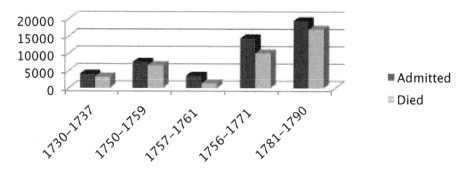

Figure 6.1. Foundling Hospital admittants and deaths.

between 1757 and 1761 is in part due to the fact that the numbers reflect only residents of the Hospital and contain no information about children in foster care, while the numbers for 1756 to 1771 reflect only those children who are in foster care.[59] The noticeable decline in the death rate for those years can also be attributed to the work of Lady Arbella Denny, who began visiting the Hospital in 1758.

As Figure 6.1 demonstrates, the years leading up Lady Arbella's intervention were exceptionally bad for the Foundling Hospital. The death rate was at its highest, over 88 per cent. Of 7,382 children admitted to the Hospital, 6,545 were already dead by 1759. Reports of poor conditions in the Hospital led to a public outcry, particularly after a 1758 report from parliament became public. The citizens of Dublin were treated to stories of an institution with a death rate so high that dead children were 'chucked' into mass graves nine or ten at a time with little ceremony.[60] Infants lay dead in their cribs unnoticed by nurses, children were ill dressed and malnourished and few were well enough to work efficiently.[61] The officers were openly accused of murder and corruption.[62] Institutional corruption was a continuous problem for the Hospital, the Lords investigation of 1737 having found evidence that the butler and the registrar had conspired to steal from the supplies. When two foundling boys exposed this corruption the butler and registrar arranged to have them convicted on false testimony and transported to the West Indies.[63] In 1758 the registrar, Joseph Purcell, was accused of conspiring with the butler to create an atmosphere

---

[59] Robins, *The lost children*, pp. 22, 24, 25, 29; *Journals of the House of Lords of the Kingdom of Ireland*, iii, 429.

[60] Wodsworth, *A brief history of the ancient foundling hospital of Dublin*, p. 33.

[61] Robins, *The lost children*, p. 20.

[62] Wodsworth, *A brief history of the ancient foundling hospital of Dublin*, p. 33.

[63] *Journals of the House of Lords of the Kingdom of Ireland*, iii, 424.

of terror. He attempted to rape a seamstress, but kept his post owing to his friendship with the governors of the house. After his dismissal, following the public scandal, it was discovered that he had stolen £1,700 pounds from the Hospital's funds.[64]

The high death rate was, however, not solely the result of corruption. Foundling hospitals and workhouses as a whole tended to have very high death rates, particularly for the very young. In London workhouses in the 1760s children who were born there or admitted under the age of one year had a 93 per cent chance of dying before the age of three. The London Foundling Hospital's death rate was about 66 per cent.[65] This is, nevertheless, significantly lower than that of the Dublin Hospital. In attempting to explain the high death rate and poor conditions governors and investigators pointed to a number of factors, such as the health of the children when they arrived and the health of their parents. In a 1792 investigation, a surgeon who attended at the Hospital reported that in one year the Hospital received 788 children infected with venereal disease most of whom died within a month of admission. Furthermore, most of the children who arrived from the country were in an exceptionally poor condition. A nurse attributed this to poor treatment received on the journey; many children were dosed with liquor to keep them quiet and others were roughly treated during transport in carts or on foot.[66] This had also been the situation previously: according to a 1743 report, many children arrived at the Foundling Hospital 'half-starved' and 'greatly distempered'.[67]

Aside from issues such as these, most contemporaries blamed the problems of the institution on a lack of funds. The Foundling Hospital was supporting far more children than was practical on their usual revenues and as a result was racking up enormous debts. The Hospital had several sources of revenue, including rents, taxes on houses in Dublin and on coaches, carriages and sedan chairs for hire, and also, of course, charitable subscriptions.[68] However, none of these was sufficient to support the large number of children placed in its care. The House of Commons felt obliged to grant large sums of money to help offset the Hospital's debts. Attempts were also made to secure additional sums from England. Lady Arbella, upon taking on the role of patroness of the Foundling Hospital in 1757, made use of her considerable connections with the peerage of Ireland and England to win support and funds for the Hospital.

---

64 Robins, *The lost children*, p. 22.
65 Ibid.
66 House of Commons Ireland, *Report of the committee appointed to enquire into the state and management of the foundling hospital* (Dublin, 1792), pp. 4–6.
67 *Journals of the House of Commons of the Kingdom of Ireland* (19 vols, Dublin, 1796), iv, 490.
68 *Journals of the House of Lords of the Kingdom of Ireland*, iii, 424.

She clearly believed that lack of money was its greatest problem, resulting in the poor quality of care. In 1761 she wrote to John Russell, duke of Bedford, requesting funds from the British parliament. She felt she had to present this matter or 'I should esteem myself accessory to the death of those infants who in my conscience I believe are lost for want of money to support the number of nurses that are necessary.'[69] The duke was unable to assist Denny, though he did promise to make the king aware of the issue. He felt that the current state of the Hospital was the fault of the Irish parliament, which had required by statute that the Hospital must take in all children but had not provided adequate funds, and advised that steps be taken in the future to limit the number of children admitted.[70] The duke followed through on his promise to inform the king, and a month later wrote to Denny that the king was granting the Hospital £1,000, free from all deductions, to help support the children.[71] The monarchy stepped in again in 1774, this time granting £10,000 to the Hospital to assist in paying off its debts.[72]

Denny also organized charity sermons to raise additional funds for the Hospital. To make up the shortfalls faced in recent years the Hospital had been forced to mortgage several properties and to rely on parliamentary grants.[73] Charity sermons, as noted, were a well-established part of philanthropic fundraising in eighteenth-century Dublin. Most charities held them regularly, both to raise funds and to keep themselves in the public eye. Charity sermons on behalf of the Foundling Hospital proved difficult, however. Denny arranged for a charity sermon to be preached on behalf of the Hospital in parishes all across the city on 27 April 1760.[74] This unprecedented city-wide appeal certainly raised public awareness of the Hospital, but was a disappointment in terms of fundraising.[75] Ministers who preached on behalf of the Hospital faced the usual rhetorical challenge associated with charity sermons. They had to convince the audience of the worthiness and efficacy of their cause, but also needed to persuade the public that donations were needed to support an organization funded by their taxes. Other charities received regular grants of money from parliament, but they had been established privately. The Workhouse and Foundling Hospital had both been established by the government and from its inception were funded with a special tax on houses. This was for some a source of resentment, and many households refused to pay.[76]

---

[69] P.R.O.N.I. T2915/11/8.
[70] P.R.O.N.I. T2915/11/26.
[71] P.R.O.N.I. T2915/11/35.
[72] T.N.A. T1/507/121.
[73] P.R.O.N.I. T2915/11/9.
[74] P.R.O.N.I. T2915/11/9.
[75] P.R.O.N.I. T2915/11/8.
[76] *Journals of the House of Commons of the Kingdom of Ireland*, iv, 490.

In his sermon on behalf of the Hospital Reverend William Henry took special care to refer to it as a charity undertaking an essential public service and not an offshoot of local or national government. He acknowledged its reliance on special grants from the Commons, while stressing that the Hospital still lacked funds to improve the basic level of care it provided. As Henry noted, there was nothing the Hospital could reasonably do to cut its expenses. 'In this distress what is to be done? Shall we abandon above two thousand infants in town and country, whom we have taken under our protection? Shall we leave them to perish? ... The only refuge we have left is to fly to your charity.' Henry expressed confidence in the 'unbounded liberality' of the citizens of Dublin.[77] By 1760, however, a number of other philanthropic causes were also laying claim to Dublin's 'liberality', making it difficult for the Foundling Hospital to adequately supplement its revenue with private charity.

There does not appear to have been any serious consideration given to limiting the number of infants accepted. One auditor of the accounts in 1751 argued instead that the governors should ask parliament to grant them funds from an additional tax. Since the Foundling Hospital provided a service to the entire nation, it ought to be funded by a tax levied on the entire nation.[78] There is evidence that the Hospital unwittingly took in children from England as well as Ireland: a significant number of children in the Hospital were the offspring of soldiers stationed in Ireland; in addition, in the 1760s, the children of soldiers and sailors from Britain were sent to Ireland and wound up in the Foundling Hospital.[79] Had each child remained in its home parish its father would have had to pay for its support. Instead, women were employed to transport these children across the Irish Sea. The *Freeman's Journal* complained that, 'our masters on the other side of the water are not satisfied at the vast sums drawn from this poor kingdom but are resolved that we should maintain their illegitimate offspring as well as their whores'.[80]

Eventually, the original role of the Workhouse became entirely subsumed by the task of caring for abandoned children. Not that all of these children lived in the house itself; the vast majority were cared for by nurses in the countryside. Figure 6.2 below, analyses the numbers of children and others under the care of the Foundling Hospital in 1784. By that time the Workhouse was almost entirely dedicated to the care of children and only a few adults were resident, classified as either 'aged poor' or 'vagabonds'. There were still enormous problems with the nursing system, which lacked sufficient oversight to ensure that children were well looked after. For one thing, the general practice by the

---

77 Henry, *The cries of the orphans*, pp. 14–15.
78 D.C.L. Robinson Mss-MS 31.
79 Henry, *The cries of the orphans*, p. 11.
80 Quoted in Robins, *The lost children*, p. 27.

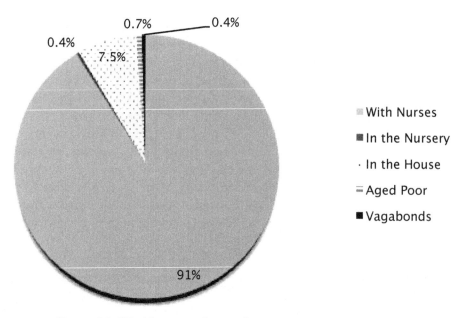

Figure 6.2. Workhouse and Foundling Hospital inmates, 1784.

late eighteenth century was to leave children with their nurses until they were nine years old. Once they turned nine they returned to the house for education and eventual apprenticeship. The governors began to complain that children were being returned with poor habits ingrained in them that proved difficult to break. In addition, most of the country nurses were Catholic, and the children were being returned to the Hospital with an attachment to the Catholic faith as well as 'vicious habits' such as theft and lying.[81]

These issues undermined some of the practical goals of the Hospital. The Foundling Hospital was not meant solely to care for the many orphaned and abandoned children around the city of Dublin. It was also meant to contribute to the broader goals of the improvement of Ireland. Saving the lives of these children, in and of itself, aided improvement by increasing the population. From an Anglo-Irish perspective, it was also positive that the wards of the Foundling Hospital were brought up as Protestants and educated in a trade, which was seen as contributing to the general welfare of the kingdom. William Henry argued that 'If the riches and flourishing estate of a country depends on the number and industry of its inhabitants, how great an emolument must it be to our dear country, already too thinly peopled, to preserve thousands of infants; to train them up in virtuous industry, and enable them to make ample

[81] T.N.A. PRO 30/9/138/13–22.

returns to their country for that early pity shewn to them.'[82] The Foundling Hospital maintained close ties with the Incorporated Society. Both organizations placed special emphasis on making sure that the children in their care became self-sufficient adults who contributed to the nation's economy. Lady Arbella devoted considerable energy towards establishing manufactures at the Foundling Hospital, both to train the children in such industries as lace manufacturing and to provide an additional source of income for the Hospital. The children were being taught a skill that 'they were to get their bread by'. Denny was particularly concerned with the girls of the Hospital. In general, girls at the Hospital and at the charter schools had few opportunities, and most wound up as maids. Denny felt that by teaching lace-making to the girls she was expanding their opportunities. 'It was hoped they might by their lace making be taken as school mistresses, or by ladies to make lace at home … it might get them husbands in some of the lower trades', all of which was preferable to the life of a kitchen maid. She also noted that these endeavours helped to encourage the general manufacture of such products in Ireland, contending that the lace manufacture at the Workhouse, 'if judiciously nursed[,] would make ample returns to Ireland'.[83] Denny's willingness to combine philanthropy towards orphaned girls with the economic development of Ireland is one reason why the Dublin Society eventually made her an honorary member.

As the Dublin Workhouse became more and more focused on the problem of homeless children in the course of the eighteenth century, the problem of adult poverty remained. In 1766 the lord mayor of Dublin complained that the city had 'become the common receptacle of objects disfigured and frightful, as well as pretending to be miserable from all parts of the kingdom'.[84] He commanded the city's constables to apprehend all non-licensed beggars and other 'idle vagrant persons, who will not betake themselves to labour, and have no visible way of getting a livelihood'. These men and women were to be sent to Bridewell, while any children were sent to the Foundling Hospital.[85] Such proclamations did not actually bring about much in the way of action. A year later the mayor, Edward Sankey, again complained that the streets of Dublin were 'infested with idle vagrants and sturdy beggars', and promised a reward of 2s. for every beggar brought before him.[86] To deal with the problem, parliament eventually stepped in and established the Corporation for the Relief of the Poor in the City of Dublin. In 1773 a House of Industry opened on the north side of Dublin under the supervision of the corporation. The act creating the House

---

[82] Henry, *The cries of the orphans*, p. 16.

[83] P.R.O.N.I. D563/2747.

[84] Gilbert, *Calendar of ancient records of Dublin*, xi, 523–4.

[85] Ibid.

[86] Ibid., xi, 525.

of Industry actually went a step farther than simply addressing the problem of poverty in the capital, setting up similar corporations in every county, city, and town in Ireland.

The idea behind this legislation was obviously to address the growing number of beggars besetting the country. The general belief was that while many had been forced to turn to begging by circumstances others did so solely out of laziness and were relying on the injudicious almsgiving of citizens. According to contemporaries, Ireland had an unusually high number of mendicants. One estimated that if Ireland had 2.5 million people in 1776 then, assuming that at most one in every 500 people was born blind, lame, or suffering from some other disability that prevented them from supporting themselves, Ireland ought to have 5,000 'real objects' of charity. Assuming that half of those objects were born to families who could support them, then there ought to be only 2,500 genuine objects of charity in the entire country. However, before the legislation of 1772 Dublin County alone had 2,000 beggars and Queen's County, where the writer was stationed and served on a poor relief corporation, had 300. Assuming those numbers held for all thirty-two counties, Ireland would be supporting 9,600 beggars, more than four times the number the writer felt it should be.[87] There were several reasons for this, one of which was that 'a natural turn to industry hath never been the general character of the natives of this kingdom'.[88] To a poor cottager struggling to support a family on only 'sour milk and potatoes', the life of a beggar would be attractive, since 'the strong beggar wallows in gluttony every day, and from the superfluity of victuals he receives gets money enough to carouse at the ale house'.[89] Corporations for Poor Relief were intended to regulate this charity. Citizens were encouraged to donate only to properly licensed beggars, while all others were to be forcibly taken up and confined in houses of industry.

Visitors to Dublin complained about the numerous 'insulting' beggars who obstructed passers-by. Indeed, many commentators seemed to feel that the real problem with poverty was the nuisance it posed to the better-off. Most famous among Dublin's nuisance beggars was the so-called 'king of the beggars', Hackball. Unable to walk, Hackball 'rides triumphantly in his Chaise drawn by an Ass, begging tho' the Streets'; according to other sources, he rode in a small cart that was drawn by two large dogs.[90] Regardless of his means of transportation, Hackball, alias Patrick Corrigan, exemplified the problem of beggars in the city of Dublin. Between the 1720s and the 1770s he was a

---

[87] First annual report of the corporation instituted for the relief of the poor, and punishing vagabonds and sturdy beggars, in the queen's county (Kilkenny, 1776), p. 28.

[88] Ibid., p. 13.

[89] Ibid., p. 29.

[90] A letter from an English gentlemen in Dublin, to his friend in England (Dublin, 1767), p. 10.

well-known Dublin character, announcing his presence with a small trumpet as he rode along. Despite being paralysed, he managed for decades to elude the authorities, who were seeking to place him in either the Workhouse or the House of Industry. Indeed, his battles with the authorities brought him such notoriety that he was dubbed 'His Lowness, Prince Hackball' or, as noted, 'the King of the Beggars'.[91] After the House of Industry opened a cart manned by armed men patrolled the streets of the city every evening collecting vagrants and beggars. In 1774 one beadle actually managed to capture Hackball and attempted to take him to the House of Industry, but was attacked by a 'riotous mob' who rescued the famous 'Lord Hackball'. In response, the governors of the house offered five guineas to any beadle who managed to capture Hackball and £5 to anyone who discovered and prosecuted those who had been involved in the mob.[92] As a paraplegic, Hackball was not a 'sturdy beggar', the particular objects of irritation for authorities in this period. Indeed, he qualified by most conventional standards as an appropriate object of almsgiving. However, as the attempts to capture him suggest, Dublin citizens by the 1770s had become tired of all beggars and even those who were not guilty of any particular laziness were to be confined to houses of industry. They were not treated as 'sturdy beggars' in these institutions, but they were to be removed from the sight of the more prosperous citizens.

Houses of industry faced the challenge of serving several roles: on the one hand they were to be 'a terror and place of punishment to the sturdy and idle'; on the other they were to serve as a 'comfortable asylum for the aged, infirm and helpless'.[93] The Dublin Workhouse retained its role as a Foundling Hospital, but was relieved of most duties relating to the adult poor. The House of Industry consisted of several hospitals catering to the poor of the city as well as a workhouse where 'sturdy beggars' were put to hard labour. The corporations for poor relief were a follow-up to Richard Woodward's earlier scheme for erecting county poorhouses around Ireland, a scheme that had been supported by the Dublin Society. Woodward published several pamphlets relating to the issues of poverty in Ireland and how to address it. Early in his clerical career he took a special interest in the plight of Ireland's poor and the lack of national provision for them. The passing of the Poor Relief Act of 1772 and the subsequent establishment of the House of Industry were a direct result of his work. Shortly after first publicizing his county poorhouse scheme, Woodward published *An argument in support of the right of the poor in the kingdom of Ireland to a national*

91 Gilbert, *History of the city of Dublin*, i, 326.

92 Charles Ribton-Turner, *A history of vagrants and vagrancy, and beggars and begging* (London, 1887), p. 412.

93 Corporation for the Relief of the Poor in the City of Dublin, *Observations on the state and condition of the poor, under the institution, for their relied, in the city of Dublin* (Dublin, 1775), p. 6.

provision in 1768. He argued that the poor had a right to some degree of support from the national government. However, he drew a sharp distinction between the deserving and undeserving poor. 'Those idle vagrants who are a pest to society' were not the objects of his compassion; instead, he referred to those who 'though willing to work, cannot subsist by labour'.[94]

The Corporations for Poor Relief were founded by Act of Parliament and were intended to serve the same purpose as the Workhouse, but did not operate on the same funding model. As proposed by Woodward, the Corporations subsisted on a combination of subscriptions, donations, and funds from charity sermons. As they were legally incorporated, they were permitted to collect inheritances and to receive bequests in land. For the first few years of their existence they survived entirely on such donations. After 1776 they became the regular recipients of grants from parliament. Each Corporation was to build a building to provide shelter for the needy poor and to forcibly confine beggars and vagabonds. They were also to supervise the badging of approved beggars, who were free to beg for money in certain parishes or cities. To be granted a licence to beg one had to be resident in an area for at least one year and receive the approval of the Corporation. Most licences were not intended to be long-term; the permanently indigent were destined for confinement in houses of industry. Licensed beggars were usually granted the privilege for a prescribed period of time to help them recover from either sickness or misfortune.[95] Badging also served to allow citizens and relief corporations to distinguish between those classified as deserving poor and those 'sturdy beggars' considered such a nuisance to the community as a whole. However, even licensed beggars were not above suspicion, and many were accused of indolence. On its formation the Dublin Corporation for Poor Relief licensed 970 people to beg in the city of Dublin. When the House of Industry opened they were all invited to enter it and 'accept the comfortable provision made for them'. Only 235 chose to accept this generous offer of being indefinitely confined in a workhouse, which the corporation attributed to laziness. 'It being certain, that few among so many hundreds who rejected convenient lodging, food and raiment, had any reason for do doing but merely this, that they foresaw that they must in their situation, go to work, according to their abilities, and by a reasonable degree of labour contribute to their own maintenance.'[96]

---

[94] Richard Woodward, *An argument in support of the right of the poor in the kingdom of Ireland, to a national provision* (Dublin, 1768), p. 11.

[95] 'An act for badging such poor as shall be found unable to support themselves by labour, and to otherwise provide for the, and for restraining such as shall be found able to support themselves, by labour or industry from begging' in *Acts and statutes, made in a parliament begun at Dublin, the seventeenth day of October 1769* (Dublin, 1772), pp. 550–53.

[96] Corporation for the Relief of the Poor, *An Account of the Proceedings, and State of the Fund of the Corporation Instituted for the relief of the Poor*, pp. 13–14.

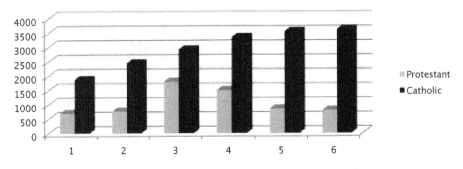

Figure 6.3. Religion of House of Industry inmates.

Inmates in the House of Industry were expected to work and to learn a trade during their confinement. The Corporation stressed that the labour of the inmates would never be a prominent source of income for the House, a lesson probably learned from the Incorporated Society's failed attempts at creating self-supporting charity schools. The inmates' work was intended to teach them a particular trade and to habituate them to labour. Of the 1,338 inmates in the Dublin House of Industry in 1775, only 596 were there at their own request. The remaining 742 were compelled to be there, having been captured by beadles. The majority of residents – 56 per cent – were women, and, as was the case with the Workhouse, most were older – 54 per cent were over the age of sixty and only 12 per cent were under thirty. Religious affiliations were not recorded for the residents of the Workhouse, who were ministered to only by the Church of Ireland, regardless of their faith. Residents of the House of Industry enjoyed more religious freedom and could be attended to by a Catholic priest. By the 1770s the sectarian fears that had dominated early eighteenth-century thought had relaxed enough that the inmates of the House of Industry were considered a threat because of their poverty, not their religion. The Corporation recorded that Catholics made up 70 per cent of the inmates,[97] a percentage that did not change drastically in the 1780s. Figure 6.3 shows the admissions data from 1784 to 1789 and illustrates the consistently higher proportion of Catholics to Protestants in the House of Industry.[98]

For the purposes of their work, the Dublin Corporation for Poor Relief divided the poor under their supervision into four distinct classes. These distinctions not only reflected contemporary attitudes towards the poor but were used for administrative purposes. The different classes were housed and fed differently depending on their situation. First were the industrious poor: they

---

[97] Corporation for the Relief of the Poor, *Observations on the state and condition of the poor*, p. 13.
[98] P.R.O.N.I. T3719/c/31/60.

resided in the Workhouse learning a trade and producing items that could be sold to further support the charity. Accordingly, they were fed the most: twelve ounces of bread a day and meat for Sunday dinner, and fish on Fridays. They also received potatoes, leeks, rice, buttermilk, beer, and pottage. Second were the aged, infirm or decrepit poor. This group was unable to work. Accordingly, their diet was much the same as the first class, but in smaller quantities: they received only eight ounces of bread, for instance. Third were the diseased poor. They were also housed in the infirmary. As the House of Industry expanded, this eventually became an entirely separate building, but in 1775 it was merely a separate ward. Aside from their daily allowance of eight ounces of bread, they subsisted on a largely soft diet – buttermilk, pottage, gruel, or rice milk. The final group were the stubborn or lazy poor, the 'sturdy beggars' who were such a source of annoyance to the authorities. They were housed entirely apart from the rest in debtor's prison, as the corporation intended to punish them in the hopes of discouraging others from taking to begging. Accordingly, they were fed the least. They received no allowance of meat or fish, and lived off eight ounces of bread, pottage, and buttermilk, and a pint of beer on Sundays.[99]

The operation of the House of Industry demonstrates some of the changing attitudes towards poor relief since the opening of the Workhouse in 1703. The fact that residents of the House of Industry enjoyed the freedom to practise their religion was indicative of widely changing attitudes among Protestants about the threat that Catholicism posed. Aside from this religious concession, it is significant that the House of Industry was funded on a model different from that of the Dublin Workhouse and Foundling Hospital, despite serving essentially the same social purpose. It demonstrates how ideas regarding the funding of social reform had evolved over the eighteenth century. Neither the Workhouse and Foundling Hospital nor the House of Industry were merely institutions of confinement directed at the lowest rungs of society. They were also institutions of improvement; governors firmly believed that residents could be transformed into hard-working industrious members of society. Foundling Hospital children were ideally to become hard-working Protestant adults, and adult residents in the House of Industry were at the very least to become practitioners of trades that were deemed economically useful. By the 1770s, thanks primarily to the many difficulties encountered by the Foundling Hospital, property taxes were no longer considered the best way to fund social reform. The corporations for the relief of the poor established in Dublin and around Ireland are examples of how social reform movements had changed by the 1770s. They were corporations established from above by Act of Parliament, but funded in the same manner as earlier voluntary societies through donations and subscriptions.

---

[99] Corporation for the Relief of the Poor, *Observations on the state and condition of the poor*, p. 14.

Like other organizations, they also relied on parliamentary grants to help fund their endeavours. Government sponsorship of social reform initiatives was no more successful than government grants for economic development or internal improvement projects, but these projects demonstrate the willingness of the Irish parliament in the eighteenth century to use public money to address contemporary social problems. Funding for these initiatives represented an improvement agenda as clearly as did the funding of canal-building or the development of industries.

Conclusion

Philanthropy and Improvement in Eighteenth-Century Ireland and Beyond

To Anglo-Irish improvers their work was a form of patriotic action. Involvement in charity movements was a way to combine the Christian obligation to aid the less fortunate with their civic duty to the Irish state. Yet committed improvers did not represent the Anglo-Irish ruling class as a whole. There were many members of the gentry and aristocracy who through their lifestyle and actions expressed a profound indifference towards the fate of Ireland and its people.[1] The sermons and pamphlets produced by charitable societies regularly exhorted their audience to perform their Christian duty towards the less fortunate,[2] but were not always successful. In 1717 Dean Rowland Davies of Cork told his listeners that charity was not only necessary for salvation; it was also a civic duty. 'That it is out greatest prudence, as well as Christian Duty, to manage our present Fortune in order to our future happiness; and so to dispose of these transitory enjoyments, as that we may purchase by them an everlasting habitation.'[3] Concern over personal salvation, a sense of religious obligations, and paternalism towards the lower classes were all a part of the philanthropic mindset. While Anglo-Irish anxieties over security lay behind many of the philanthropic endeavours examined in this book, the activities of those who did work for improvement reflect an Enlightenment-era optimism about the perfectibility of society. Philanthropists and improvers believed that by addressing the roots of social problems they could eradicate them.

This book has examined several different organizations, each focusing on different social or economic difficulties affecting eighteenth-century Ireland. While these organizations varied with regards to methods and focus they shared many common goals. The charity movements examined here illustrate a shift in philanthropic activity and the aims that motivated it. These organizations were meant to serve the interests of the state as well as the interests of society and religion. Some philanthropists, such as John Putland and Lady Arbella Denny, were clearly motivated by sincere religious conviction, but even they also saw their endeavours as serving the practical interests of the nation in concrete

---

[1] Barnard, *Improving Ireland?* p. 170.

[2] Karen Sonnelitter, '"To unite our temporal and eternal interests": sermons and the charity school movement in Ireland, 1689–1740' in *Eighteenth-century Ireland*, 25 (2010), p. 71.

[3] Rowland Davies, *The right use of riches. A sermon preach'd in the parish church of St. Peter's, Corke on Sunday August the 11th, 1717* (Dublin, 1717), pp. 10–11.

ways. Many improvers were motivated more by rational self-interest then by any genuine charitable principle. In 1787 Richard Lewis wrote favourably of the Magdalene Asylum not because of the good it did, but because it helped to keep poor women out of sight of the well-to-do residents of the city. According to Lewis, 'An institution of this kind was greatly wanted for Dublin, where our sight was constantly struck with objects disgraceful to human nature; with wretched strumpets, tricked out in tawdry apparel, or covered with tattered weeds; and where our ears were continually assaulted with vociferations that would startle deafness, and appal blasphemy.'[4] Thomas Campbell, who visited the city in 1775, complained of the 'wretched harridans who ply for hire' that populated the city. Campbell recognized that these women were a symptom of the poverty of the city, but he was still offended by their 'midnight orgies'.[5] To both Lewis and Campbell, therefore, the primary benefit of the Magdalene Society was not that it helped poor women forced to turn to prostitution but that it helped the better-off residents of Ireland by removing prostitutes from their sight. Similar rationales were used to support the Dublin Workhouse, the Foundling Hospital, and the House of Industry. In 1695 the citizens of Dublin complained of vagrant children 'crying at their doors, at unseasonable houres in the night to excite them to give them reliefe'.[6] To many residents of eighteenth-century Dublin, the greatest problem they had with poverty was looking at it.

Leaving aside the individual motivations of improvers, eighteenth-century philanthropy was not defined by the actions of individuals, but by the actions of organizations. Personal charity became largely subsumed by voluntary societies run on the same joint-stock model that was sweeping the business world. These organized charities elected governors and directors, met regularly, and solicited subscriptions. They combined the associational and consumer cultures of the period to develop a new methodology of philanthropy. Subscribers were free to give as much or as little as they saw fit and could discontinue their subscriptions if the organization ceased to be effective. This new approach to philanthropy struck many as both enlightened and practical. It enabled the foundation of a number of charity societies, each of which assumed that they would be able to achieve their goals based on the income of regular subscribers. They were wrong, however; charity societies were regularly short on funds and were unable to meet their operating costs from subscriptions alone. Joint-stock charities did enable many people to participate in charity work who previously had not, but they did not provide a stable financial base. In Ireland, however, they were also able to rely on a varying amount of financial support from the

4 Lewis, *The Dublin guide*, p. 51.
5 Thomas Campbell, *A philosophical survey of the south of Ireland, in a series of letters to John Watkinson, MD* (London, 1777), p. 49.
6 Gilbert, *Calendar of ancient records of Dublin*, vi, 90.

Irish parliament, which provided necessary funds to charities; its involvement meant that voluntary societies were held accountable to the state, as well as their subscribers.

Individual private benevolence persisted, but was increasingly frowned upon. Injudicious almsgiving was derided as an encouragement to the sturdy beggars that infested Ireland's cities. The rational, enlightened method of easing poverty was through subscription to voluntary societies which addressed the root causes of poverty. Reverend John Garnett, in a 1758 sermon, called for citizens to show 'discernment' in their benevolence and to 'fix upon the proper objects'. Garnett argued that the principal difficulty facing Irish philanthropists was determining how best to distribute their beneficence.

> If we give encouragement to sloth, we counteract the scheme of providence; yet if we discourage the wretched, and the unhappy, we counteract the principle of humanity. If we leave them to nakedness and starving we lose so many useful hands to the publick; yet it we place them in a rank, superior to the regards of industry, or economy, it is not charity, but ill-judged commiseration; a distinction, which it may be proper to keep in view, in this day's, as well as in every project of public charity.[7]

Garnett fixed upon the widows and children of clergymen as proper and deserving objects of charity. The basic principles he expressed were widely echoed by other charities. Irish citizens had a responsibility to aid the poor that stemmed from a 'principle of humanity' and from religious conviction. Aiding the poor also served the economic and political interests of the nation. As the earl of Chesterfield warned in 1746, the Anglo-Irish were in as much danger from 'poverty' as from 'popery'.[8]

This book has investigated several different charitable responses to eighteenth-century Ireland's social problems. Despite their different emphases and concerns there were a variety of connections between each of the institutions. The Church of Ireland struggled to balance its desire to play a leadership role in the emerging movement for improvement with its position as an organization in need itself of both charity and improvement. It also worked in close contact with a variety of voluntary societies. The Incorporated Society was first proposed by the archbishop of Armagh, Hugh Boulter, and the church episcopate always played an important role in the society's government. The Incorporated Society was not merely a tool for large-scale proselytism, but also focused on instructing students in vocational trades that would improve the economy. The intention was to teach Irish Catholic children English religion, language, and culture; therefore, proselytizing the Irish served multiple goals.

---

[7] John Garnett, *A sermons preached at the ordinary visitation of the two dioceses of Ferns and Leighlin. Recommending a subscription for clergymens' widows* (Dublin, 1758), p. 10.

[8] P.R.O.N.I. T3228/1/26.

It was believed that spreading Protestantism would secure the state politically and improve the economy. Catholicism was, after all, associated with rebellion and indolence.

Medical charities, meanwhile, addressed the same problems of economic and political stability but less directly; they sought to address the health concerns of the working poor. The charters of voluntary hospitals frequently expressed an Enlightenment-inspired aversion to traditional folk medicines, and the professionalized and scientific medical care offered by voluntary hospitals was strictly contrasted with traditional medicine, which was seen as backwards and uncivilized, as an inappropriate way for a modern nation to treat its medical problems. Providing medical care to the poor was not simply a way to demonstrate that Ireland was scientifically and medically in step with the rest of Europe, however; it was also about addressing a pressing social concern – the poor of Ireland represented a potential danger to the Anglo-Irish Ascendancy. In addition, they were essential to the nation's economy and therefore had to be in good health; political economists observed that a nation's population was directly related to its wealth, so, by providing medical services to the working poor, voluntary hospitals were making a concrete contribution to the nation's economic health.

The Dublin Society was partly focused on demonstrating scientific accomplishments, but it worked too to find other practical applications for Enlightenment-inspired knowledge. Its goals were to encourage agriculture and industry in Ireland with the aim of addressing the country's economic difficulties. By making Ireland more prosperous the members also believed that they were strengthening the position of the Anglo-Irish state. The Dublin Society worked closely with the state to foster economic development[9] and in concert with the established Church to encourage the spread of Anglicanism through premiums offered to Protestant settlers.[10] The Society conceived of its economic agenda in philanthropic terms; like the Incorporated Society and voluntary hospitals, it saw itself as performing a service that would better the lives of many in Ireland.

Other charities discussed here had similarly complex agendas. They each focused on a single social problem, as the wide variety of social ills afflicting Ireland seemed to require a focused, small-scale approach. They also worked closely with state, municipal, and religious authorities.[11] While each voluntary society addressed only a single small social problem, they all argued for the large-scale implications of addressing and correcting that issue. The Dublin Magdalene Asylum, for example, hoped to reform penitent prostitutes and

9   Livesey, 'The Dublin Society in eighteenth-century Irish political thought', pp. 615–16.
10 *Premiums offered by the Dublin Society*, p. 18.
11 Kelly, 'Charitable societies', p. 107.

offered a basic education and vocational training. The asylum argued that it did more than simply help the women they admitted, however; the proliferation of prostitution was thought to be damaging to the national economy, primarily through its role in spreading venereal disease. The Magdalene Asylum argued that their small attempts to reform these women had the potential to better society on a large scale. The Dublin Foundling Hospital was created to address the nuisance issue of abandoned children but it stressed that all abandoned children in their care would be brought up as Protestants and taught a trade. Abandoned children, meanwhile, had the potential to become unruly adults prone to rebellion. The Foundling Hospital, like the Incorporated Society, promised that political stability would be a natural side effect of their activities. Each of these institutions served the interests of the Anglo-Irish state. At the same time, they were all inspired by Enlightenment values. Improvers believed in the transformative abilities of education, and that a rational and scientific approach to philanthropy was the best way to address social and economic problems.

Many of these institutions were modelled on organizations in England. Charity schools, voluntary hospitals, and Magdalene Asylums were founded first in England. The Dublin Society was inspired by the Royal Society in England. Of the institutions examined here, only the Dublin Foundling Hospital was not based on an organization already established across the Irish Sea.[12] Aside from inspiration, encouragement and funding from England was important to many Irish charities. Irish 'improvers' did not operate in a vacuum and the connections with Great Britain and the continent are apparent in the activities of many organizations. At the same time, each of the organizations studied here was adapted to address specifically Irish concerns. The Dublin Society focused on economic development in a nation that was seen as economically backward. The Incorporated Society focused on proselytism in a nation that was predominantly Catholic. Improvers were energized by the belief that Ireland would become truly peaceful and prosperous only once the Irish had been culturally assimilated. Mercer's Hospital and the Magdalene Asylum did not set out to convert those they helped, but, as with other organizations, they contained a strongly Protestant ethos.

By the end of the eighteenth century charitable institutions had become so ingrained within Ireland that most received assistance and funding from the Irish parliament. To oversee the government's investment in these institutions, the Society for Promoting the Comforts of the Poor established a sub-committee which made regular reports on the state of the charitable institutions of Dublin. In 1800 they made one of their last reports to the Irish parliament. In it they

---

12   The London Foundling Hospital was founded by Thomas Coram in 1741.

commented on the insufficiency of Irish charities compared with those of London. London's charities were three times as extensive as Dublin's, even taking into account the difference in population. The sub-committee hoped that these facts would 'awaken the attention of the public'; 'generous emulation will animate the citizens of Dublin to view with the sister kingdom in establishments of such utility'.[13] The comparison with London was significant to Anglo-Irish philanthropists. The improvement movement was inspired by a nascent sense of Anglo-Irish patriotism and the relationship between Anglo-Irish improvers and their English counterparts varied between cooperative and competitive. However, improvement was also a reflection of Anglo-Irish desires to make Ireland more like England.

The impact and success of each organization varied and, in many cases, is impossible to quantify. In the course of the eighteenth century, improvers were successful in many of their overall goals for Ireland. The population rose steadily, the island remained peaceful, the government was stable, and trade increased. The city of Dublin was in the midst of a transformation. Streets were widened and impressive new buildings and houses were constructed in the Georgian style. Anglo-Irish concern over incipient rebellion eased in the second half of the eighteenth century. Below the surface, however, Ireland was still beset by a number of problems. Repeated political crises after 1778 demonstrated the tensions both within Ireland and between Ireland and England, and the relaxation of Poynings' Law did not ease the tensions that energized Henry Grattan's parliament. Improvers may have succeeded in some of their goals, but their successes were also countered by a number of public and private failures that reveal the flaws in their approach to philanthropy and humanity. To the bewilderment of Lady Arbella Denny, former Magdalenes regularly 'fell back into vice'.[14] Hospitals and schools were built, but proved difficult and expensive to maintain and many fell into disrepair. Incorporated Society children frequently ran away or reunited with their Catholic families. Schools were publicly condemned for their poor conditions. The Dublin Society's many economic schemes, from raising bees to growing hops, either failed to materialize or failed to transform Ireland's economy. The popular enthusiasm for new charities eventually faded into popular indifference. Every charity saw subscription rates decline over time. In fact, the improvers' mission was flawed in ways they could not recognize. Population growth, cited as a benefit of the voluntary hospital movement, was seen as a sign of strength, but the growing population prefigured the crisis of the Great Famine. Improvers focused on

---

[13] *First part of the report of the sub-committee of the society for promoting the comforts of the poor, on the charitable institutions of Dublin* (Dublin, 1800), pp. 15–16.
[14] R.C.B.L. 551–1-1.

religious conversion through the Incorporated Society; meanwhile, Catholics and nonconformists remained excluded from political life. Energized by revolutionary philosophies, some rebelled in 1798. This event precipitated the end of self-government in Ireland.

The Act of Union had major ramifications for Irish philanthropy. The United Kingdom parliament was far less likely to allot public funds for social reform projects in Ireland. In this context, the definition of improvement began to evolve. Population growth no longer seemed to provide a way to economic growth. In the nineteenth century voluntary societies remained the primary agents of benevolence; however, their focus changed. Eighteenth-century philanthropists believed that through associational philanthropy they could conquer the social ills affecting their nation. In the nineteenth century charity did not cease or even decline, but there was a shift in the aspirations of charitable organizations. Nineteenth-century philanthropy focused less on eradicating social problems and more on relieving them. It was still thought possible to reform the minds of the labouring poor, but the emphasis shifted towards teaching them sobriety and economy.[15] State involvement came to be frowned upon: charity worked best as an entirely voluntary endeavour. All aid that was assured actually did more harm than good. John Holroyd, earl of Sheffield, argued that 'Great is the mischief that has arisen from the system of compulsory charity: it destroys the connecting feelings between the several ranks of society, and their mutual dependence on each other; it has ruined the morals of the people, rendered them odious and insolent, and independent of character.'[16] It was no longer believed that the nation would experience tangible economic benefits from charity. Economies would only improve through investment in new industries. This shift in attitudes had a strong impact on the organizations examined in this project. Magdalene Asylums, which had formerly focused on reforming fallen women into contributing citizens, became Magdalene Laundries, where disgraced women were confined and controlled.

Throughout the course of the eighteenth century Irish philanthropy changed in tangible ways. As the seventeenth century drew to a close traditional philanthropy motivated solely by social or religious obligation was no longer seen as adequate to meet the needs of society, and in some cases 'injudicious' giving was seen as harmful. Philanthropy motivated by sympathy or religious conviction alone was impractical. Instead, the focus shifted towards rational and constructive charity that would address and correct the roots of social problems. Sympathy and religion were never entirely removed from the

---

[15] William Allen, *The philanthropist: or, repository for hints and suggestions calculated to promote the comfort and happiness of man* (7 vols, London, 1811–1819), i, 215.

[16] John Holroyd, earl of Sheffield, *Observations on the impolicy, abuses, and false interpretation of the poor laws* (London, 1818), p. 4.

philanthropic equation, however; this was not the goal. On an individual level many improvers were motivated by some degree of genuine religious conviction and honest sympathy for the objects of their charity. However, the corporate philanthropy that characterized this period was defined not by individual compassion but by pragmatism. Philanthropic societies cited tangible benefits to the nation that would come from each of their schemes. Education would end religious division and bring about political stability, hospitals would aid the essential working poor and reinforce the social bonds between rich and poor, Dublin Society premiums would foster economic innovation. At the core of many of these schemes was an Anglo-Irish concern over political stability, a concern which eased as the century continued but never entirely disappeared.

Bibliography

Archival Sources

Armagh Public Library
Lodge Manuscripts

Dublin City Library and Archive
Robinson Manuscript

Marsh's Library, Dublin, Ireland
Dublin Workhouse Manuscripts
Letters Concerning the Society for Promoting Charity Schools
Reports Concerning Linen Manufacture

National Archives of Ireland, Dublin, Ireland
Mercer's Hospital Records
Mercer School Records
Pembroke Estate Papers

National Archives, Kew
Charles Abbot Papers
Public Records Office Domestic Records
Treasury Department Papers

National Library of Ireland, Dublin, Ireland
Adlercron Family Papers
Egmont Papers
Rowan Papers
The Dublin Hospitals

Public Record Office of Northern Ireland, Belfast, Northern Ireland
Armagh Diocesan Registry Papers
Cole Papers
Duke of Bedford, Lord Lieutenancy Papers
Earl of Northumberland, Irish Viceregal Papers
Foster/Massereene Papers
Granard Papers
Harrowby Papers
Hort Papers

Normanton Papers
Perceval-Maxwell Papers
Sheffield Papers
Sir Robert Wilmot Papers

Representative Church Body Library, Dublin, Ireland
Magdalene Asylum Dublin Records

Royal Dublin Society Library, Dublin, Ireland
Royal Dublin Society Minute Books

Trinity College, Dublin, Ireland
Incorporated Society for Promoting English Protestant Schools in Ireland
    Records

Published Primary Sources

*A copy of His Majesty's royal charter, for erecting English protestant schools in the
    kingdom of Ireland* (Dublin, 1733).
*A copy of His Majesty's royal charter for incorporating the governors and guardians of
    the hospital for the relief of poor lying-in women, in Dublin: dated the second day
    of December, 1756* (Dublin, 1757).
*A correct copy of the registry of private licensed sedan chairs, in the city of Dublin,
    as they appear on the collector's books, 25th March, 1786. Published pursuant
    to order of the governors of the foundling and lying-in hospitals* (Dublin, 1786).
Adam, James, *Practical essays on agriculture: containing an account of soils, and the
    manner of correction them* (2 vols, London, 1789).
*A letter from a gentleman in the country to his son at the university, dissuading him
    from going into holy orders* (Dublin, 1737).
A letter from a layman, to the clergy of Ireland (Dublin, 1749).
A letter from a lord to a commoner, concerning the two church bills lately rejected
    (2nd ed., Dublin, 1732).
A letter from an English gentleman in Dublin, to his friend in England (Dublin,
    1767).
Allen, William, *The philanthropist: or, repository for hints and suggestions calculated
    to promote the comfort and happiness of man* (7 vols, London, 1811–1819).
An account of charity schools in Great Britain and Ireland (London, 1712).
'An act for badging such poor as shall be found unable to support themselves
    by labour, and to otherwise provide for the, and for restraining such as shall
    be found able to support themselves, by labour or industry from begging' in
    *Acts and statutes, made in a parliament begun at Dublin, the seventeenth day of
    October 1769* (Dublin, 1772).

'An act to prevent the destroying and murdering of bastard children' in *Acts and statutes made in a parliament begun at Dublin the twenty first day of September, Anno Dom. 1703* (Dublin, 1728).

A new scheme for increasing the Protestant religion and improving the kingdom of Ireland (Dublin, 1756).

An epistle to the fair-sex on the subject of drinking (London, 1744).

A Protestant's address to the Protestants of Ireland (Dublin, 1757).

A representation of the present state of religion, with regard to infidelity, heresy, impiety and popery: drawn up and agreed to by both houses of convocation in Ireland (Dublin, 1711).

Baker, John Wynn, *A plan for instructing youths in the knowledge of husbandry, published at the request of the Dublin Society* (Dublin, 1765).

—, *Experiments in agriculture, made under the direction of the right honourable and honourable Dublin Society, in the Year 1764* (Dublin, 1765).

—, *To his excellency, the right honourable, Lord Viscount Townshend, lieutenant general, and general governor of Ireland, president, his grace, the duke of Leinster, his grace, the right reverend archbishop of Armagh, vice-presidents. And to the rest of the lords composing the Dublin Society, the following remonstrance is most humbly addressed by John Wynn Baker* (Dublin, 1769).

Bayly, Edward, *A sermon preached on the opening of the chapel of the Magdalene asylum for female penitents* (Dublin, 1768).

—, *A sermon preached on the opening of the new chapel of the Magdalen asylum, in Leeson-Street, Dublin* (Dublin, 1770).

Bellers, John, *An essay towards the improvement of physik. In twelve proposals. By which the lives of many thousands of the rich, as well as of the poor, may be saved yearly* (London, 1714).

Boulter, Hugh, *Letters written by his excellency Hugh Boulter, D.D. Lord Primate of all Ireland, to several ministers of state in England* (2 vols, i, Dublin, 1770).

Boyle, Robert, *The works of the honourable Robert Boyle* (5 vols, v, London, 1744).

Brady, John, 'Remedies proposed for the church of Ireland' in *Archivium Hibernicum*, 22 (1959), pp. 163–73.

Brooke, Henry, *A brief essay on the nature of bogs, and the method of reclaiming them. Humbly addressed to the Dublin Society* (Dublin, 1772).

By-laws and ordinances of the Dublin Society. For the good government of the corporation (Dublin, 1769).

Carpenter, Andrew (ed.), *Letters to and from persons of quality* (Dublin, 1976).

Corporation for the Relief of the Poor in the City of Dublin, *An account of the proceedings, and state of the fund of the corporation instituted for the relief of the poor* (Dublin, 1774).

—, *Observations on the state and condition of the poor, under the institution, for their relied, in the city of Dublin* (Dublin, 1775).

Cox, Richard, *A letter from Sir Richard Cox, bart. To Thomas Prior, esq.; shewing, from experience, a sure method to establish the linen-manufacture; and the beneficial effects, it will immediately produce* (Dublin, 1749).

—, *An essay for the conversion of the Irish shewing that 'tis their duty and interest to become Protestants: in a letter to themselves* (Dublin, 1698).

—, *Some thoughts on the bill depending before the right honourable the House of Lords, for prohibiting the exportation of the woollen manufactures of Ireland to foreign parts. Humbly offer'd to their lordships. Written in the year, 1698* (Dublin, 1740).

Dalrymple, Sir John, *Memoirs of Great Britain and Ireland* (2 vols, ii, London, 1773).

Davies, Rowland, *The right use of riches. A sermon preach'd in the parish church of St. Peter's, Corke on Sunday August the 11ᵗʰ, 1717* (Dublin, 1717).

Debates relative to the affairs of Ireland, in the years 1763 and 1764 (2 vols, ii, London, 1766).

Delany, Patrick, *Eighteen discourses and dissertations upon various very important and interesting subjects* (London, 1766).

Dodd, William, *An account of the rise, progress, and present state of the Magdalen charity. To which are added, the Rev. Mr. Dodd's sermon, preached before the president, vice-presidents, and governors, &C. his sermon preached before His Royal Highness the duke of York, &C. and the advice to the Magdalens; with the hymns, prayers, rules, and list of subscribers* (London, 1761).

—, *The Magdalen, or, history of the first penitent prostitute received into that charitable asylum. With anecdotes of other penitents* (London, 1799).

Downes, Henry, *A sermon preach'd in the parish church of St. Warbrugh, Dublin: May the 7th 1721* (Dublin, 1721).

Falkiner, Sir Frederick Richard, *The foundation of the hospital and free school of King Charles II., Oxmantown Dublin: commonly called the Blue Coat School: with notices of some of its governors, and of contemporary events in Dublin from the foundation, 1668 to 1840, when its government by the city ceased* (Dublin, 1906).

First annual report of the corporation instituted for the relief of the poor, and punishing vagabonds and sturdy beggars, in the queen's county (Kilkenny, 1776).

First part of the report of the sub-committee of the society for promoting the comforts of the poor, on the charitable institutions of Dublin (Dublin, 1800).

Fitzmaurice, Edmond George Petty, *Life of William, earl of Shelburne, afterwards first marquess of Lansdowne. With extracts from his papers and correspondence* (3 vols, i, London, 1875).

Foster, Edward, *An essay on hospitals. Or succinct directions for the situation, construction and administration of country hospitals* (Dublin, 1768).

Foy, Nathanael, A sermon preached in Christs Church Dublin; on the 23rd of October 1698. Being the anniversary thanksgiving for putting an end to the Irish Rebellion (Dublin, 1698).

Garnett, John, A sermons preached at the ordinary visitation of the two dioceses of Ferns and Leighlin. Recommending a subscription for clergymen's widows (Dublin, 1758).

Gilbert, J. T. (ed.), Calendar of ancient records of Dublin in the possession of the municipal corporation of that city (18 vols, Dublin, 1896).

—, A history of the city of Dublin (2 vols, Dublin, 1854).

Hanway, Jonas, A plan for establishing a charity-house, or charity-houses, for the reception of repenting prostitutes. To be called the Magdalen charity (London, 1758).

Hely-Hutchinson, John, The commercial restraints of Ireland considered (Dublin, 1779).

Henry, William, The cries of the orphans. A sermon preached in the parish church of St Michael, on Sunday April 27th for the support of the orphans in the foundling hospital (Dublin, 1760).

Holroyd, John, earl of Sheffield, Observations on the impolicy, abuses, and false interpretations of the poor laws (London, 1818).

Hort, Josiah, Sixteen sermons by Josiah, lord bishop of Kilmore and Ardagh (Dublin, 1738).

House of Commons Ireland, Report of the committee appointed to enquire into the state and management of the foundling hospital (Dublin, 1792).

Hovell, John, A discourse on the woollen manufactory of Ireland and the consequences of prohibiting its exportation (Dublin, 1698).

Howard, John, An account of the principal lazarettos in Europe, etc. (Warrington, 1789).

Howard, Robert, A sermon preached in Christ-Church Dublin before the Incorporated Society for Promoting English Protestant schools in Ireland (Dublin, 1738).

Hutchinson, Sir Francis, A bill for raising and establishing a fund for a provision of the widows and children of the clergy of the church of Ireland (Dublin, 1783).

Hutchinson, Francis, Advices concerning the manner of receiving popish converts (Dublin, 1729).

—, A letter to a member of parliament, concerning the imploying and providing for the poor (Dublin, 1723).

—, A sermon preached in Christ-Church Dublin, on Thursday the 30th of January 1723. Being the anniversary fast for the martyrdom of King Charles the First (Dublin, 1723).

—, The church catechism in Irish (Belfast, 1722).

Incorporated Society in Dublin for Promoting English Protestant Schools in Ireland, A brief account of the proceedings of the Incorporated Society in Dublin, for Erecting and Promoting English Protestant Schools in Ireland. To which is prefix'd, an abstract of His Majesty's royal charter (London, 1735).

—, An account of the proceedings of the Incorporated Society in Dublin, for Promoting English Protestant Schools in Ireland, from February 6th. 1733, on which day the royal charter was opened, to the 6th. of March following. In two letters published by order of the Society (Dublin, 1734).

—, A brief review of the rise and progress of the Incorporated Society in Dublin, for Promoting English Protestant Schools in Ireland. From the opening of His Majesty's royal charter, February 6th, 1733, to November 2d. 1748 (Dublin, 1748).

—, A continuation of the proceedings of the Incorporated Society in Dublin, for Promoting English Protestant Schools in Ireland, from the 25th of March, 1740, to the 25th of March, 1742. To which is annexed, an account of the benefactions received by the Society, from the 25th of March, 1740, to the 25th of March, 1742 (Dublin, 1742).

—, An abstract of the proceedings of the Incorporated Society in Dublin, for Promoting English Protestant Schools in Ireland: from the opening of His Majesty's royal charter, on the 6th day of February, 1733. To the 25th day of March, 1737 (London, 1737).

—, Rules established by the Incorporated Society, in Dublin, for Promoting English Protestant-Schools in Ireland (Dublin, 1734).

Instructions for managing bees. Drawn up and published by order of the Dublin Society (Dublin, 1733).

Instructions for planting and managing hops, and for raising hop-poles. Drawn up and published by order of the Dublin Society (London, 1733).

Johnson, Robert, Some friendly cautions to the heads of families: containing ample directions to nurses who attend the sick and women in child-bed (London, 1767).

Journals of the House of Commons of the kingdom of Ireland (19 vols, Dublin, 1792).

Journals of the House of Lords of the kingdom of Ireland (8 vols, Dublin, 1779–1800).

King, Charles Simeon (ed.), A great archbishop of Dublin William King D.D., 1650–1729. His autobiography, family, and a selection from his correspondence (London, 1908).

King, William, The state of the Protestants of Ireland under the late King James's government in which their carriage towards him is justified, and the absolute necessity of their endeavouring to be freed from his government, and of submitting to their present Majesties is demonstrated (London, 1691).

Lansdowne, Marquis of (ed.), The Petty Papers: some unpublished writings of Sir William Petty, edited from the Bowood papers (2 vols, New York, 1967).

Lewis, Richard, The Dublin guide: or, a description of the city of Dublin, and the most remarkable places within fifteen miles (Dublin, 1787).

Madden, Samuel, *A letter to the Dublin Society on the improving of their fund; and the manufactures, tillage, etc. in Ireland* (Dublin, 1739).

—, *Reflections and resolutions proper for the gentlemen of Ireland, as to their conduct for the service of their country, as landlords, as masters of families* (Dublin, 1738).

Mandeville, Bernard, *The fable of the bees, or private vices, publick benefits* (2 vols, Indianapolis, 1924).

Maule, Henry, *God's goodness visible in our deliverance from popery. With some fit methods to prevent the further growth of it in Ireland. In a sermon preached at Christ-Church, Dublin, &C. on the twenty-third day of October, 1733. By Henry, lord bishop of Dromore* (London, 1735).

Maxwell, Henry, *An essay upon an union of Ireland with England: most humbly offered to the consideration of the queen's most excellent majesty, and both houses of parliament* (Dublin, 1704).

Molyneux, William, *The case of Ireland's being bound by acts of parliament in England, stated* (Dublin, 1698).

Nelson, Robert, *An address to persons of quality and estate* (Dublin, 1752).

Nicholson, Edward, *A method of charity-schools, recommended, for giving both a religious education, and a way of livelihood to the poor children in Ireland* (Dublin, 1712).

On faction; a poem occasionally wrote by a member of the Spiritual Society; and inscribed to Mr. John Putland (Dublin, 1753).

Petty, Sir William, *Tracts; chiefly relating to Ireland. Containing: I. A treatise of taxes and contributions. II. Essays in political arithmetic. III. The political anatomy of Ireland. By the late Sir William Petty. To which is prefixed his last will* (Dublin, 1769).

Pierson, Samuel, *A dissertation on the inlargement of tillage, the erecting of public granaries, and the regulating, employing, and supporting the poor in this kingdom* (Dublin, 1741).

Pool, Robert and John Cash, *Views of the most remarkable public buildings and monuments in the city of Dublin* (Dublin, 1780).

Premiums offered by the Dublin Society, in the year 1766, for the encouragement of agriculture, manufactures, and useful arts, in Ireland (Dublin, 1766).

Prior, Thomas, *A list of the absentees of Ireland, and the yearly value of their estates and incomes spent abroad. With observations on the present state and condition of that kingdom* (Dublin, 1729).

—, *An essay to encourage and extend the linen-manufacture in Ireland, by premiums and other means* (Dublin, 1749).

—, *A proposal to prevent the price of corn from rising too high, or falling too low, by the means of granaries. By Thomas Prior, Esq.* (Dublin, 1741).

—, *Observations on coin in general. With some proposals for regulating the value of coin in Ireland. By the author of the list of the absentees of Ireland* (London, 1730).

Reports of the committee of St. Mary's parish on local taxation (Dublin, 1823).

'Report on the state of popery in Ireland, 1731' in *Archivium Hibernicum*, 4, no. 10 (1915), pp. 131–77.

'Report on the state of the Protestant charter schools of the kingdom, reported by the Right Honourable Mr Secretary of State' in *Journals of the House of Commons of the Kingdom of Ireland from the Eighteenth of May 1613 to 1794*, 25 (Dublin, 1788).

Richardson, John, *A proposal for the conversion of the popish natives of Ireland, to the established religion* (Dublin, 1711).

—, *A short history of the attempts that have been made to convert the popish natives of Ireland, to the established religion* (London, 1712).

—, *The great folly, superstition, and idolatry, of pilgrimages in Ireland* (Dublin, 1727).

Rules and regulations for the asylum of penitent females: with an account of receipts and disbursements (Dublin, 1796).

Rundle, Thomas, *A sermon preached in Christ-Church Dublin, on the 25th Day of March 1736. Before the Incorporated Society for Promoting English Protestant Schools in Ireland* (Dublin, 1736).

Slator, Lionel, *The advantages, which may arise to the people of Ireland by raising of flax and flax-seed, considered. Together with instructions for sowing and saving the seed, drawn up and published by the direction of the Dublin Society* (Dublin, 1732).

Smyth, Edward, *An account of the trial of Edward Smyth, late curate of Ballyculter, in the diocese of Down* (Dublin, 1777).

Some remarks occasion'd by the Reverend Mr. Madden's scheme, and objections rais'd against it (Dublin, 1732).

Some thoughts on the tillage of Ireland: humbly dedicated to the parliament (London, 1737).

Steven, Robert, *An inquiry into the abuses of the chartered schools in Ireland* (2nd ed., London, 1818).

Swift, Jonathan, 'A proposal for giving badges to the beggars in all the parishes of Dublin' in Temple Scott (ed.), *The prose works of Jonathan Swift* (12 vols, vii, London, 1905), vii, 325–35.

—, 'Some reasons against the bill for settling the tyth of hemp, flax, etc by a modus' in *The prose works of Jonathan Swift* (London, 1898), iii, 227–30.

Synge, Edward, *A brief account of the laws now in force in the kingdom of Ireland, for encouraging the residence of the parochial clergy, and erecting of English schools* (Dublin, 1723).

—, *A charitable address to all who are in communion with the church of Rome* (London, 1727).

—, An account of the erection, government and number, of charity-schools in Ireland (Dublin, 1717).

—, A sincere Christian and convert from the church of Rome, exemplified in the life of Daniel Herly, a poor Irish peasant (London, 1707).

—, Methods of erecting, supporting & governing charity-schools: with an account of the charity-schools in Ireland; and some observations thereon (Dublin, 1721).

—, The reward of converting sinners from the error of their ways. A sermon preached in the parish church of St. Bridget, Dublin (Dublin, 1719).

The groans of Ireland, in a letter to a member of parliament (Dublin, 1741).

The histories of some of the penitents in the Magdalen-House, as supposed to be related by themselves (2 vols, Dublin, 1760).

The Magdalen: or, dying penitent, exemplified in the death of F.S. who died April 1763, aged twenty-six years (Dublin, 1789).

The medical museum, or, a repository of cases experiments, researches and discoveries, collected at home and abroad by gentlemen of the faculty (3 vols, i, London, 1763).

The pedlar's letter to the bishops and clergy of Ireland (Dublin, 1760).

The present state of Doctor Steevens's hospital; together, with a scheme to enlarge the fund, for the maintenance and cure of 300 sick persons (Dublin, 1735).

The royal charter of the Dublin Society. To which are added, the Society's by-laws and ordinances, for the good government of the corporation (Dublin, 1766).

The statutes at large, passed in the parliaments held in Ireland: from the third year of Edward the Second (21 vols, vii, Dublin, 1786).

The statutes at large passed in the parliaments held in Ireland (21 vols, xi, Dublin, 1769).

Warburton, John, History of the city of Dublin, from the earliest accounts to the present time (2 vols, London, 1818).

West, Matthew, Charity the seal of Christian perfection, a sermon preached before his excellency, the lord lieutenant, and the vice-patroness, governesses, and guardians of the asylum for penitent women (Dublin, 1777).

Wilcocks, Joseph, A sermon preach'd before the society corresponding with the Incorporated Society in Dublin, for Promoting English Protestant Working-Schools in Ireland, at their anniversary meeting in the parish-church of St. Mary Le Bow, on Saturday, March 17. 1738–9 (London, 1739).

Wodsworth, William Dudley, A brief history of the ancient foundling hospital of Dublin, from the year 1702 (Dublin, 1876).

Woodward, Richard, An argument in support of the right of the poor in the kingdom of Ireland, to a national provision (Dublin, 1768).

—, A scheme for establishing county poor-houses, in the kingdom of Ireland. Published by Order of the Dublin Society (Dublin, 1766).

—, The present state of the church of Ireland: containing a description of its precarious situation; and the consequent danger to the public (5th ed., Dublin, 1787).

Young, Arthur, *Arthur Young's tour in Ireland 1776–1779*, ed. Arthur Hutton (2 vols, ii, London, 1892).

—, *A tour in Ireland; with general observations on the state of the kingdom* (London, 1780).

Newspapers and Periodicals

British Evening Post
Faulkner's Dublin Journal
Lloyd's Evening Post
Morning Chronicle and London Advertiser
Morning Herald and Daily Advertiser
Pue's Occurrences

Secondary Sources

Ahern, Michael, 'Clonmel Charter School' in *Tipperary Historical Journal*, 5 (1992), pp. 148–52.

Andrew, Donna T., *Philanthropy and police: London charity in the eighteenth century* (Princeton, 1989).

Barker-Benfield, G. J., *The culture of sensibility: sex and society in eighteenth-century Britain* (Chicago, 1992).

Barnard, T. C., *A new anatomy of Ireland: the Irish Protestants, 1649–1770* (New Haven, 2003).

—, 'Gardening, diet and "improvement" in later seventeenth-century Ireland' in *Journal of Garden History*, 10, no. 1 (1990), pp. 71–85.

—, 'Improving clergymen, 1660–1760' in Alan Ford, James McGuire, and Kenneth Milne (eds), *As by law established: the church of Ireland since the Reformation* (Dublin, 1995), pp. 136–51, 257–65.

—, *Improving Ireland? Projectors, prophets and profiteers, 1641–1786* (Dublin, 2008).

—, *Making the grand figure: lives and possessions in Ireland, 1641–1770* (New Haven, 2004).

—, 'Protestants and the Irish language, c. 1675–1725' in *Journal of Ecclesiastical History*, 44 (1993), pp. 243–72.

—, 'The Dublin Society and other improving societies, 1731–85' in James Kelly and Martyn J. Powell (eds), *Clubs and Societies in Eighteenth-Century Ireland* (Dublin, 2010), pp. 53–88.

—, 'The eighteenth-century parish' in Elizabeth Fitzpatrick and Raymond Gillespie (eds), *The Parish in Medieval and Early Modern Ireland* (Dublin, 2006), pp. 297–324.

—, *The kingdom of Ireland, 1641–1760* (New York, 2004).

—, 'The Hartlib Circle and the cult and culture of improvement in Ireland' in Michael Leslie, Mark Greengrass, and Timothy Raylor (eds), *Samuel Hartlib and the universal reformation: studies in intellectual communication* (Cambridge, 1994), pp. 281–98.

—, 'The uses of 23 October 1641 and Irish Protestant celebration' in *English Historical Review*, CVI, CCCCXXI (1991), pp. 889–920.

Bartlett, Thomas, *The fall and rise of the Irish nation: the Catholic question 1690–1830* (Savage, MD, 1992).

Beckett, J. C., *The Anglo-Irish tradition* (Ithaca, NY, 1976).

—, *The making of modern Ireland: 1603–1923* (new ed., London, 1981).

Berry, Henry, *A history of the Royal Dublin Society* (London, 1915).

Borsay, Peter, 'The culture of improvement' in Paul Langford (ed.), *The Eighteenth Century, 1688–1815* (Oxford, 2002), pp. 183–212.

Borsay, Peter, and Lindsay J. Proudfoot, *Provincial towns in early modern England and Ireland: change, convergence and divergence* (Proceedings of the British Academy, 108, Oxford, 2002).

Bradshaw, Brendan, 'Sword, word, and strategy in the Reformation in Ireland' in *The Historical Journal*, 21, no. 3 (1978), pp. 475–502.

Brady, Ciaran, *James Anthony Froude: an intellectual biography of a Victorian prophet* (Oxford, 2013).

Briggs, Asa, *The age of improvement 1783–1867* (New York, 1959).

Bright, Kevin, *The Royal Dublin Society, 1815–1845* (Dublin, 2004).

Brown, Michael, 'Was there an Irish Enlightenment? The case of the Anglicans' in Richard Butterwick and Simon Davies (eds), *Peripheries of the Enlightenment* (Oxford, 2008), pp. 49–63.

Browne, Alan, 'Bartholomew Mosse, 1712–1759, founder and first master' in Alan Browne (ed.), *Masters, midwives, and ladies-in-waiting: the Rotunda Hospital 1745–1995* (Dublin, 1995), pp. 1–20.

Butler, B. B., 'Lady Arabella Denny, 1707–92' in *Dublin Historical Record*, 9 (1947), pp. 1–20.

Cavallo, Sandra, *Charity and power in early modern Italy: benefactors and their motives in Turin* (Cambridge, 1995).

Chojnacka, Monica, 'Charity and community in early modern Venice: the Casa Delle Zitelle' in *Renaissance Quarterly*, 51, no. 1 (1998), pp. 68–91.

Clare, Liam, 'The Putland family of Dublin and Bray' in *Dublin Historical Record*, 54 (2001), pp. 183–209.

Clark, Peter, *British clubs and societies 1580–1800* (Oxford, 2000).

Clarke, Desmond, *Thomas Prior 1681–1751, founder of the Royal Dublin Society* (Dublin, 1951).

Connolly, S. J., *Divided kingdom: Ireland 1630–1800* (Oxford, 2008).

—, 'Eighteenth-century Ireland' in D. George Boyce and Alan O'Day (ed), *The making of modern Ireland: revisionism and the revisionist controversy* (London, 1996), pp. 15–33.

—, 'Religion and history: review article' in *Irish Economic and Social History*, 10 (1983), pp. 66–80.

—, *Religion, law and power: the making of Protestant Ireland 1660–1760* (Oxford, 1992).

Coughlan, Patricia, 'Natural history and historical nature: the project for a natural history of Ireland' in Michael Leslie, Mark Greengrass, and Timothy Raylor (eds), *Samuel Hartlib and the universal reformation: studies in intellectual communication* (Cambridge, 1994), pp. 298–317.

Craig, Andrew Gordon, 'The movement for reformation of manners' (Ph.D. thesis, University of Edinburgh, 1980).

Crawford, E. Margaret (ed.), 'William Wilde's Table of Irish Famines, 900–1850' in Crawford, E. Margaret (ed.), *Famine: The Irish Experience 900–1900* (Edinburgh, 1989), pp. 1–30.

Crawford, W. H., 'The influence of the landlord in eighteenth century Ulster' in L. M. Cullen and Thomas Christopher Smout (eds), *Comparative aspects of Scottish and Irish economic and social history, 1600–1900* (Edinburgh, 1977), pp. 193–203.

Davidoff, Leonore and Catherine Hall, *Family fortunes: men and women of the English middle class, 1780–1850* (Chicago, 1987).

Dickson, David, *Arctic Ireland: the extraordinary story of the great frost and forgotten famine of 1740–41* (Belfast, 1997).

—, *New foundations, Ireland 1660–1800* (Dublin, 2000).

—, 'The gap in famines: a useful myth?' in Margaret Crawford (ed.), *Famine: the Irish experience, 900–1900. Subsistence crises and famines in Ireland* (Edinburgh, 1989), pp. 96–111.

—, 'The other great Irish famine' in Cathal Poirteir (ed.), *The Great Irish Famine* (Cork, 1995), pp. 50–59.

Dickson, David, Cormac Ã. Grada, and S. Daultrey, 'Hearth tax, household size and Irish population change 1672–1821' in *Proceedings of the Royal Irish Academy, section C* (1982), pp. 125–81.

Diefendorf, Barbara B., *From penitence to charity: pious women and the Catholic Reformation in Paris* (New York, 2004).

Dinan, Susan E., *Women and poor relief in seventeenth-century France: the early history of the daughters of charity* (Aldershot; Burlington, VT, 2006).

Dudley, Rowena, 'The Dublin parish, 1660–1730' in Elizabeth Fitzpatrick and Raymond Gillespie (eds), *The Parish in Medieval and Early Modern Ireland* (Dublin, 2006), pp. 277–96.

—, 'The Dublin parishes and the poor, 1660–1740' in *Archivium Hibernicum*, LIII (1999), pp. 80–94.

Elliott, D. W., *The angel out of the house: philanthropy and gender in nineteenth-century England* (Charlottesville, 2002).

Fagan, Patrick, *Catholics in a Protestant country: the papist constituency in eighteenth-century Dublin* (Dublin, 1998).

—, 'The population of Dublin in the eighteenth century with particular reference to the proportions of Protestants and Catholics' in *Eighteenth-Century Ireland*, 6 (1991), pp. 121–58.

Fauske, Christopher J., *Jonathan Swift and the church of Ireland, 1710–24* (Dublin, 2002).

Flora, Peter and Jens Alber, 'Modernization, democratization and the development of welfare states in western Europe' in Peter Flora and Arnold Heidenheimer (eds), *The development of welfare states in Europe and America* (New Brunswick, NJ, 1998), pp. 37–80.

Foster, R. F., *Modern Ireland, 1600–1972* (London, 1988).

Froude, J. A., *The English in Ireland in the eighteenth century* (3 vols, London, 1872).

Gargett, Graham and Geraldine Sheridan (eds), *Ireland and the French Enlightenment, 1700–1800* (London, 1999).

Gay, Peter, *The Enlightenment: an interpretation, the rise of modern paganism* (2 vols, New York, 1967).

Geary, Laurence M., *Medicine and charity in Ireland, 1718–1851* (Dublin, 2004).

—, '"The whole country was in motion": mendicancy and vagrancy in pre-famine Ireland' in Jacqueline R. Hill and Colm Lennon (eds), *Luxury and austerity* (Dublin, 1999), pp. 121–36.

Ginzberg, Lori D., *Women and the work of benevolence: morality, politics, and class in the nineteenth-century United States* (New Haven, 1990).

Hayton, D. W., 'Anglo-Irish attitudes: shifting perceptions of national identity' in D. W. Hayton (ed.), *The Anglo-Irish experience, 1680–1730: religion, identity, and patriotism* (Woodbridge, 2012), pp. 25–48.

—, 'Creating industrious Protestants: charity schools and the enterprise of religious and social reformation' in D. W. Hayton (ed.), *The Anglo-Irish experience, 1680–1730: religion, identity, and patriotism* (Woodbridge, 2012), pp. 149–73.

—, 'From barbarian to burlesque: the changing stereotype of the Irish' in D. W. Hayton (ed.), *The Anglo-Irish Experience, 1680–1730: religion, identity, and patriotism* (Woodbridge, 2012), pp. 1–24.

—, 'Did Protestantism fail in early eighteenth-century Ireland? Charity schools and the enterprise of religious and social reformation, c.1690–1730' in Alan Ford, James McGuire, and Kenneth Milne (eds), *As by law established: the church of Ireland since the Reformation* (Dublin, 1995), pp. 166–86.

—, 'Parliament and the established church: reform and reaction' in James Kelly,

David Hayton, and John Bergin (eds), *The eighteenth-century composite state: representative institutions in Ireland and Europe, 1689–1800* (Basingstoke, 2010), pp. 78–106.

—, 'The long apprenticeship' in David Hayton (ed.), *The Irish parliament in the eighteenth century: the long apprenticeship* (Edinburgh, 2001), pp. 1–26.

Hayton, D. W. and James Kelly, 'The Irish parliament in european context: a representative institution in a composite state' in James Kelly, David Hayton, and John Bergin (eds), *The eighteenth-century composite state: representative institutions in Ireland and Europe, 1689–1800* (Basingstoke, 2010), pp. 3–16.

Hill, Jacqueline R., *From patriots to unionists: Dublin civic politics and Irish Protestant patriotism 1660–1840* (Oxford, 1997).

Himmelfarb, Gertrude, *The roads to modernity: the British, French and American Enlightenments* (New York, 2004).

Hoppen, K. Theodore, *The common scientist in the seventeenth century: a study of the Dublin Philosophical Society, 1683–1708* (London, 1970).

—, 'The Dublin Philosophical Society and the new learning in Ireland' in *Irish Historical Studies*, XIV (1964), pp. 99–118.

Hufton, Olwen, *The poor of eighteenth-century France 1750–1789* (Oxford, 1974).

Johnston-Liik, Edith Mary, *History of the Irish parliament, 1692–1800: commons, constituencies and statutes* (6 vols, Belfast, 2002).

Jones, Colin, *The charitable imperative: hospitals and nursing in Ancien Regime and Revolutionary France* (New York, 1989).

Jones, M. G., *The charity school movement: a study of eighteenth century puritanism in action* (Cambridge, 1938).

Kelly, Patrick, 'Conquest versus consent as the basis of the English title to Ireland in William Molyneux's *Case of Ireland Stated*' in Ciaran Brady and Jane Ohlmeyer (eds), *British Interventions in Early Modern Ireland* (Cambridge, 2005).

—, 'The Irish Woollen Export Prohibition Act of 1699: Kearny re-visited' in *Irish Economic and Social History*, VII (1980), pp. 22–44.

Kelly, James, 'Charitable societies: their genesis and development' in James Kelly and Martyn J. Powell (eds), *Clubs and Societies in Eighteenth-Century Ireland* (Dublin, 2010), pp. 89–108.

—, 'Infanticide in eighteenth-century Ireland' in *Irish Economic and Social History*, XIX (1992), pp. 5–26.

—, *Poynings' Law and the making of law in Ireland, 1660–1800* (Dublin, 2007).

—, 'The emergence of scientific and institutional medical practice in Ireland, 1650–1800' in Greta Jones and Elizabeth Malcolm (eds), *Medicine, Disease and the State in Ireland, 1650–1940* (Cork, 1999), pp. 21–39.

—, 'William Burton Conyngham and the north-west fishery of the eighteenth century' in *Journal of the Royal Society of Antiquaries of Ireland*, CXV (1985), pp. 64–85.

Kelly, James and Martyn J. Powell, 'Introduction' in James Kelly and Martyn J. Powell (eds), *Clubs and Societies in Eighteenth-Century Ireland* (Dublin, 2010), pp. 17–35.

Kennedy, Maire, 'Reading the Enlightenment in eighteenth-century Ireland' in *Eighteenth-Century Studies*, XLV, no. 3 (2012), pp. 355–78.

Kiernanh, T. J., *History of the financial administration of Ireland to 1817* (London, 1930).

Kidd, Colin, *British identities before nationalism: ethnicity and nationhood in the Atlantic world, 1600–1800* (Cambridge, 1999).

—, 'Gaelic antiquity and national identity in Enlightenment Ireland and Scotland' in *The English Historical Review*, 109, no. 434 (1994), pp. 1197–214.

Landa, Louis A., *Swift and the church of Ireland* (Oxford, 1954).

Lecky, W. E. H., *A history of Ireland in the eighteenth century: abridged and with an introduction* (Chicago, 1972).

—, *A history of Ireland in the eighteenth century* (5 vols, London, 1892).

Leerssen, Joseph, *Mere Irish and Fior-Ghael: studies in the idea of Irish nationality, its development and literary expression prior to the nineteenth century* (Cork, 1996).

Livesey, James, 'The Dublin Society in eighteenth-century Irish political thought' in *The Historical Journal*, 47, no. 3 (2004), pp. 615–40.

Lowe, William C., 'Conway, Francis Seymour-, first marquess of Hertford (1718–1794)' in Lawrence Goldman (ed.), *Oxford Dictionary of National Biography* (online ed., Oxford, <http://www.oxforddnb.com/view/article/6121>) Accessed 14 July 2010.

Luce, J. V., *Dublin societies before the R.D.S.* (Dublin, 1981).

Luddy, Maria, *Women and philanthropy in nineteenth-century Ireland* (Cambridge; New York, 1995).

Lyons, J. B., *The quality of mercer's: the story of Mercer's Hospital, 1734–1991* (Dublin, 1991).

Magennis, Eoin, 'Coal, corn and canals: parliament and the dispersal of public moneys 1695–1772' in David Hayton (ed.), *The Irish parliament in the eighteenth century: the long apprenticeship* (Edinburgh, 2001), pp. 71–86.

Malcolm, Elizabeth, *Swift's Hospital: a history of St. Patrick's Hospital, Dublin, 1746–1989* (New York, 1989).

Malcomson, A. P. W., *John Foster: the politics of the Anglo-Irish ascendancy* (Oxford, 1978).

McCartney, Donal, *W.E.H. Lecky: historian and politician, 1838–1903* (Dublin, 1994).

McCormack, W. J., *Ascendancy and tradition in Anglo-Irish literary history from 1789 to 1939* (Oxford, 1985).

McCracken, J. L., 'The ecclesiastical structure, 1714–1760' in T. W. Moody and W. E. Vaughan (eds), *A new history of Ireland: vol. 4: eighteenth-century Ireland 1691–1800* (Oxford, 1986), pp.

—, 'The political structure 1714–1760' in T. W. Moody and W. E. Vaughan (eds), *A new history of Ireland: vol. 4: eighteenth-century Ireland 1691–1800* (Oxford, 1986).

McDowell, R. B., 'Colonial nationalism and the winning of parliamentary independence, 1760–1782' in T. W. Moody and W. E. Vaughan (eds), *A new history of Ireland: vol. 4: eighteenth-century Ireland 1691–1800* (Oxford, 1986).

—, 'Ireland on the eve of the famine' in R. D. Williams and T. D. Edwards (eds), *The Great Famine: Studies in Irish History, 1845–52* (Dublin, 1994), pp. 3–86.

McGrath, C. I., 'Parliamentary additional supply: the development and use of regular short-term taxation in the Irish parliament, 1692–1716' in David Hayton (ed.), *The Irish parliament in the eighteenth century: the long apprenticeship* (Edinburgh, 2001), pp. 27–54.

—, *The making of the eighteenth-century Irish constitution: government, parliament and the revenue, 1692–1714* (Dublin, 2000).

Meenan, James, and Desmond Clarke (eds), *RDS: The Royal Dublin Society 1731–1981* (Dublin, 1981).

—, 'The RDS 1731–1981' in *RDS: The Royal Dublin Society 1731–1981* (Dublin, 1981).

Melling, Joseph, 'Welfare capitalism and the origins of welfare states: British industry, workplace welfare and social reform, c. 1870–1914' in *Social History*, 17, no. 3 (1992), pp. 453–78.

Milne, Kenneth, *The Irish charter schools 1730–1830* (Dublin, 1997).

Mulligan, Fergus, *The founders of the Royal Dublin Society* (Dublin, 2005).

Murray, Catherine, 'English schools in Ireland in the seventeenth and eighteenth centuries' (M.A. thesis, Queen's University Belfast, 1954).

O'Brien, Eoin, '"Of vagabonds, sturdy beggars and strolling women": the house of industry hospitals in the Georgian and Victorian eras' in Lorna Browne, Eoin O'Brien, and Kevin O'Malley (eds), *The house of industry hospitals, 1772–1987: the Richmond, Whitworth and Hardwicke (St Laurence's Hospital) a closing memoir* (Dublin, 1988), pp. 1–62.

O'Brien, George, *The economic history of Ireland in the eighteenth century* (Dublin, 1918).

O'Brien, Gerard, 'Scotland, Ireland, and the antithesis of Enlightenment' in Sean Connolly, Allan Houston, and Robert Morris (eds), *Conflict, Identity and economic development: Ireland and Scotland, 1600–1939* (Preston, 1995).

O'Ciardha, Eamonn, *Ireland and the Jacobite cause, 1685–1760: a fatal attachment* (Dublin, 2004).

Owen, David, *English philanthropy 1660–1960* (Cambridge, 1964).

Paquette, Gabriel B., *Enlightenment, governance, and reform in Spain and its empire, 1759–1808* (New York, 2008).

— (ed.), *Enlightened reform in southern Europe and its Atlantic colonies, c. 1750–1830* (Burlington, 2009).

Peacocke, Joseph Irvine, 'Anthony Dopping, bishop of Meath' in *The Irish Church Quarterly*, 2, no. 6 (1909), pp. 120–33.

Pocock, J. G. A., 'Post-puritan England and the problem of the Enlightenment' in Perez Zagorin (ed.), *Culture and politics: from puritanism to the Enlightenment* (Berkeley, 1980).

Porter, Roy, *Blood and guts: a short history of medicine* (1st American ed., New York, 2003).

—, *English society in the eighteenth century* (New York, 1982).

—, *The greatest benefit to mankind: a medical history of humanity* (1st American ed., New York, 1998).

Porter, Roy, and Mikuláš Teich, *The Enlightenment in national context* (Cambridge, 1981).

Prochaska, F. K., *Women and philanthropy in nineteenth-century England* (Oxford, 1980).

Proudfoot, Lindsay J., 'Landownership and improvement ca. 1700 to 1845' in Lindsay J. Proudfoot and William Nolan (eds), *Down: History & Society. Interdisciplinary Essays on the History of an Irish County* (Dublin, 1997), pp. 203–37.

Pullan, Brian, 'Catholics, Protestants, and the poor in early modern Europe' in *Journal of Interdisciplinary History*, 30, no. 3 (2005), pp. 441–56.

—, *Rich and poor in Renaissance Venice: the social institutions of a Catholic state to 1620* (Cambridge, 1971).

—, *Poverty and charity: Europe, Italy, Venice 1400–1700* (Aldershot, 1994).

Raughter, Rosemary, 'A discreet benevolence: female philanthropy and the Catholic resurgence in eighteenth-century Ireland' in *Women's History Review*, 6, no. 4 (1997), pp. 461–84.

—, 'A natural tenderness: the ideal & the reality of eighteenth-century female philanthropy' in Maryann Gialanella Valiulis and Mary O'Dowd (eds), *Women & Irish history: essays in honour of Margaret Maccurtain* (Dublin, 1997), pp. 71–88.

Ribton-Turner, Charles, *A history of vagrants and vagrancy, and beggars and begging* (London, 1887).

Robins, Joseph, *The lost children: a study of charity children in Ireland, 1700–1900* (Dublin, 1980).

Ryan, Michelle, 'Divisions of poverty in early modern Dublin' in Augusteijn Joost and MaryAnn Lyons (eds), *Irish history: a research yearbook* (Dublin, 2002), pp. 131–6.

Sheehan, Jonathan, 'Enlightenment, religion, and the enigma of secularization' in *American Historical Review*, 108, no. 4 (2003), pp. 1061–80.

Slack, Paul, *From reformation to improvement: public welfare in early modern England* (Oxford, 1999).

—, *Poverty and policy in Tudor and Stuart England* (London, 1988).

Smyth, James, '"Like amphibious animals": Irish Protestants, ancient Britons, 1691–1707' in *The Historical Journal*, 36, no. 4 (1993), pp. 785–97.

Sneddon, Andrew, 'Bishop Francis Hutchinson (1660–1739): a case study in the eighteenth-century culture of "improvement"' in *Irish Historical Studies*, 35, no. 139 (2006), pp. 289–310.

—, '"Darkness must be expell'd by letting in the light": Bishop Francis Hutchinson and the conversion of Irish Catholics by means of the Irish language, c. 1720–4' in *Eighteenth-Century Ireland*, 19 (2004): pp. 37–55.

—, 'Legislating for economic development: Irish fisheries as a case study in the limitations of "improvement"' in James Kelly, David Hayton, and John Bergin (eds), *The eighteenth-century composite state: representative institutions in Ireland and Europe, 1689–1800* (Basingstoke, 2010), pp. 136–59.

Sonnelitter, Karen, '"To unite our temporal and eternal interests": sermons and the charity school movement in Ireland, 1689–1740' (M.A. thesis, Queen's University Belfast, 2006).

—, '"To unite our temporal and eternal interests": sermons and the charity school movement in Ireland, 1689–1740' in *Eighteenth-Century Ireland*, 25 (2010), pp. 62–81.

Spaeth, Donald, *The church in an age of danger: parsons and parishioners, 1660–1740* (Cambridge, 2000).

Stearns, Peter N., 'Prostitution and charity: the Magdalen hospital, a case study', in *Journal of Social History*, 17, no. 4 (1984), pp. 617–28.

Teich, Mikulas, 'Afterword' in Roy Porter and Mikulas Teich (eds), *The Enlightenment in national context* (Cambridge, 1981), p. 216.

Virgin, Peter, *The church in an age of negligence: ecclesiastical structure and problems of church reform 1700–1840* (Cambridge, 1989).

Wall, Maureen, *The penal laws, 1691–1760: church and state from the Treaty of Limerick to the accession of George III* (Dundalk, 1961).

White, Terence De Vere, *The story of the Royal Dublin Society* (Tralee, 1955).

Wilde, William, 'Illustrious physicians and surgeons in Ireland: Bartholomew Mosse, M.D. surgeon' in *Dublin Quarterly Journal of Medical Sciences*, 2 (1846), pp. 565–96.

Woodward, John, *To do the sick no harm: a study of the British voluntary hospital system to 1875* (London, 1974).

Index

Act of Union (Britain-Ireland, 1801), 146–7, 176
Act of Union (Scotland-England, 1707), 14
Adlercron, Meliore, 122, 128
agriculture: improvements, 34, 106–8, 113, 117
Ahern, Michael, 47–8
Anglo-Irish: and Enlightenment values, 1, 3; as ruling elite, 1, 12; and improvement, 2, 12, 18, 170, 175; aspire to Irish independence, 8, 18; identity, 13, 15–16; on woollen Act, 16; aim for Anglicization, 18; on Presbyterians, 22; religious conviction, 39; found Dublin Society, 99, 103; threatened by poor, 173; concern for political stability, 177; see also Protestants
apothecaries, 96–7
Arran, Charles Butler, 1st earl of, 104

Baker, John Wynne, 116–17; *Some hints for the better improvement of husbandry*, 116
Barnard, Toby C., 18–19, 31
Bayly, Edward, 128–9
Bedford, John Russell, 4th duke of, 160
bees, 114
beggars: in Dublin, 78, 153; children, 153, 171; badging, 166; numbers, 166; see also poor, the; vagrants
Bellers, John, 79
Berkeley, George, 101
Blue Coat School see Hospital and Free School of Charles II
Boland, Thomas, 72
Borsay, Peter, 17
Botanic Gardens, Dublin, 120
Boulter, Hugh, archbishop of Armagh, 30, 32, 34, 48, 52–3, 104, 172
Boyle, Robert, 41

Boyne, Battle of the (1690), 25
Boyton, William, 94
Brereton, Ann, 142
Britain (and England): and government of Ireland, 7–8; view of Irish, 13; trade with Ireland, 14, 59, 109; early mortality rates, 79; parliament fails to issue grants to charities, 147; charitable organizations as model for Irish, 174
Brooke, Henry, 106
Butler, Edward, 94

Caldwell, Sir James, 76
Campbell, Thomas, 171
canals and waterways: government funding, 151
Carey, William, 76–7, 97–8
Castlebar school, County Mayo, 71
Castletown House, 5
Catholic Church: survives penal laws, 11; strength, 48
Catholics: unrest, 1–2, 10; Tory affiliation, 9; status and rights in Ireland, 10–12, 176; as objects of charity, 22; attempted conversion to Protestantism, 37–42, 44–6, 48, 50–5, 58, 172; numbers, 37–8; bishop Hutchinson on, 41; despised by Foy, 42; Richardson condemns, 43; equated with ignorance, 45–6; children educated in charter schools, 50–2, 62–4, 74; schools prohibited by penal laws, 51–2; accused of indolence, 61; women in charity work, 124; political restrictions, 148–9, 176; nurses, 162; in House of Industry, 167
Caugh, Elinor, 139
cesses (taxes), 154
Chadwick, Charles, 68, 71–2

197